IN SEARCH OF
WILLIE MORRIS

ALSO BY LARRY L. KING

Non-Fiction

. . . And Other Dirty Stories (1968)

Confessions of a White Racist (1971)

The Old Man and Lesser Mortals (1974)

Wheeling & Dealing: Confessions of a Capitol Hill Operator (with Bobby
Baker: 1978)

Of Outlaws, Con Men, Whores, Politicians & Other Artists (1980)

That Terrible Night Santa Got Lost in the Woods (1981)

The Whorehouse Papers (1982)

Warning: Writer at Work (1985)

None but a Blockhead (1986)

True Facts, Tall Tales & Pure Fiction (1997)

Larry L. King: A Writer's Life in Letters,
or, Reflections in a Bloodshot Eye (1999)

Novel

The One-Eyed Man (1966; Reissued, 2001)

For Children

Because of Lozo Brown (1988)

Stage Plays

The Best Little Whorehouse in Texas
(with Peter Masterson & Carol Hall: 1978)

The Kingfish (with Ben Z. Grant: 1979)

Christmas: 1933 (1986)

The Night Hank Williams Died (1988)

The Golden Shadows Old West Museum
(based on a story by Mike Blackman: 1989)

The Best Little Whorehouse Goes Public
(with Peter Masterson & Carol Hall: 1994)

The Dead Presidents' Club (1996)

LARRY L. KING

IN SEARCH OF
WILLIE MORRIS

The Mercurial Life
of a Legendary
Writer and Editor

PublicAffairs
New York

Published in the United States by PublicAffairs™,
a member of the Perseus Books Group.

Book design by Jane Raese
Text set in 11-point New Baskerville

Library of Congress Cataloging-in-Publication Data
King, Larry L.
In search of Willie Morris : the mercurial life of a legendary writer and editor /
by Larry L. King.
p. cm.
Includes bibliographical references and index.
ISBN-13: 978-1-58648-384-5
ISBN-10: 1-58648-384-6
1. Morris, Willie. 2. Mississippi—Intellectual life—20th century. 3. Authors,
American—20th century—Biography. 4. Editors—United States—Biography.
5. Mississippi—Biography. I. Title.
PS3563.08745Z75   2006
813'.54—dc22
[B]
2005045643

FIRST EDITION

10 9 8 7 6 5 4 3 2 1

This book is for
DAVID HALBERSTAM

No better colleague,
No better friend

Scars . . . in perpetuity

"A writer's life, the totality of it, is at best bizarre, and at worse horrendous. There are human reasons for this. You live through each book, and each book in signal retrospect represents and evokes for you the particular period in which you wrote it, the especial tribulations and compulsions of, as the Nixon people said, that point in time.

"That is why most writers choose, whenever possible, to forget the books they have written, because each takes a specific piece out of you, a big chunk of your own personal history. It is reported that William Faulkner, among others, always got the drunkest between books.

". . . any book has the writer's surreptitious scars on it in perpetuity. Unlike members of various modern-day professions, a writer more than most others must be left forever with what he did do, or didn't."

—WILLIE MORRIS

in the Foreword to the 1994
Louisiana State University Press
paperback edition of his 1973 novel,
The Last of the Southern Girls

CONTENTS

CONTENTS

CONTENTS

WORDS OF THANKS

MANY PEOPLE HELPED WITH THIS BOOK. JoAnne Prichard Morris, widow of Willie Morris, a fine editor and writer herself, never once dodged a question or tried to censor me. She was helpful also in winnowing the "best truth" from conflicting testimony and also permitted—along with Willie's son, David Rae Morris—my use of many of the papers in the Willie Morris Collection, now reposing in the Department of Archives and Special Collections, John Davis Williams Library, University of Mississippi, Oxford.

David Rae Morris, a stickler for facts, was otherwise helpful in many ways. An accomplished photographer, he never hesitated when I asked many questions about his recollections of his father—with whom he worked on their book *My Mississippi.*

Also of great help was Dr. Celia Buchan Morris, ex-wife of Willie and mother of David Rae, who permitted liberal use of quotes from her revealing memoir, *Finding Celia's Place* (Texas A&M University Press), and who responded candidly to my many questions.

Larry Wells and Dean Faulkner Wells, writers as well as owners of Yoknapatawpha Press in Oxford, were instrumental in Willie Morris's return from "exile" on Long Island in late 1979 to teach at Ole Miss and to serve as its first writer-in-residence. They published several of Willie's books, both originals and reprints, and probably did more for him in Mississippi than anyone save JoAnne Prichard. I cannot overstate the help Larry and Dean gave me.

Author-academician Edwin M. Yoder, Jr., a Rhodes Scholar with Willie Morris, and among his closest friends for forty-three years, provided many enlightened observations. David Halberstam, my colleague at *Harper's* when Willie Morris was our editor-in-chief as well as our friend, shared many valuable insights and memories.

Other writers who shared their personal recollections include Barry Hannah, Winston Groom, Herman Gollob, Jill Conner Browne, Norman Mailer, Edwin (Bud) Shrake, Sally Quinn, Robert Kotlowitz, Jim Dees, Joseph Goulden, and Barbara Howar, the latter also being Willie's lover in the 1970s and for several years a prime influence.

Political cartoonist Patrick Oliphant and artist William Dunlap—a native of Mississippi—both of whom had worked with Willie Morris, shared their stories. I am indebted, too, to the late Malcolm McGregor, a long-time friend of Willie's from his early Texas years; to Taddy McAllister of San Antonio and Washington, once engaged to Willie Morris; to Ron Shapiro, Charles Henry, Rocky Miskelly, and U.S. Senator Thad Cochran, all of Mississippi, and to numerous sources there who prefer anonymity.

A bow also to Evan Smith, top honcho of *Texas Monthly,* whose suggestion in 2001 that I write a Willie Morris article for his magazine led to my winning the Texas Institute of Letters O. Henry Award and, indirectly, also led to this book.

Barbara S. Blaine, my wife-lawyer-agent, risked my wrath when suggesting that all was not perfect in my manuscript—as was her job—and also contributed her own helpful personal memories of Willie Morris.

You would not be reading this except for Peter Osnos, who chose to publish *In Search of Willie Morris,* and David Patterson, a good and patient editor.

Last but not least I was greatly assisted by Jack Bales, an editor and writer who also serves as Reference and Humanities Librarian at the University of Mary Washington in Fredericksburg, Virginia. In the last years of Willie's life, Jack Bales became very close to him, a relationship that started with a "fan letter" from Bales. On subsequent visits to Mississippi, Bales was given Willie's self-described

"$64 tours" of Jackson, Oxford, and Yazoo City. I feel certain that Willie Morris wanted Jack Bales to become his biographer, but Bales urged me to assume that role because of my longer association with Willie—even as he edited two books, *Conversations with Willie Morris,* and a collection of Willie's essays he chose, *Shifting Interludes,* both published by the University Press of Mississippi. Jack Bales gave me the run of his enormous Willie Morris files and assisted in other ways. "Brother Jack's" willingness to help another writer—a thing Willie Morris often did—would make Willie mighty proud, I am sure, just as it makes me mighty grateful.

—Larry L. King
Washington, D.C.
July 8, 2005

INTRODUCTION

EVERYONE THOUGHT THEY KNEW HIM. Few did. Willie Weaks Morris was a man of many parts. What was it Churchill said of Russia? "A riddle wrapped in a mystery inside an enigma." My friend Willie was a little like that.

The private Willie Morris—the brooder, the loner, the man who could lose himself in sleep because wakefulness was too painful, the man who preferred whiskey oblivion to facing problems, the Willie Morris who hid his telephone in the stove or refrigerator to muffle its rings and who called it an instrument of torture, the Willie Morris who couldn't bear to say "no" to writers, friends, or supplicants and so would over-promise and then have to dodge or fudge or run away, the editor who assigned magazine articles and—should they go wrong—might avoid the erring writers rather than convey bad news, the Willie Morris who having hired both Norman Mailer and David Halberstam to cover the 1968 Democratic National Convention in Chicago for *Harper's* could not bring himself to tell either of the proud writers that they must *share* the only press pass he had been able to obtain, the Willie Morris who could stick his head in the sand and think himself invisible, the man who for a time became known (in plain ugly language and in more than one place) as the town drunk, the man who could be as stubborn and unyielding as any mule his idol William Faulkner ever owned—well, that fellow was a complex and puzzling man his adoring public never met.

No way to rhyme that private, haunted, sometimes terribly diffi-cult soul with the public Willie Morris of legend: the boy-wonder youngest editor-in-chief, at age thirty-two, of America's oldest maga-zine, the glad-hander and shoulder-hugger, the merry-eyed Good Old Boy from Mississippi equally at home in Texas saloons and New York salons, the editor who not only was near-perfect in matching writer-to-subject but so adroit a copy editor—pruning excesses, changing a serviceable word to one of more clarity or originality—that writers felt chagrin they hadn't written it that way. Willie was the pal of presidents and poets, the enthusiastic fellow-reveler of profes-sional athletes and rough-and-tumble trial lawyers, a telephone joker who could imitate almost anyone well enough to fool and gleefully embarrass his famous friends and other contemporaries into making self-serving or pompous statements, an editor who could—and often did—write better than most who wrote for him, a man generous with gifts even when short of funds, the kind and playful "Uncle Willie" on whom kiddies doted and who himself loved kiddies and dogs and cats and all manner of improbable strays, whether they had four legs or two.

Yet Willie Morris himself was something of a stray, a wanderer given to showing up on friends' doorsteps unannounced at all hours, one who required an extraordinary amount of care and look-ing after, one who seemed to *expect* his friends and/or associates not only to serve him as needed but also to forgive the many social sins that hard drinkers inflict: everything from endlessly repeating the same story to profane utterances to half-baked arguments shorn of proof to occasional physical rowdiness or foolish lies. But if Willie Morris expected others to happily receive him in the wee hours or otherwise accommodate him when he felt a need, he had no trou-ble hiding himself from friends or loved ones should he want to avoid them for whatever reasons. And his knowledge that they might be seeking him for good reasons of their own cut no ice; in-deed, it might drive Willie to seek even deeper cover. I knew Willie Morris for almost forty of the sixty-four years he lived: worked with him, drank with him, laughed with him, cried with him, traveled with him, visited in his various homes as he visited in mine, loved him and admired him and once had a drunken fistfight with him over which of us owned the affections of a certain fickle socialite in Washington, it turning out that neither of us did. I thank such gods as be that despite our mutual imperfections, causing occasional tiffs, we were fast friends when Willie Morris died suddenly on August 2, 1999, or otherwise I could not have borne it. I will miss the man so long as I have breath.

But I must admit that sometimes I spoke sharply to my editor and friend, many of my sentences starting, "God*dammit*, Willie . . ." In such moments I wanted to grab and shake him and hold him to account. Willie had such intelligence and talent that I always expected more of him; his aura when I knew him best was that of the athlete almost certain to drive in the winning run, score the deciding last-second basket, kick the vital field goal from a difficult angle as time ran out; he simply wasn't supposed to have bad moods or sub-par days like the rest of us. I didn't pause to reflect that perhaps too many of us put too many demands on Willie and made him overly aware of our great, and sometimes selfish, expectations—not the least being his ever-hectoring old Mississippi mama.

And maybe that is why Willie Morris sometimes had to flee from us, and from events, and from life. He was not well-suited to positions of power, it turned out, for—among other reasons—he truly hated to say "No," would procrastinate, and leave matters hanging. This had the effect of complicating not only his life but the lives of others. And he had no patience with the administrative duties attending a top editor's job: most correspondence, just about all business telephone calls, staff meetings, office politics. Nor was he always candid with those of us who worked with him: When he said, "Don't worry about that, I've got it covered," or words to that effect, we learned, in time, that the opposite was likely true.

Those of us close enough to know the private Willie would eventually learn that several Willies existed and that sometimes it seemed we hardly knew any of them. "We've got our own Bridey Murphy," Marshall Frady joked, referring to a best-selling nonfiction book of the 1950s about a young woman—one Ruth Simmons—with multiple personalities, one of which, under hypnosis, danced an Irish jig, spoke in a thick Irish brogue, and claimed to be "Bridey Murphy" of nineteenth-century Cork and Belfast. Of those making the exhilarating—if sometimes strange or puzzling—journey with Willie Morris, most who walked closest to him were writers whose careers he enhanced during his glory years at *Harper's*; he was widely credited with having turned that dull and ponderous magazine into "the hottest book in the business"; a half dozen of us were around not only to see it happen but to help make it happen as Willie's personal choices: David Halberstam, Marshall Frady, John Corry, Bob Kotlowitz, Midge Decter, poet John Hollander, myself. Outside the small *Harper's* staff, on the New York scene Willie then was perhaps closest to the writers James Jones, William Styron, and Norman Mailer; the latter two, particularly, along with a dozen other top-drawer writers of the 1960s–1970s period helped to brighten and upgrade "America's Oldest Magazine," as *Harper's* was billed, and, unfortunately, had begun to read like. Its veteran editors had perhaps become too satisfied with the status quo and their own seats of influence and comfort, too enamored of their movers-and-shakers pals—or men who had been movers and shakers—who congregated almost daily to lunch in the staid old Century Club; men who perhaps had become too accepting of official versions of events and public policies. *Harper's* no longer either afflicted the comfortable nor comforted the afflicted; it failed, often, to question received opinions, or the decisions or the reasoning behind them.

Whatever else may be said of Willie Morris, he turned *Harper's* around, regained much of its lost respect, and attracted men and women who delivered lively, informative prose much superior to that of the retired State Department officials, experimental diet faddists, wordy academicians, holders or seekers of public office, and a few senior writers—some of whom had lost a step or two—that had begun to dominate its pages. It seemed to Willie Morris, young, vibrant, and ambitious to the core when he joined the magazine as a young editor, that *Harper's*—as he later told me—"wallowed dead in the water." When he became its editor-in-chief in 1967, thirty-two-year-old Willie Morris almost immediately moved to jettison old baggage.

Those of us who worked with Willie regularly learned that no matter whether we were dealing with the gleeful big-kid Willie, the distant hard-to-reach Willie, or the Willie who wore his huge sentimental heart on his sleeve so that he might cry at song lyrics, midnight poetry, the talent of Babe Ruth, or the memory of a dog long dead, he was *real,* warts and all—not a man of artifice or strategic bobs-and-weaves or stuffed-shirt pretentiousness. His emotions were as primitive, genuine, and changeable as the weather.

He was, indeed, just about the worst I ever saw at hiding his true feelings; "a thundercloud expression" became not a cliché but a live storm brewing in your face, one just short of crackling lightning bolts; when something pleased him or he was amused his eyes danced jigs, his face beamed sunshine. I never played poker with Willie, but if I had I imagine that by watching his face when he looked at his cards I could have won his billfold, his car, and his next three paychecks.

Such a demonstrative face was not a good weapon in the deadly game of office politics, where runaway ambitions and sudden slashings were better served by artful concealments or attacks from ambush. Willie simply had little talent for these darker and subtle duplicities or sly wicked dirkings—a trait that ultimately helped cost him the job he then cherished above all other things in his life.

One might argue that Willie Morris was not helpless when it came to in-fighting—he could plot intrigue, as the record will show—but he was not, somehow, very adept at following through. No matter the fight, there generally would come a day when he inexplicably lost interest in the battle. Then he became the classic head-in-the-sand ostrich: Suddenly, whatever problem had existed seemed to have magically disappeared. It had not of course; usually it continued to fester unattended, to the ultimate disadvantage of Willie Morris or one of his causes.

We learned, too, that—for all his goodness and greatness—Willie was . . . well, yes, Mr. Churchill. A riddle. Wrapped in a mystery. Inside an enigma. Halberstam and I, and sometimes Marshall Frady, privately talked about Willie's presumed "missing part," to which we assigned blame for his puzzling disappearing acts, brooding spells, evasions, incommunicative periods.

Budd Schulberg asked in his famous 1940s novel *What Makes Sammy Run?*—and we asked "What Makes Willie run?"—the difference being that the novel's Sammy Glick was a 100 percent ratfink, while our Willie had many redeeming qualities and much of the time was great fun. We learned, however—in time—that he wasn't the simple Tom Sawyer or Huck Finn figure of his classic mid-life memoir, *North Toward Home,* or in any other of his numerous lyrical books. No, the "real-life" Willie Morris was much more complex and sophisticated than the country innocent revealed in his own works, and he also had a dark side few suspected. If he had no poker face in person, at the typewriter he became much better at concealment and camouflage.

Willie was an editor who urged his writers to write it *true* and helped them do it—but who, when himself writing, had trouble revealing any but his sunnier parts; to be fair, he extended that generosity to almost everyone he wrote about. Under the influence of bottled 90-proof midnight truth serum, I sometimes complained to Willie that, when writing, he viewed a world greener than God had made it; one night he said, softly, "Yes, I lie a lot." I was shocked, didn't know what to say, and never again chastised him about that because there was in the glance he gave me and his voice a hint of a cry: *I'm sorry but I have to! I must!* Willie's son, David Rae Morris, thinks Willie only meant what he often had told him: "Sometimes, in order to tell the truth, a writer must lie a little." After his death, Willie's widow and editor, JoAnne Prichard, offered her explanation: "Willie had greatly mellowed in the years since he had been the young crusading editor of *The Texas Observer* and *Harper's.* He wanted to write of people, places and things he remembered with affection and to use the wisdom he'd accumulated. I believe he was glad to leave his old wars behind, to perhaps be a little protective of himself and others."

Willie had *long* felt, I think, a need to be protective; perhaps much of that dated from a childhood much more demanding and far less sunny than is pictured in his work. And some of that need no doubt stemmed from the rapidity with which he had fallen from being "Mr. Big" to a neglected and disappeared "has-been" almost in the blink of an eye, following his sudden and unexpected resignation in March of 1971 during a dispute with management, an act that caught all of Willie's sub-editors and writers by surprise. "He's become Judge Crater," Marshall Frady said of Morris only a few weeks after the *Harper's* fiasco—alluding to a famed New York jurist who went out to dinner one night in 1930 and disappeared without a trace. Willie Morris not only had dropped out of the spotlight and headlines but had gone into such deep cover even old friends and colleagues couldn't contact him. Protecting himself, as he saw it. And, at the same time, sticking his head in the sand.

And so Willie sometimes "pulled his punches" or glossed over certain matters or simply left them out or, yes, greened up the world God had made. Larry Wells, the Mississippi publisher and a writer of novels and screenplays, who knew Morris for more than twenty years, said of him, "He turned out much fine writing. Poetical. Lyrical. Almost like music. And he made worthy comments about home, roots, the human heart and much more. But there were two Willies: the one who wrote a life and the one who lived a life, and if they had met in public, standing on a subway platform shoulder to shoulder, say, there's a good chance neither would have recognized the other." Of all the things I have heard said about Willie Morris, that strikes me as possibly the most accurate.

Morris waited until his final book, published posthumously—a novel, not his usual nonfiction—to write his most self-revealing work. Halberstam, who knew Willie Morris to the bone if anyone did, who worked with him as I did and loved him as I did, and was puzzled by him as I often was, has said, "*Taps* is Willie's most honest book about himself, his time and his place."

I think it no accident that such a book was published posthumously. *Taps* was in Willie's mind for more than thirty years; he worked on that novel over at least a twenty-five-year period: fussing with it, tinkering with it, making it fat, slimming it down, fattening it anew, then throwing it in a trunk or box or desk drawer for long periods, perhaps to simmer or marinate. Once he even gave away his only copy, to a Mississippi pal, Charles Henry; Henry pressed him to take it back, many months later, and attack it anew. So, once more, Willie repeated the painful creative cycle of massive rewrites followed by equally massive cuts—and then, after agonizing re-evaluations, repeated that process yet again, ad infinitum it seemed. Perhaps five years before he died I asked how many times he had rewritten *Taps*. "I don't think I can count that high," Willie said with a rueful laugh.

Though he variously referred to *Taps* as "my baby" or said, "It will contain all I know" or confided to friends that his ultimate literary reputation likely depended on that book, he never seemed able to let it go. On the day he would die, shortly after being stricken, Willie told JoAnne Prichard, "Get *Taps* in shape."

I wasn't in Willie's head on that final day, but what I know of his history and his apprehensions leads me to believe he thought, even if only subconsciously, *I won't be here to face the consequences of this book so it's time to let it rip.* Not that the consequences would have been all that dire, but Willie almost always feared or shied away from the personal judgments of others; he seemed to think they would be harsher than he ultimately found them on most occasions, though he did take some few floggings—as any writer will: Critics are, after all, paid to criticize.

What people thought of him was more important to Willie, I believe, than he pretended. God knows he been made aware almost from the cradle of "what people think" by a socially insecure Mississippi mother who gave evidence of having believed that she had married beneath herself and somehow seemed to fear that her private secrets would be shouted by a town crier in the Yazoo City square. Early on Willie recognized his mother's fears; I have no doubt she passed shadowy portions along to her son. Willie tried to give the impression that he cared not a whit for the judgments of others, but I saw too many times when he was wounded, angered, or otherwise troubled by critical comments or perceived slights.

As Willie's body lay in state in the Old Capitol in Jackson—only the third in Mississippi's history to do so—his friends laughed and told funny stories about him even in the presence of his still form.

Some of the best ones, perhaps, were not published by the University Press of Mississippi in a fine little book of final tributes, *Remembering Willie*. No, many murmured stories that day were of the private Willie, the brooding Willie, the "mystery" Willie, the Willie who drank a bit much and stumbled into misadventures. Of the manuscript written by Peter Benchley—pre *Jaws* and fame and big money—that Willie left in a taxicab but, not wanting to admit that, paid Benchley's agent for it—and then for two years had to toe-dance around questions as to why it had not been published or when it would be. Of the time he cut his credit cards up late in the evening, to curtail his rash spending, and then the next day desperately, futilely tried to glue them back together. Of the lovely he picked up in a cocktail lounge, after his divorce, and took to his apartment before she admitted to being a call girl who required $200, and how—when Willie dozed off on the couch in the wee hours, his passion still unfulfilled—she stole many of his clothes, his shoes, his alarm clock, and a treasured silver bauble given to him by one of his heroes, Gordon McLendon, "The Old Scotsman," whose re-creations of major league baseball games on network radio Willie had cherished as a boy. Some of the tales were excellent black comedy, but they did not qualify to go public on a day when, traditionally, the record is swept clean of all save one's virtues.

I have thought for many hours about Willie Morris since his sudden death—of the magic and the mystery and the misery in the man. He touched and influenced my life as much as any other single individual and stirred within me a wider range of emotions, over a longer period of time, than has anyone else. Much the same was said of Lyndon B. Johnson by those who knew him well, but, as one who knew them both, I would make a few key distinctions: LBJ often used a hatchet; Willie at the top of his game was a gifted rapier man; LBJ often was sadistic in his blows; Willie seldom, if ever, in his thrusts; LBJ was no stranger to jealousy and malice in politics; Willie literally had none, in a profession where jealousy and malice often appeared to grow on trees: In his personal life, Willie did hurt some people—but the person he most often hurt, I believe, was himself.

What all that thinking and speculation has led to is this search for

Willie Morris, made on behalf of my personal curiosity and perhaps as a surrogate seeker for all who knew Willie and admired him or loved him—or both—but who came to realize that they didn't always understand him. And also for readers who did not know him but perhaps had heard of him or had at least a passing familiarity with his work.

I FIRST WROTE AN ARTICLE about Willie Morris, more than two years after his death, for *Texas Monthly* magazine. It was published in May of 2001; Evan Smith, chief editor of *Texas Monthly,* had asked for 5,000 words. I couldn't quit at that. I had become obsessed with "getting it all and getting it right"—an instruction Willie repeated to writers with some frequency—and so I wrote more than 19,000 words, many more than the astonished editor could use when my manuscript clunked heavily on his desk. Almost immediately—assisted by the suggestions of a few writer friends—I decided to write this book.

In the course of interviewing people and searching documents for the *TM* article, I had discovered numerous facts previously unknown to me and had heard rumors or bare-bones accounts of other stories I desperately wanted to use but couldn't develop in time to meet the *Texas Monthly* deadline or space restrictions. I was, frankly, surprised to learn that I was ignorant of, or had been oblivious to, many facts about a man I long had presumed to know better than I knew some of my blood kin.

I also began to realize that while Willie Morris had made numerous whiskey confessions of his fears and obstacles to Mississippi intimates in Oxford, especially during his last years as writer-in-residence at Ole Miss, when much had gone sour in his life, he had been more circumspect with those of us from his past. We were busy crafting our own books, stage plays, lectures, TV or movie scripts, whatever; we no longer saw Willie frequently, and so knew few details of his contemporary Mississippi life; we probably made no more than perfunctory inquiries into how Willie *really* was doing, that not seeming necessary because he reported himself to be doing well on his native ground. Had we probed deeper, as the reporter's instincts in us should have pushed us to do, we might have been appalled at what had become his "normal" conduct.

We knew, from Willie and others, that he originally had loved his return "home," that he had been re-energized by it, that most at Ole Miss were happy with Willie and he with them. He was, we thought, more in the saddle than since his best days at *Harper's*. It is now obvious, alas, that when talking with us Willie had painted much rosier pictures of his condition than the facts supported—especially during his last three years of the decade he spent at Ole Miss; our careless inattentions, however, had permitted Willie to hide the pea under any one of several shells.

It is something of an irony, I guess, that such belated reports drove me to attempt the sort of "truth with the bark off," dirt-under-the-fingernails approach to the Willie Morris story of the kind Willie himself encouraged from those of us who wrote for him at *Harper's* more than three decades ago.

So I have gone to Mississippi to scratch its dust in search of Willie's boyhood tracks, have questioned those who knew him there in his childhood and teen years, some who knew him in Texas during his college days and after at *The Texas Observer.* I have talked to a scarce few who knew him in England during his four-year Rhodes Scholar period (an experience about which he wrote very little) and have checked the memories and impressions of many who shared his company in Manhattan, as I did, when Willie "owned" it for a few heady seasons. Willie's main companions and fellow writers on Long Island, where he lived in self-imposed exile after his brilliant magazine career abruptly ended—James Jones, John Knowles, and Truman Capote—are dead, but I found others who had observed him in that time and place and who shared helpful recollections; life there was not always a bowl of cherries, as we shall see, though you will hear few rumbles of troubles or discontent in Willie's reports on that period in his books.

And, finally, I quizzed again people in Mississippi where Willie Morris spent his final twenty years, in Oxford and Jackson, where— with the help, the love and support of JoAnne Prichard—he in his final decade blessedly made a comeback as a writer, as a cheerful and lively raconteur and where, all too soon, his life ended only a few blocks away—though many travels, honors, battles, adventures, and worlds away—from where it began on November 29, 1934.

Some warts turned up, yes, most of them in a period covering Willie's exile to the Hamptons on Long Island after his world blew up at *Harper's* and, again, during his last couple of years at Ole Miss, in a time when he found little satisfaction in his work, when—often—the words simply wouldn't come; when he drank even more excessively than was his wont and began to show, quite often, a darker side than most knew he had; when he felt forgotten and something of a failure; when he felt bereft of friends and so conducted himself that it sometimes was hard to *be* his friend. "He had real problems then," recalls a friend who had urged him to come home to Mississippi from his lengthy and often lonely Long Island exile, "and he made problems for others."

I am not at all comfortable being the instrument of revelations, the bearer of bad tidings, about my old friend and mentor, but I set out to write this book with my eyes open—knowing that Willie Morris was an imperfect man in an imperfect world. And I truly think that, despite some moments of personal discomfort, at bottom the best editor I ever had would not have wanted me to pull my punches.

One thing I have learned for certain, and with that new knowledge came a certain pain: I was not Willie Morris's "best friend," as I for so many years considered myself, but maybe one of one hundred people—perhaps even more—who, at different times, thought they were closer to him than anyone else. Willie was, simply, a near-genius in making people feel they had earned that designation. It was a form of deception, yes, the kind good politicians are adept at in getting others to rally 'round their flags, basically harmless in most cases, and can be sustained by those practicing it so long as they care to make the effort. Those of us persuaded of our closeness to Willie could not fathom his having any troubles or problems he would not share with us: Surely he would want our advice! It is evident now that the opposite was true: Willie took special care to conceal problems, setbacks, or other misadventures from those of us who had known him best at the pinnacle of his *Harper's* years—so, in truth, we were the last to know. The man had a real talent for compartmentalizing himself.

When Ann Richards was governor of Texas she told a "Willie story" in a speech at the dedication in 1992 of the Southwestern Writers Collection at Texas State University, San Marcos, that seems appropriate here. Ms. Richards spoke of when she had joined a few old friends paddling down the Rio Grande separating Texas from Mexico. Willie, she noted, was not famed as an outdoorsman so he was placed in the charge of a state legislator (who would later become a district judge), Neil Caldwell, who did the paddling in his and Willie's canoe without mishap. They camped that night on the banks of the river.

"The next morning," Governor Richards said, "I saw Willie at the water's edge with a collapsible toothbrush, performing his cleansing in the Rio Grande river. And I said, 'My God, Willie, don't you realize that all the effluent of Mexico and a number of houses that should go unmentioned is coming directly into this river and you are putting it in your *mouth?*' Willie was horrified at the lack of the pristine nature of the out-of-doors. I wanted to tell you that story so you would know that we must not deify these people"—and here Governor Richards motioned toward a section where most of the attending writers sat—"because they are, after all, fallible."

My search for Willie Morris has not unlocked all the mysteries, but I hope it helps us better understand the complexities, fears, and drives of a man who contributed in so many ways to the world of American letters.

PART ONE

A BIG DUCK
IN A SMALL POND
PREPARES FOR
DEEPER WATERS

"I was an ambitious little son-of-a-bitch."

—WILLIE MORRIS

in an interview with Dr. Orley B. Cordell
of the University of Southern Mississippi, 1979

CHAPTER 1

Taps, published posthumously, provided the first public clues from Willie Morris that all had not been well in the modest home where he grew up in Yazoo City, Mississippi, that town—in Willie's words— "perched on the edge of the delta, straddling that memorable divide where the hills end and the flatlands begin."

The novel's young protagonist, Swayze Barksdale, is driven about half bonkers by a nagging, prattling, smothering mother. Since the life of Willie's fictional counterpart so closely resembles Willie's own in so many other ways, it is fair to assume that Swayze's old Mississippi Mama bears more than a slight resemblance to Willie's real-life one.

Some who had visited Yazoo with Willie, who had met his mother and talked a bit with the town's old-timers about his late father— and I was one of those—had earlier come to believe that the Henry Rae and Marion Morris home was a household with too little love between its partners, too many restrictions about what one might or might not say or do, too many fearful concerns about what "people might think," too many secrets, too many problems unspoken, unacknowledged and unresolved.

Though he wrote little about it, Willie Morris in later years said that going to church so often—twice on Sunday, Wednesday night prayer meeting, at least one week-long summer revival, Vacation Bible School—"became a dreadful weight." It was, he said, oppressive and boring; he heard too many visiting, shouting evangelists using the same language in threatening parishioners with damnation to eternal hellfire. Willie's father seldom attended church at all—excepting a few Easter Sundays when he shifted impatiently in his pew, according to Willie's recollection—while Mrs. Morris, Willie felt, attended largely because in her time and place it was the proper thing to do; she also served as church pianist for thirty-two years.

Sometimes Willie spoke of the church ritual with humor, saying he ultimately quit going "because of an itchy tail bone," and sometimes he spoke of it with anger in his voice. Why, then, did he march down the aisle to get "saved" about "fifteen times" before reaching age fourteen? Some of it may have been emotional follow-the-leader, youngsters tending to react in bunches and clusters and finally finding comfort in being part of the crowd. But probably, I think, Willie "witnessed" in public mainly to please his mother. Getting saved was, Willie wrote, "the proper thing to do." And who in the Morris family so cherished "the proper thing"? (Willie's widow, JoAnne Prichard Morris, believes that Willie "wasn't entirely honest" in writing of his religious experiences. She thinks he was "saved" so many times as a youngster "to deal with hurt"—the same way he later used alcohol—"and because there was an intimacy" not otherwise available in his life.)

Not everything in the Morris home was quite so "proper." Rae Morris was said to often get solitarily, quietly drunk while his wife, for all her life-long lectures to her only child against the evils of demon rum, was said by one of Willie's favorite schoolteachers (and later, after his mother's death, by Willie himself) to have been a secret nipper. It was a thing Willie had suspected for some years, though he told me had never found—nor sought—corroborating evidence; it is probable that he stuck his head in the sand. David Rae Morris says, however, that he recalls his father having a conversation on the phone with his mother in the mid-1970s when it appeared that she reached out to him because she suspected she had a drinking problem. Willie told her, David said, to "talk to so-and-so, who I assumed was the minister of her church. My dad may not have actively sought out the information, but he did try to help when my grandmother asked for help."

At any rate, when Willie Morris returned to Yazoo City to dispose of his mother's worldly goods and sell the family homestead on Grand Avenue, following her death in April of 1977, he found evidence that his mother had, indeed, been a secret drinker: empty vodka bottles in many secret caches. They were in shoeless shoeboxes neatly stacked in bedroom closets; under beds, where the telltale bottles had been further concealed by covering rugs; under the kitchen sink behind cleaning materials; hither and yon. Such pathetic stowings are enough to arouse some sympathy even for a fearful and often difficult woman.

Some of Willie's oldest friends recall that Marion Morris provided little in the way of creature comforts at home. Willie himself told Larry and Dean Faulkner Wells that he often went to friends' homes about mealtime to insure that he would eat well. And he told me that until he married JoAnne Prichard late in his life, "I never really had a home where I felt at ease." (That claim to some extent runs contrary to other testimony and my own observations: In Austin Willie's and Celia's home was a center for liberal/artistic social life, and much the same may be said for their homes in Manhattan and their country place in Brewster County, New York, during the *Harper's* years until they divorced in late 1969.)

A sensitive and intelligent youngster growing up in a world where he was told to live by one set of rules but observed lives being lived by quite another—including in his own home—would have had to find a way to live with so many contradictions. Young Willie Morris chose fantasy and he used that escape hatch for the rest of his life.

NOT NEARLY ALL OF WILLIE'S WRITINGS about his boyhood were escapist fantasies. That became clear in May of 2001—about twenty-one months after his death—when a number of his old friends gathered in Yazoo City for a "Remembering Willie" weekend. Among his childhood pals were several wearing tags bearing the nicknames Willie had awarded them decades ago: "Honest Ed" Upton, now a Methodist preacher in Texas; "Big Boy" Wilkinson, a dentist in Memphis; "Muttonhead" Shepherd, a retired teacher and coach in

North Carolina. From the same stage where they had been in school plays with Willie Morris or sang songs with him during their elementary and grammar school days, they fondly remembered him for his pranks—many of which he had himself reported in his books.

Yes, Willie *had* taught his dog Skip to carry a deflated football in his mouth and follow Willie's blocking in sandlot games; he *had* propped Skip behind the wheel of an automobile and, crouched down so as to work the gas pedal and brake with his hands, had permitted the dog to "drive" the car to the astonishment of witnesses; he *had* found on shortwave radio a re-creation of major league baseball games (by the aforementioned "Old Scotsman," Gordon McLendon) that ran about two innings ahead of the delayed broadcast reaching most of Yazoo and had then called the fire station as "The Phantom" to amaze local firemen by telling them precisely what would happen to the next few batters, down to ball-and-strike counts. Yes, he *had* employed a $2 gadget ordered from a mail order house, called an "ultra mike," that when properly grounded could break in on real radio broadcasts and, with the same tone, make anything that one said appear to be part of that broadcast. "Big Boy" Wilkinson recalled how Willie had slouched down in a car Wilkinson was driving in downtown Yazoo and using his "ultra mike"—for the benefit of an acquaintance idling on a street corner—said something like, "And in Washington today the Pentagon announced that the first name drawn from a hat, to be drafted into an Army being rapidly expanded to fight the latest Communist menace, was that of Such-and-So of Yazoo County, Mississippi. Military officials said they would activate young Such-and-So and ship him to basic training within two weeks." As Wilkinson told it, the chosen victim—about sixteen years old—immediately ran home yelling for his mama.

That his boyhood chums still remembered Willie kindly, even loved him, was evident in several ways. One old chum almost broke down and had to stop for long moments to regain his composure. "Muttonhead" Shepherd walked with a cane, wore an oxygen apparatus, and had to be helped on and off the stage, but his old eyes sparkled in recalling boyhood exploits involving Willie. "Honest Ed" Upton, who chose not to speak from the stage, said afterwards, "We had to make our own fun back then in a little town like this. But that was no problem with Willie among us."

It was a bit disconcerting to see what time and gravity had done to the faces and hairlines of Willie's old pals, because one who had read Willie's books and heard him spin barroom yarns of "Muttonhead" and "Big Boy" and "Honest Ed" and "Bubba" Barrier and others still saw them—in his mind's eye—as perpetual youngsters. That surreal experience aside, however, Willie's boyhood chums provided valuable testimony for one searching the dust for his tracks: Even if Willie's youth had not been all Tom Sawyer or Huck Finn, certainly there had been Twain-like elements in it, enough that Willie's reports of his early life somehow took on a new legitimacy, a new authority.

WILLIE MORRIS FIRST CAME to widespread public attention as the crusading editor-in-chief of the campus newspaper, *The Daily Texan*, in 1955–56 at the University of Texas. In that era, children, there was only one UT campus, and it was in Austin. An unlikely figure—Willie's late father—was wholly responsible for getting him there.

Rae Morris, a service station operator who also delivered gasoline by truck to large plantations in the Mississippi Delta, appears to have been a distant and remote man not much engaged with people or events around him; his daughter-in-law, Celia Buchan Morris, thought him "a sad man." His only child wrote very little about him and said little more. Scarce letters from Willie to his father run along the lines of "Dad, thanks for the sports report"; no emotion shows through.

Willie said his father taught him the basics of baseball and to appreciate the Mississippi woods, but we see only random snapshots: Rae Morris hiding in tall weeds in an alley behind his house, chain-smoking cigarettes, to outwait the visits of parsons; railing against "hypocritical" churchgoing businessmen who made their living by gambling, selling bootleg whiskey, or charging usurious interest rates to poor Negroes. Rae's preference for wrinkled khaki britches and a stained old hat, as well as his avoidance of social small talk, indicate that he did not share his wife's thirst for upward mobility. His father was, Willie told a few intimates, "as common as dirt"; Willie did not deliver that line as a pejorative so much as a matter-of-fact description, as a writer whose mind's eye was at work. Willie also said his father was "as reluctant to socialize as a cave-dwelling hermit" and that liquor loosed his tongue not at all. "He was *Country*, in the way that he was tuned to its rhythms and cycles," Willie wrote. "He and his Tennessee people were simple, trustworthy, straight forward, and as good as grass."

Yet there is some evidence—from what Willie told his wife JoAnne—that Willie often felt abandoned by his father, a man who would not face down his wife even as Willie felt she was smothering him or screaming at him when his father was the only person on earth who could have come to his rescue. It is significant, perhaps, that the young protagonist of *Taps*, Swayze Barksdale, has no fa-ther—only a big-brother–like friend, Luke, who helped young Swayze get away from home and stand up to his mother, and who talked to him about life and personal matters the way a father ide-ally might have. Rae Morris, on the other hand, dealt with his wife by *not* dealing with her, in Willie's recall: shutting the door and climbing into bed to read detective magazines, playing cards with the boys at the fire station, drinking more than just a bit in solitary repose, usually remaining as silent as the grave as he imbibed; I can-not recall one instance of Willie quoting conversations between his parents, either in person or in his work.

Still, that rather common and uncommunicative man rose above his near-recluse instincts and rode a Continental Trailways bus 500 miles to Austin to inspect the University of Texas campus in the summer of 1952; it almost surely was the only college campus Rae Morris ever visited, but he apparently inspected it closely: He would return home to tell his son of its impressive campus tower, dorms, classrooms, and athletic facilities. "I think you oughta go to school out there," he told seventeen-year-old Willie Morris. "Can't nothin' in *this* state match it."

Willie was reluctant to leave his pals, the sweet-lipped teenaged daughter of a Delta planter, the comfortable niche he had carved for himself locally not only as Class Valedictorian and Most Likely to

Succeed but also as Most Versatile (an athlete as well as a scholar, he was a mainstay on the baseball and basketball teams) and Wittiest among his contemporaries at Yazoo High School #1—which is to say the "white" high school; Yazoo High #2 was attended only by blacks in those racially segregated days.

Willie was old-shoe comfortable in Yazoo, an up-and-coming youngster with a hand in many pies: editor of the school newspaper, *The Flashlight;* disk jockey, news reader, and sports announcer at 500-watt radio station WFAZ, "1230 on your dial, with studios high above the Taylor and Roberts Feed and Seed Store, in downtown Yazoo City, the Gateway to the Delta"—the official in-house spiel Willie gave during station breaks. He also began writing sports for the weekly *Yazoo Herald* at age twelve, "using a strange argot that must have been incomprehensible to the occasional dirt farmer who might have followed my white-hot dispatches from the playing fields of Eden, Satartia, Flora, and Bentonia." He was elected a delegate to Boys State, a mock state government that annually convened in the State Capitol in Jackson, where real legislators cautioned against introducing too many mock bills because some of them might, inadvertently, "interfere with the Mississippi way of life"—an instructive if coded caution to the young that racial segregation must be maintained, that one could not be too careful in the official preservation of old customs and familiar rituals. "I was full of the regional graces and was known as a perfect young gentleman," Willie wrote of his formative years in *North Toward Home,* his self-styled "autobiography in mid-passage," published when he was thirty-two years old. Meaning no disrespect, but Willie as a youngster also was pissant ignorant in the ways of the world.

Morris told John Carr, interviewing him for Carr's 1972 book exploring a dozen Southern writers (*Kite-Flying and Other Irrational Acts),* "When I was seventeen, I was deeply in love with this blond majorette from a plantation out there in the country, and I wanted to go to Ole Miss. I wanted to play baseball for Ole Miss, and I had visions of coming back and marrying the belle of the plantation and spending the rest of my life lazing around on the banks of the Yazoo River and fighting the NAACP and the rest of it."

Young Morris had lived in Yazoo City all save his first six months; he knew its every pothole and pebble, its streets and sidewalks and alleys. Though he was not unaware of its shacks and a few chinked log cabins on the wrong side of town—mainly where the poorest of the black citizens lived—and knew its downtown business district was largely pedestrian, Willie in 1970 proudly wrote: "The Northern visitor is invariably surprised when he comes to my home town to find it is not the raw little hill town that the name may deserve—not a Canton, say, or a Philadelphia in Neshoba County—but a substantial town with many broad old streets and beautiful homes peopled by an extremely large number of college-educated whites for this part of the country. The trees and vegetation are lush and green most of the year; in springtime there is no more beautiful place in America."

One of Willie's favorite places was Yazoo City's green old Glendale Cemetery, where he roamed with his beloved fox terrier, Skip. "There was something about that cemetery that comforted me," Willie said. "It was restful. It provoked thought." And he wrote, "I loved to walk among the graves and look at the dates and words on the tombstones. I learned more about the town's past here, the migrations, the epidemics, the old forgotten tragedies than I ever could have learned in the library." Sometimes Willie carried a sack lunch to his restful haven, usually choosing to sit under a shade tree near the graves of two of John Hancock's sons, who had died of some mysterious disease while passing through Delta country; there he would eat ham sandwiches washed down with Nehi strawberry soda, giving his scraps to Skip.

That burial ground was the first place Willie took me when I first visited Yazoo City with him in 1967, and he immediately matched a foot race between my thirty-eight-year-old legs and those of his spry seven-year-old son, David Rae. Willie delighted in my gasping and wheezing and the muscle pull I suffered in catching the youngster, who had been given a fifteen-yard head start, and at David Rae's clear astonishment that such an old fat man had run him down; David Rae agitated for years for a rematch I never granted.

It was not the first time Willie had used the cemetery for his own amusement; he liked to set up his youthful companions for unexpected ghostly wails, indescribably scary to most of the victims, in the burial grounds after nightfall. He once arranged for William Styron to find Styron's novel *Lie Down in Darkness* reposing "on the grave of one James Dillard, who had died on February 9, 1909, and whose likeness [on his headstone] blazed out for all to see, a John Brown visage, wild beard and fearsome eyes. On the flyleaf of [Styron's] novel my son had written *To William Styron. Come lie down in darkness with us. It is not as bad as it has been made out. From James Dillard and the Bethel dead.*"

Willie elaborated on a local legend in his book *Good Old Boy* about a "witch" buried in that local cemetery; she allegedly had broken out of her grave in 1904 and burned down the whole town as an act of revenge for supposed ill treatment at the hands of townspeople; he made effective use of a broken chain by an old grave, citing it as "evidence" of "the witch" having escaped her grave. The Yazoo City Chamber of Commerce, hoping to bolster tourism, erected a tombstone for the witch. Willie was delighted to have a book signing in the cemetery at the unveiling of the marker.

Willie not only knew the physical Yazoo City as a youngster but also the movers and shakers of his hometown, had seen them in action, had heard behind-the-hand reports of certain conduct not meant to break into print in the friendly local newspaper, and had observed some few of those community hypocrisies his father railed against.

When his father told him, not long before scouting the University of Texas, that Willie should "get the hell out of Mississippi" in search of more and better opportunities, he was taken aback; intimate or revealing chats were not usual. Willie would not inherit a plantation or a thriving business or for that matter much of anything at all, his father explained. And so he could not presume admittance to the ruling inner circles of Mississippi's "closed society"—a phrase more likely Willie's than Rae's, or even more likely to have been borrowed by Willie from a "Yankee" interloper who taught at Ole Miss, James

Silver, and who was ostracized after publication in 1962 of his book *Mississippi: The Closed Society.*

At any rate, Rae Morris told his son, he therefore must seek the best education possible. This was an honest, perceptive, and intimate analysis coming from the distant or indifferent figure most folks thought Rae Morris to be. Willie himself was surprised. "I was then blind to many imperfections," about the culture around him, he said in later years.

The degree of Willie's social astigmatism isn't clear: He had been surprised by his father's private declaration, "The niggers pay taxes, don't they? If they pay taxes they have the right to vote. It's just that simple." Certainly that was neither a majority opinion nor a popular one in the Mississippi of the 1950s. Willie also recalled a surprising speculation by his beloved maternal grandmother Mamie, who once said, "Well, maybe when we get to Heaven they'll be white and we'll be black." More than likely the teenager Willie Morris didn't dwell on racial segregation much at all, merely accepted it as the way things were, would probably remain, and perhaps *should* remain; he did, after all, presume that he would, as an adult in his beloved Delta, fight "the NAACP and the rest of it."*

We do know that Willie sent mixed messages in his tales of youthful relationships with blacks in Yazoo City. He told writer-editor Jack Bales that he and his contemporaries sometimes drove by a certain

---

*One cannot be too sure, however, exactly what Willie thought about many things; he loved to pose as more of a wide-eyed know-nothing than was actually the case, a life-long affectation should it strengthen a story or an impression he wanted to bolster. He enjoyed saying, for example, that when he visited a faculty member's home as a University of Texas newcomer, there were so many books in the parlor he wondered if they might be for sale. Not likely: Willie was a reader even then—though he did not begin to read Faulkner until turned on to it by a native of Mississippi, Frank Lyell, who taught him freshman English at UT; we know, however, that Willie had a well-used library card in Yazoo City dating back to when he was a young boy and that on several occasions the local librarian quizzed him as to whether he actually read some of the more advanced books he checked out—and whether he perhaps should *not* read some. She did, in fact, tell young Willie Morris that Thomas Wolfe wrote "bad books" Willie should not waste his time reading. The youngster had been led to seek Wolfe's works by an unlikely source—the actress Linda Darnell—when he read in a movie magazine that the North Carolinian was her favorite writer.

sidewalk ledge where blacks allegedly sat to chat, spit, and whittle and—by opening car doors—knocked them from their perches. Bales thought it would be "a stretch," physically, to accomplish that; a Yazoo businessman thinks the tale likely is fanciful; though a contemporary of Willie's he never heard of such harassments and no one else I talked to professed to know of the "nigger knocking"—as Willie sometimes put it when telling the tale.

Willie told Jack Bales that when his father advised him to "get out of Mississippi," Rae Morris was concerned that Willie's "liberal" racial views might get him in trouble. I very much doubt that, never having heard Willie Morris make that claim to anyone else and there is nothing *I* can find to indicate that seventeen-year-old Willie Morris took any actions, or said anything, that would have set him apart from his contemporaries when it came to "supporting the Southern way of life." Surely, if he had, in that time when the sap was rising for civil rights wars not far in the Southern future, his heresy would have been long remembered and harshly remarked on—not only in the society at large, but by his fearful Mississippi mother—something that simply didn't happen. JoAnne Prichard Morris thinks that Bales may have misunderstood Willie and believes that Willie was talking of his father's concern at a later time, when Willie came home from the University of Texas with more progressive racial ideas, after the Supreme Court's decision in *Brown v. Board of Education.*

But Willie's immediate predecessor on *The Daily Texan,* a young woman named Shirley Strum, from deep East Texas—almost as Southern as Mississippi—editorialized for racial integration much more forcefully than did Willie Morris; Ronnie Dugger, another *DT* editor who preceded Willie and later became founding editor of *The Texas Observer,* outshined Willie in that regard, too.

And it is a matter of record that in his junior year at UT Willie wrote in the December 5, 1954, issue of *The Daily Texan* that—despite the Supreme Court's order in *Brown v. Board of Education* that the nation's public schools should be integrated "with all deliberate speed"—a go-slower policy should be followed. Three juxtaposed columns (written by UT students Tom K. Barton, Carl Burgen, and

Willie Morris) addressed public school integration in that issue of *The Daily Texan* respectively slugged "Now," "Tomorrow," or "Someday." Willie wrote, under "Someday," that "this question of actual equal political and social rights for Negroes involves such fundamental changes not only in superficial customs and manners, but in inbred ideas and ideals, that only a patient and comradely approach to the problem can be of permanent good." Although that was the most reactionary view expressed in the three articles, one must remember the temper of the times: Even Willie's go-slow position as expressed in his article would have brought down on him great castigations, and perhaps physical threats, had it been so openly expressed in his native Mississippi or in other die-hard Southern states where "Never!" was the battle cry.

It is a fact, indeed, that Willie Morris while visiting home attended at least one White Citizens' Council meeting, though let me hasten to add it was as an observer rather than a participant. The WCC was organized after the *Brown* decision. The White Citizens' Councils were made up of so-called good whites—businessmen, community leaders, many of them soft-spoken and genteel. But they were united in a basic cause with people they likely would not have welcomed to their homes—rednecks, the unwashed, screamers and shouters and Ku Klux Klan members or sympathizers. That cause was, in acceptable social language of the period, "the preservation of the Southern way of life" and, in harsh reality—to quote Alabama's Governor George Wallace— "segregation forever." Hard to say whether at that point in his life Willie Morris was more disposed toward racial integration than his writings then revealed, whether—as sometimes happened in his later works—he used words to conceal as much as to reveal.

CHAPTER 2

STEPPING OFF THAT TRAILWAYS BUS in Austin in 1952, Willie Morris entered a far larger and more complex world than he previously had set foot in: "Everything around me was brisk, burgeoning, *metropolitan*. It was bigger than Memphis when I was twelve."

Willie's portrait of himself as a seventeen-year-old who was "frightened . . . desperately homesick . . . unbearably displaced and alone" probably isn't too far off the mark given his tender years and his limited experience outside of Yazoo precincts.

But, Willie-like—I believe—he probably exaggerated the bumpkin impression he purportedly made on three "frat rats" who met him at the Austin bus station, probably because he had looked good on paper and they hoped to get a leg up on other fraternities that might be inclined to rush him. They were severely put off, by Willie's account, "because of my green trousers and the National Honor Society medal on my gold-plated watch chain" and, later, by his table manners. That simply is not of a piece with the recollections of others—nor of his own early actions, which show a single-minded intent to attain and achieve in his new surroundings that simply could not have been possible from a gravy-slurping bumpkin in green britches.

Willie immediately started making a place for himself: trying out for—and winning—a position on *The Daily Texan* staff (and being given a by-line column, something that just *never* happened with lowly frosh). His first by-lined story appeared in the school newspaper dated September 17, 1952, and far from revealing a bashful bumpkin—though he admitted to "a forlorn feeling of homesickness"—it was largely a take-the-bull-by-the-horns piece. The over-line above the headline ran, "Well, Here I Am"—as if, perhaps, he had been eagerly awaited by more than the few frat rats who had met him at the Austin bus station. "In time"—young Willie wrote—"I will be as important as the next fellow. . . . I will make my way, confident and unafraid, into the world. . . . I have made my way from one life to another, and now I am ready to lick this old world."

Willie involved himself in much of campus life: playing intramural baseball and touch football; joining everything from the Freshman Council to student government to the ROTC band; offering his hand and a grin to everyone while working the room as efficiently as a professional politician. In Austin, as in so many other places, his friendly quips, funny stories, and merry eyes made it appear that he was interested in you and *only* you.

"I was an ambitious little son-of-a-bitch," Willie blurted to Dr. Orley B. Caudill, conducting an oral history interview for the University of Southern Mississippi in 1979. So ambitious, indeed, that he opted as a sophomore to enroll in what eventually became twenty-one hours of journalism courses in order to qualify as a candidate for editor-in-chief of *The Daily Texan* his senior year. (Those journalism courses were "an enormous waste," Willie said, "except for one very basic course taught by old Mr. Owen Hinkle in copy reading, copy editing; just the fundamental core . . . which meant a lot to me. When I went to work at *Harper's* magazine, those basics were valuable.")

By the beginning of his junior year Willie was keeping a private ledger in which he tallied potential supporters toward his becoming editor-in-chief of *The Daily Texan,* taking pains to solicit "frat rats" and sorority girls that he claimed not to have enjoyed or associated with—until he needed their votes. Little happened by accident in Willie's determined climb. Marion Morris would have been proud of the way her son selected his goals and relentlessly pursued them, while managing not to look grasping or unbecomingly ambitious in the eyes of others.

I have found no one—not a soul—who recalls thinking of Willie at this time as "disenchanted . . . progressively more lonely . . . bitter . . . with cynicism in my heart," though that is how he recalled himself in Texas in *North Toward Home*. Others, including the studious University Sweetheart he would marry, recall him almost as an exciting amalgam of Superman, Edward R. Murrow, and maybe John F. Kennedy.

Speed Carroll, a fellow student, remembers young Willie Morris as the only person he met at UT "who seemed larger than life." Sam Blair, who would go on to a solid career in journalism, has recalled that when Willie first joined *The Daily Texan* staffers passed around an earnest letter one of his Yazoo High teachers had written to the campus newspaper's editor, calling Willie her brightest and most gifted student ever, and asking that he be given a chance to prove himself. This could have caused great misery for the outlander from Mississippi had his peers been inclined to dish it out, but in Sam Blair's words, "we soon realized Willie was a quick study and the years proved that behind his baby blues thrived a brilliant, creative mind, a fierce pride and a tough will."

"He had a natural gaiety when he was young and when 'gay' didn't mean what it does today," wrote Willie's ex-wife, Celia Buchan Morris, in her informative memoir, *Finding Celia's Place*. She recalls meeting at an intramural football game "a lanky, loose-jointed guy from Mississippi with a thatch of light brown hair and a face that belonged behind a tall ice cream soda," a teasing youngster who almost immediately asked her out for coffee. She accepted. "I'd read his column in *The Daily Texan*, and I not only liked the wry way he ridiculed our pieties but thought the rhythms of his prose now and again sensational."

Celia Morris (she still retains Willie's last name, though she had a second marriage to—and a divorce from—the late Texas Congressman Bob Eckhardt) recalls that at UT Willie "drew people to him whose spirits were heightened by his company, so that our lives often felt more charged and delicious when he was around." And again: "He seemed so much less parochial than the rest of us . . . he could talk knowledgeably about the blight of Senator Joe McCarthy or the mess the British were getting into at Suez. He could make politics come alive with spicy anecdotes, and if you add to all that the fact that he had a passion for books and spoke of certain authors as though they were related, if distantly, you have a truly interesting person. He was biding his time in the boondocks, but nobody I knew doubted he would end up in the very midst of the action."

It is amazing how much alike are the comments when old friends or associates speak of the youthful years of Willie Morris and, in a later time, of another bright-eyed, personable, talkative young man out of a southern small town, one William Jefferson Clinton. And David Halberstam says of Willie Morris and of another son of Mississippi a generation older, Turner Catledge, who rose to power at *The New York Times,* "In another time both Willie and Turner probably would have become governors or United States senators, given their adroit ways with people, their intelligence, their interest in the public welfare, their obvious personal ambitions and their instincts to lead or at least influence events."

But because, as Mississippi men in a time when that state often elected the worst possible choices—such vitriolic, crude die-hard racist spokesmen as the Vardamens, the Bilbos, the Eastlands—men like Willie Morris and Turner Catledge, as political candidates, would have had to pander to segregationists and neither was willing to take that low road. Thus, they chose to participate in the big world as journalists. Bill Clinton, of course, had the good luck to come along in a calmer time, after the civil rights wars and attendant violence had been stilled.

WILLIE APPLIED THE SAME APPROACHES to establishing himself at UT that he had used to become a Big Duck in the small pond that was Yazoo City. He used his native intelligence, a gift of gab, a talent for knowing how to reach others. Though later Willie would agitate many of those in power, not many originally failed to receive his respectful greetings or handshakes. He paid particular court to his academic instructors, as he had to his high school teachers, and of course they loved that.

Sounds pretty calculating, huh? Well, if so, the original strategy must be credited to Willie's mother. Surely she presumed that her tireless ministrations and admonitions to her son (no less insistent than Fagin's in training his London street urchins as thieves, one dares suggest) gave him valuable guidance; she was only being the kind of "good mother" that every boy deserves. She was the instigator.

What Mrs. Morris seemed unaware of, however—then or later—was how harassing or smothering her constant attentions, drills, and orders must have seemed to a kid struggling to grow up and find his own identity. As one of several friends who accompanied Willie to Yazoo City in early 1967, for his speeches and readings from the then-unpublished manuscript of *North Toward Home,* I saw his agitated, worry-wart mom in action and frankly wondered how a younger and more dependent Willie had kept from going mad.

Mrs. Morris made us hide in her kitchen to drink and urged us to rinse our mouths with Listerine before going into the parlor, where she taught music to local children on her baby grand Steinway piano, to greet callers coming to see Willie and to meet his visiting friends. Even though we complied and were mannerly, Willie's mother's hands shook, and at times she seemed in a near-catatonic daze; in other moments she darted from here to there and back again without apparent purpose. She grew so upset when Norman Podhoretz and I told a questioning young reporter that yes, surely, we favored racial integration in the South as well as in the rest of the nation, that she literally poured more coffee on her parlor carpet than into her visitors' cups—and seemed not to notice. Until Willie chided his mother that we had a right to speak for ourselves, she had begun to say to the scribbling reporter, "Now I think what these boys really *mean* is . . ."

Terribly disconcerted when she learned that Willie would read and speak at Yazoo High #2—the Negro school—as well as at all-white Yazoo High #1, she took to her bed with a "sick headache" that conveniently gave her an excuse not to attend. Prior to suddenly taking ill, however, she had cut Willie out of the visiting herd long enough to implore him not to speak at "#2" because it might offend the local powers-that-be.

Although Willie rejected his mother's advice, it was her *attempt* to so influence him that caused Willie to retreat to the Yazoo Motel for almost all of the remainder of his visit, having those of us gathered with him to say during his mother's repeated calls, "No Ma'am, Willie's not here right now and I don't know where he is." It was during Willie's dark brooding in that motel room that I correctly guessed he absolutely never returned home without bringing one or more friends along to interpose themselves between himself and his mother. "Don't leave me alone with her," he once whispered to me in his boyhood home on Grand Avenue.

During that trip, Willie said his mother had pinned on him, when he was very young, a hated nickname: *"Winkie!"* Willie said, twisting his lips in an expression of distaste. When he ran for a class office, young *William* Weaks Morris—his birth name—came up with a campaign slogan: "Don't be Silly/Vote for Willie!" Mrs. Morris hated "Willie"; it was undistinguished, she told her son, and not a "nice boy's" name; she fought a determined battle to retire it. Her son, however, campaigned incessantly with everyone he knew—kids and grown-ups alike—to call him "Willie"; he introduced himself as such, wrote that name on his schoolbooks and on school papers. Long after most people had forgotten that he had ever been called anything but Willie, his mother continued to fight a rear-guard action. Almost until her death in 1977, she wrote to her son as "Winkie" or "Winks" on occasion or, most of the time, "Dear WM." (Willie did not object, years later, when his wife JoAnne called him "Winkie Mo," and David Rae Morris thinks his father even signed a few letters that way.)

"I never understood exactly what my mother was afraid of," Willie once told me. "Everything, it seemed. Once I said in my monthly call from England that I had spoken to the Young Socialists League at Oxford—on politics in the United States—and her reaction was, 'Oh, Son, don't have your picture made with any of them!'"

So I was not surprised, years later, in reading Willie's *Taps* to meet its youthful Mississippi protagonist at times being driven half bonkers by his mama's suffocating tutelage—so much so that he once locked her in a closet and fled the house. It is not, I think, a thing that Willie did in real life, though it well could have represented a fond wish.

"The original draft of *Taps* was harder on the fictional mother than she wound up after many rewrites," says Larry Wells. "Willie softened her considerably."

Still, as Celia Morris has said, remember this about Mama: She was in Willie's early years an effective coach and guide; she instilled ambition and a desire to excel and started him on his way. And, yes, it was an eventful journey not without its thrills, satisfactions, and real accomplishments.

WILLIE MORRIS CAME TO *The Daily Texan* at a time when much of America seemed pretty well satisfied with the status quo. In those bland Eisenhower years it seemed that people wanted only material changes, not social changes: new cars with bigger fins, larger houses, more work-saving kitchen gadgets, better roads in the burgeoning suburbs. Veterans who had given vital young years to World War II service were intent on making up for lost time; they were serious about college, jobs, establishing careers, getting ahead. Men not long out of olive-drab uniforms seemed not to mind wearing another in the era of the gray flannel suit, so long as it helped them "fit in."

Business was brisk enough that Republicans could brag "Everything is booming but the guns"—never mind that the boom included backyard bomb shelters, an arms race with the Soviet Union, and a National Highway Program that was advertised as primarily a "national defense" necessity: More and bigger bombs could be moved faster over the new roads system, which also would assist as a speedy evacuation route if-and-when we got into the expected nuclear exchange with the Soviet Union. In that time when school kids were taught to crouch under their desks with their arms wrapped around their heads as a "defense" against atomic bombs, "You could pass just about anything in Congress if you gave it a 'National Defense' tag," recalls former Texas Congressman Charles (Good Times) Wilson. "And that was true for thirty years or more. The

Cold War was a God-send to most politicians. Not only could they place military bases and payrolls in their districts, they could wrap themselves in the flag."

The 1950s was a time when "national security" considerations prohibited known homosexuals from holding government jobs, because they allegedly were fair game for blackmail and thus might reveal official secrets, and a time in which Wisconsin's Republican Senator Joe McCarthy, a drunken bully and congenital liar who had no special knowledge of Communists in government or otherwise, stumbled on the notion of becoming the arbiter of patriotism and loyalty in the United States. Soon he terrorized the State Department, paralyzed the timid Eisenhower White House, and was feared by his colleagues in Congress, especially after he campaigned against—and helped to defeat—Maryland Senator Millard Tydings, who'd had the temerity to cross McCarthy. In time, Senator McCarthy and his chief counsel, Roy Cohn, purged government libraries of "dangerous" books and even challenged the U.S. Army's commitment to "fighting Communism." Senate Majority Leader Lyndon Johnson told intimates that McCarthy at the moment was "too powerful to challenge," though he confided that the Wisconsin demagogue was a drunk barely able to tie his own shoes. Many money men in Texas who supported LBJ—largely because he supported the oil depletion allowance, which made the first 27.5 percent of oil profits tax free (a boondoggle if ever there was one), and often sided with conservatives in their intra-party fights with Texas liberals for the good political reason that he knew the conservatives would win—also were white-hot McCarthyites. Indeed, Texas was a hotbed of McCarthy supporters; when the Texas legislature invited "Tail Gunner Joe"—as he liked to be called—to speak to it, State Representative Maury Maverick, Jr., was booed and reviled when he offered an amendment seeking to include Mickey Mouse in the invitation resolution. Even when the U.S. Senate finally decided that McCarthy's excesses had weakened him enough that he could be censured—and he was, in December of 1954—LBJ was careful to conceal his masterminding of the censure effort behind the scenes, so as not to arouse the wrath of Texas money men who remained McCarthyites.

Governor Allan Shivers, a nominal Democrat, mocked Ike's opponent Adlai Stevenson's accent ("Are they likely to throw *to-mat-toes* at me in Texas?") in leading Texans into the Eisenhower camp in the 1952 election; his Lt. Governor, Ben Ramsey, the anti-labor, anti-liberal, anti-intellectual equal of Shivers, presided over the State Senate and ruled the Legislature with a whip and a glare; the first thing he asked newly elected solons was, "Are you on the team?" Unless they quickly responded in the affirmative, they received no further recognition, no favors, no breaks. "You could wind up being appointed to what we called 'the Toilet Paper and Ice Water Committee,'" recalls former State Legislator and Congressman J. T. Rutherford.

Daily newspapers in Texas were slavishly adoring of the reigning powers: *The El Paso Herald-Post* was the only big-city daily to endorse Adlai Stevenson for president. The voices of liberal Democrats in Texas were few and faint in the Texas hinterlands. In an atmosphere in which most adults were so tame and docile, if not fearful of being branded as a Red, who could expect a bunch of kids running a campus newspaper in Austin to charge the barricades?

Then, quite suddenly, it seemed, here came this baby-faced rebel from Deep East Jesus—not even a *Texan,* now—and before you could say "I Like Ike" he was making sport of the pieties and mores of the Ruling Texas Establishment. *How dare this smart-assed kid piss on the well-shod and shined feet of the mighty?*

The Powers were as surprised as they were shocked—largely because, for most of his first three years as a *Daily Texan* staffer, Willie Morris had not made much noise. His job as a freshman columnist was to read the exchange papers—i.e., other college newspapers from all across the USA—and in his column, "Neighboring News," summarize items that would reveal what was happening or being talked about on other campuses. Willie would write in later years that he had received an education from reading those exchange papers, especially comments about national and world issues. Strangely, however, he rarely shared them with his own readership; mostly he seemed to have used items that he could joke about and that helped him end with a good punch line. Frankly, those early columns if read today are not impressive. Nor was there much that distinguished Willie's sophomore columns and stories, when as the newly named intramurals coordinator, he wrote about campus sports. As a junior, writing a weekly column called "The Round-Up," Willie began to poke fun at politicians and local mores, making use of satire and parody, but little foretold the firestorms he would start as editor-in-chief.

That top job was gained by winning an election involving the entire student body. Willie Morris campaigned hard, hand-shaking and personally soliciting votes. His campaign platform promised

> Fair, hard-hitting editorials; a free thinking, tolerant, virile liberal *Texan;* conscious desire to prevent an inert, indifferent University populace; sincere effort to make *Texan* respected, if not agreed with; elimination of cliques on staff; more staff spirit and unity; complete editorial independence; daily columns by editor, managing editor; interpretive columns by campus authorities; weekly summaries of local and non-local news; sensible campaign to produce more readable interesting *Texan;* Union expansion; creation of academic atmosphere at UT; more liberal cuts system; open Regents' meetings; better student-professor relations; monthly current events forum; good-reading course; class poem contests; honor system where workable; independent platform.

Well, okay. Not much there to shake people's souls, even if they waded through all those promises: It was only a *political platform,* for God sakes, and how many of *those* were adhered to once elections were over? Besides, who gave a damn—or even knew about—cliques on *The Daily Texan* staff or the degree of spirit among staffers? And don't you know the school jocks and chronic layabouts were delighted to hear of class poem contests and a good-readings course? And what the hell did "honor system where *workable*" mean?

Maybe the Powers should have paused and pursed their lips over "Union expansion" and "complete editorial independence" and perhaps "independent platform"—but they would have had to giggle at "open Regents' meetings"—which, everyone knew, simply wasn't about to happen; maybe that promise was so foolishly unreal-istic as to negate any serious expectations of other reforms listed in Willie's platform. *Besides, the boy put somethin' in there about "interpretive articles by campus authorities," right? So maybe the kid ain't all bad. More'n likely he's just playin' politics to get elected.*

His shake-and-grin campaign got Willie Morris elected by more than 1,400 votes; he more than doubled the total received by his op-ponent. Probably Willie was the only person in the world aware of the thunderbolts he was about to let loose.

Almost immediately he began to attack the policies of Governor Allan Shivers, who had appointed most of the UT Regents. He at-tacked the oil lobbyists who controlled the Texas State Legislature and shamed the legislators for permitting rich Texas to lag near the bottom of states in care of the aged, the infirm, and the children of the poor. He excoriated UT Regents themselves for their closed meetings and for caring less about students and academic freedom than about adding more bricks and mortar to the rapidly expanding campus. He scorned the sacred 27.5 percent oil depletion allow-ance and the Harris-Fulbright Natural Gas Bill, which would free oil companies from paying *any* federal tax on gas at the wellhead. *Damn that smart-mouthed kid! Who the hell does he think he is?*

Willie had told 'em in his first editorial as editor-in-chief who the hell he was; had they paid attention they clearly would have heard his call-to-arms:

> Joseph Pulitzer once said a newspaper has no friends—to re-phrase, *The Daily Texan* has no obligations. [It] is bigger than any one man. We will protect it and its tradition with our youth and our strength, and if necessary, with our personal reputation. You will be jostled, cajoled, embarrassed. Yet, through our telescope of ideas, you will see your life here in much nobler focus. We have been appalled by the tragic shroud, which cloaks our undergradu-ates. This student apathy, this disregard of all save the most mate-rial, is a thing of the mid–20th century. If we do not kill it now, here on a thousand campuses, it will eventually kill us—an ugly cancer polluting the bloodstream of democracy.

For a while, Willie seemed to be making inroads: He actually did get UT Regents to open their meetings to *The Daily Texan;* a few weeks later the Faculty Council agreed to open theirs. Perhaps the authorities hoped to appease Morris, thinking if they opened their doors he might not criticize them so often about so much. Willie refused to be co-opted; his drummings didn't cease. Authoritative mouths began to curl down. Willie was "invited" for curative chats by faculty authorities; they did not receive much satisfaction from several meetings; Willie Morris was polite, but firm in his responses: *The Daily Texan* had certain obligations, and he intended to meet them. Alarmed, the authorities put in place what amounted to a faculty censor—an action that further roiled the waters.

If faculty "advisers" killed editorials, Willie originally retaliated with tongue-in-cheek editorials titled "Let's Water the Pansies" or "Don't Step on the Grass." But he dropped his own bomb, eventually, when a front-page editorial attacking the Harris-Fulbright Natural Gas Bill was suppressed—UT owning all those oil-rich lands throughout Texas, after all, and profiting handsomely from tax-free boondoggles. Willie's response was to leave a huge blank hole on *The Daily Texan*'s front page where the suppressed editorial should have appeared, with the eye-catching headline "This Editorial Censored." That spoke louder than any conventional protest he could have composed had he used a month of Sundays.

Other campus newspapers, and some dailies outside of the oil states, then obtained copies of the censored editorial from Willie and prominently displayed it in their own pages. Guess how much the faculty and Regents appreciated that. A big-talking Regent named Frank Voyles unwisely boasted that the Regents would soon reduce Willie's voice, and the voices of his supporters, to nothing more than "a college yell." But his comment caused more voices to rally behind Willie Morris.

J. Frank Dobie, then perhaps the most famed of Texas writers, author of many books, and a beloved former UT professor who himself had run afoul of a reactionary university administration, rushed to Willie's aid with his classic comment that the UT Regents were "as much concerned with free intellectual enterprise as a razorback sow would be with Keats's 'Ode on a Grecian Urn'"—a quip immediately picked up around the nation and still quoted a half-century later. Many of America's daily newspapers made of Willie Morris a brave young martyr—a literary David taking on a crassly commercial Goliath—while excoriating or poking fun at his tormentors. The editors of *The Nation* asked Willie to write a piece about his editorial wars; "Mississippi Rebel on a Texas Campus" became his first piece published in a national magazine. More and more Willie's detractors became less and less eager to tangle with him, which of course vastly increased his power. (A few months after Willie graduated UT, the faculty rose up against the administration's proposed regulation that would have prohibited faculty members from "public advocacy of, or opposition to, candidates for governor, lieutenant governor and the state legislature." The faculty passed a resolution of its own, supporting the "right publicly to support candidates for any public office." UT Regents, probably fearful of a greater uprising after all the battles with Willie Morris and the public relations shellacking they had taken, refrained from attempting to veto the faculty resolution.)

Still, neither Willie nor his newspaper nor his ideals escaped unscathed. Some UT students wrote angry letters to Willie or to *The Daily Texan* taking exception to all the controversy and "dividing" of the campus. Some faculty, and newspapers, asked why it was bad for the *state* university to profit from state oil properties, since benefits would accrue for many years to hundreds of thousands of Texas kids who would be well educated and then settle into jobs, businesses, or positions of leadership in their native place; so who was getting hurt? There even was a certain amount of in-fighting and hard feelings on *The Daily Texan* staff. After Willie had editorialized in favor of Adlai Stevenson being invited to the UT campus as part of a "Great Issues" program, his own managing editor—Joseph Goulden—quite pointedly wrote a column criticizing Stevenson's being invited because, he implied, the invitation politicized the Great Issues program. Just as pointedly, Willie Morris rushed to the typewriter to let everyone know who was boss: "Our columnists (Goulden, Jerry Wilson, Toxic Texan) may air any view they please, within the bounds of ethics and decency. Censorship is a nasty instrument, and we would never violate the individual dignity of any journalist by dictating his personal beliefs. We prefer rebuttal to suppression. . . . Goulden is a conservative. The editor is a liberal. That means *The Daily Texan* is liberal." In other words, partisanship *was* at work as to the newspaper's editorial policies: So what? How did that differ from the editorial policies of commercial newspapers in Texas? QED. (Goulden, to this day, thinks Willie Morris was spoiling for a public fight—and started one—without worrying about long-range consequences. "Tom Sealy, of Midland, President of the Board of Regents, got in touch with me and told me I should tell Willie that he and the other Regents were disposed to take actions assuring *The Daily Texan* wouldn't have as much power in the future, if he persisted," Goulden says. "I told Willie of Sealy's warning and said, 'Willie, you're likely to screw it up for everybody, and I don't think you want to do that.' But he paid me no mind.")

The Texas Student Publications Board of Directors, made up of five students and five faculty members, met after Willie's big run-in with the Regents and recommended—not ordered—that: (1) Morris avoid "facetiousness" in future editorials, (2) "reduce" the amount of space "given to controversy" in *The Daily Texan*, (3) "already controversial issues in sensitive areas should be avoided" in the future, and (4) "New controversial issues in the future should be handled only as news stories." The *Austin American-Statesman* headlined that story "UT Editor Gets Mild Reprimand"; the text said Willie received only "a mild spanking" and noted he was not ordered to stop his campaign. Willie was a member of that Student Publications Board of Directors, as each editor-in-chief of *The Daily Texan* has been, and he did, indeed, attend that meeting. He said little or nothing, however, and after the meeting his only comment later was, "I take note of their *suggestions.*" Maybe so, but he then pretty much ignored them.

Morris later said he regretted his reign had been so "clamorous" and said the confrontations between students and UT authorities—leading to an "official censor" being put in place to check the campus newspaper's content (one of the actions Regent Tom Sealy had threatened)—had been the opposite of what he had wanted. He also wished he had made more use of "the sharp edges of humor and satire"—he told Jack Bales in a 1997 interview—"but back then I was young and a little frightened, because this was big time stuff."

In his final editorial, however, Willie credited his policies with certain "positive gains." Never again, he wrote, would gas and oil moguls "so sanctimoniously rule the University"; college students would be more alert against state politicians corrupting university affairs; students' rights would not be so "brutally mistreated"; college journalism would not be so lightly regarded. The Board of Regents could never again bludgeon students or faculty with a bill the legislature had passed that prohibited them, really, even from expressing opinions about actions involving "political matters." There is little doubt that Willie Morris left UT feeling like a reformer who had won most of his big battles.

AND IF THE RULING POWERS at UT have remained wary of Willie Morris—even as their antecessors were—the youngsters keep reminding us that they have not forgotten his reign. Any underdog victory is long-lived because it is so rare in a world where, routinely, the big 'uns gobble up the little 'uns. And that is why even today—a half century later—youngsters writing for *The Daily Texan* consider Willie a founding father and are proud to walk in his footsteps.

In April of 2002, the newly renovated Delta Tau Delta fraternity house in Austin formerly dedicated The Willie Morris Room, housing a collection of his works and memorabilia donated by Dave Williams, chairman emeritus of Alliance Capital and a Tau Delta alumnus, spearheaded by JoAnne Prichard Morris, who attended the dedication ceremonies along with numerous of Willie's pledge class members, and by Larry and Dean Faulkner Wells of Yoknapatawpha Press of Mississippi. JoAnne Morris also arranged for a portrait of Willie to be painted, framed, and hung.

Marshall Maher, occupying Willie's old chair as editor-in-chief of *The Daily Texan* at the time of the dedication, wrote an editorial commending Delta Tau Delta's actions, "In Memory of Willie Morris," in which he said,

While Morris' efforts did help end the overt censorship of the *Texan*, the aftermath he left was quite severe. *Texan* editors lost their votes on the Texas Student Publications Board. Editors' presence at TSP Board meetings are largely symbolic without a vote. But the reputation Morris helped forge for the newspaper became the biggest insurance policy against administrative abuse. The level of leadership he established set a high bar for everyone to follow, but one we revel in maintaining every day. The spirit of Willie Morris is alive at the *Texan* today. . . .

CHAPTER 3

HARRY RANSOM, dean of arts and sciences at UT in Willie Morris's time there—and who would go on to become president, then chancellor—urged Morris shortly after the beginning of his senior year to apply for a Rhodes Scholarship. It was not a thought that had entered Willie's head. He respected Ransom, however, finding him much less aloof and remote than other faculty administrators. So with the added encouragement of a couple of his professors, Willie decided to give it a try. He thought himself a long shot on learning that the university had not produced a Rhodes Scholar in more than a decade.

In *North Toward Home* Willie recalls himself as surprised when he survived the campus and regional competition, and as full of fear and trembling when he flew to New Orleans for the Southern finals: "The interviews were held in a big hotel in the French Quarter, and I got a room in a flophouse across the street. I stayed up a good part of the night before in that cold, bare room reading W. J. Cash, and went to sleep with the most terrible visions of imminent failure." Earlier that night he had attended a party for the dozen competitors, given by the interview committee members, themselves all former Rhodes Scholars. Willie's account of his reaction to his competitors, written years later, has him uncomfortable, almost awed, and uncertain in his conversations. Most of his competitors, Willie wrote, "came from the best Eastern schools; in their carefully tailored suits and their button-down collars, I thought they were the smoothest people I ever encountered, for they could talk with an easy grace about everything from the book publishing business to the stock market to all the nuances of the objective correlative." Willie reports himself as crossing his legs and standing in awkward positions while trying to hide the cigarette burn at the cuff of his trousers and, altogether, miserably wondering how he had gotten himself into such a fix. (None of those recollections jibe with what other Rhodes Scholars of that time recall of Willie Morris; we have already seen that some thought him perhaps the most outstanding individual in an outstanding group; one Rhodes Scholar did tell JoAnne Prichard Morris that when he first met Willie he thought, *"This guy will never make it at Oxford."* But, he said, "within a few weeks Willie seemed to know everybody there and had them eating out of his hands." Another Rhodes Scholar, a West Pointer who first met Morris while sailing to England, thought him the most fascinating of an exceptional group.)

During his questioning by the interview committee in New Orleans—after he had answered questions ranging "from America's foreign policy to Eisenhower's farm program to the modern novel"—Willie found himself having to defend William Faulkner against the criticisms of the committee's chairman, owner of an Alabama lumber company. Willie began talking about the Emmett Till case in Mississippi and quoted Faulkner: "If we in America have reached that point in our desperate culture when we must murder children, no matter for what reason or what color, we don't deserve to survive, and probably won't." Then he got involved in the legal complications of that trial and "got myself in a difficult position over my interpretations of the law"—while being hectored by the chairman. Ultimately, another southerner on the panel, a lawyer, came to Willie's defense: "Mr. Morris is absolutely correct on his legal discussion. He knows the law and has presented a fair and accurate description of the trial."

When the names of the four selected as Rhodes Scholars were announced, Willie turned to a fellow candidate and asked, "Did I hear right?" He had heard right. In a twinkling he had become one of what Cecil Rhodes had called "the best men for the world's fight."

As soon as possible, Willie called home: His father—who never had made over $75 per week—had a quick, joyous, and practical reaction: "Boy, you won't *never* have to worry about getting a good job now." Afterwards, Willie "in a happy state" roamed the night streets of old New Orleans, "streets George Washington Cable and Sherwood Anderson must have walked, up Canal Street with its extravagant stores and hotels, then to the flophouse again for a night of fitful thoughts about Oxford—'to the strands of the daughters of the sunset, the apple tree, the singing, and the gold.'"

I HAVE NOT FOUND IT EASY to understand how Willie Morris truly felt about Oxford and his Rhodes Scholar experience. This man who could, and did, talk with humor and gusto and passion of almost any subject or personal experience rarely talked about Oxford of his own volition. When I tried to quiz him—and I can be a pest when curious—Willie was not forthcoming. His responses were anecdotal rather than analytical or emotional or even truly informative. In time I would come to understand that the same few Oxford anecdotes he told me were the same ones he repeated in his slim writings about that place.

One such anecdote related how Willie had escorted Robert Frost in a taxicab for the New England poet's appearance at Rhodes House. "Where you from, boy?" Frost purportedly asked. Willie replied, "Mississippi." "That's the worst state in the Union," Frost responded. Stung, Willie said, "Well, it has produced a lot of good writers." "Can't anybody down there read them," Frost is said to have grumped. Certainly that story captures the essence of the somewhat frosty poet, no pun intended.

Perhaps Willie's favorite anecdote was how, in 1956, he had stayed up all night polishing his paper for his first tutorial, which was on the Reform Act of 1832: "My next-to-last sentence said, 'Just how close the people of England came to revolution in 1832 is a question that we shall leave to the historians.' I read this to my tutor, and from his vantage point in an easy chair two feet north of the floor he interrupted: 'But Morris, we *are* the historians.'"

In *North Toward Home* Willie wrote but two pages about Oxford. In 1980—from Mississippi—he wrote for *The Texas Quarterly* an article called "The Other Oxford," giving his first detailed examination of that place. Of his first year at New College—which, Willie liked to say, hadn't been "new" since the fourteenth century—Willie's piece said: "We Americans found ourselves, quite suddenly, taking meals in those darkened medieval dining halls, surrounded by portraits of heroes and warriors and kings, princes and scholars and poets, prime ministers and parliamentarians and ecclesiastics; living for the first time amid crumbling walls and towers predating the discovery of America; eating at society dinners with silver two or three centuries old." What that says is that in myriad ways Yazoo City or Austin or the University of Texas ain't no Oxford: But how did Willie Morris *feel* about the place in his heart and in his head? In 1989, "My Two Oxfords" appeared in Willie's book *Homecomings,* with art by Mississippi native William Dunlap; it was more a comparison of two cities and cultures than anything like a gimlet-eyed examination of the English Oxford, however.

"In a Shifting Interlude," written after Willie and JoAnne Prichard had visited Oxford and New College—Willie's second visit since he had completed his four-year Rhodes Scholar stint, and his first in thirty years—was published in *American Way* magazine (and reprinted in 2002 in a book edited by Jack Bales, *Shifting Interludes,* and published by University Press of Mississippi); in it, writing of his initial days there, Willie opened up a bit:

> We encountered an England still in the ruin of war. And in Oxford we confronted one of the preeminent universities in the world, if not *the* foremost, in its inwardness and nuance and sweep, a nexus far removed from our native ground, where the measure was more languid and the aspect more subtle and evasive, a repository of the dire complexities of mankind. The sacrosanct privacy of the place, the almost studied eccentricities, the enervating fogs and rains, at first elicited a loneliness, an angst and melancholia such as I had never known before. The advanced civility of our new milieu, the weight of its history, where every

blade of grass had known a dozen drops of blood, the Old World tensions, seemed cloying and troublesome, and the mementos of mortality were everywhere, in the lugubrious graveyards, in the interminable rolls of the war dead in the college chapels, in the dampened dusks and spooky midnights.

But, earlier, had not Willie Morris loved to roam the graveyards of Mississippi even at "spooky midnights"? Had not his playing "Taps" at the funerals of Korean War dead, and visiting every Civil War battlefield he could find, somewhat equated with "the interminable rolls of the war dead in the [Oxford] college chapels"? Perhaps England's "every blade of grass" had known more blood than America's grass—England being so much older and more frequently invaded—but American blood had spilled at home in the Revolutionary War, the War of 1812, in wars against Mexico and frontier wars against Native American "Indians," and of course the Civil War: the one closest to Willie's soul and the bloodiest ever on American soil.

I can only conclude that the eternal dampness, and seizures of homesickness—which he mentioned to me more than once—accounted for Willie's loneliness, angst, and melancholy. He is, after all, noted for having said on a chill English morning when standing on a cold floor, "Oh to be in April, now that England's here."

"Yet slowly, the spell of Oxford grew"—Willie wrote—"until one was suffused with it, with its majesty and largesse and thrall. We became Oxford men, and the elegiac and lofty mosaic of it would be part of us forever, and also the ambivalent misgiving." That is about as much as he ever tells, except descriptions of the landscape and eccentricities witnessed among scholars and dons. Little or nothing is revealed of the specifics converting Willie and his colleagues into "Oxford men."

Some years later Morris attempted a novel set in Oxford in the 1950s, *The Chimes at Midnight,* but eventually bogged down. He made three or more stabs at going back to that novel but never progressed to his satisfaction; he *talked* about it fairly frequently and the more he talked about it the more it sounded as if it might be moving forward, taking shape in his mind: In a 1976 interview he said *The Chimes at Midnight* was giving him trouble because "Oxford University was such an exotic experience for me. And I've always had a difficult time trying to relate it to the stream of my whole life. Because you're there in the place, you're living in what amounts to a work of art . . . you're overwhelmed with this horrendous sense of the past . . ."—and that, presumably, made for very difficult writing.

As early as October of 1973, Willie Morris wrote to a Mississippi friend, Harriet DeCell (who, with JoAnne Prichard, wrote *Yazoo: Its Legends and Legacies*), that he was working on *The Chimes at Midnight*, saying that while the book was set in England it would be "intensely American." He added of his protagonist:

> Outside his window in his Oxford college, the American boy—the Southern boy—sees every day an old wall, 13th Century, around which the blood and anguish of civilization has transpired. Gradually it begins to teach him that all the noble things molded by the wall have derived from human suffering—and in one luminous twilight, in England in 1957, he begins to become a feeling man, to perceive that there is some ineffable link with his own violent, brooding land of the delta. . . . [A]ll of what I am telling you is not as pretentious as it sounds. It is a little tale that occupies only a few hours: 4 P.M. to just past 1 A.M.

By 1980 Willie was saying that when he got *Taps* finished—thinking, then, that wouldn't be long in the future—he felt he would be ready to return to his Oxford novel. A year later he told a reporter that he felt his "best stuff" was yet to be written, and included *The Chimes at Midnight* in his hopeful inventory. And as late as 1997, only twenty-six months before he died, Willie told Jack Bales that novel "has been bothering me a long time" and was much on his mind. The incomplete work is among the Willie Morris Papers at the University of Mississippi.

Edwin Yoder, Jr., having read the incomplete manuscript of some 100 pages, said it had "fine passages in it, though unfortunately no real story line had developed by the time Willie abandoned it."

Yoder knows what the novel was to be based upon: A friend of Willie's, a budding historian, fell from the old city wall at Oxford one night, busted his head and suffered rather severe brain damage; that incident haunted Willie, apparently, for the rest of his life. "When we were young and foolish we routinely scaled those hazardous walls, climbing in and out of various colleges," Yoder has written; the implication is that any of the reckless young men—including Willie Morris—might have been seriously injured, or killed. Willie was both touched and horrified by his young friend's accident; given his sensibilities the potential seems great for a worthy literary work to have resulted. But, alas, with respect to *The Chimes at Midnight,* we can only sigh in regret and wonder what might have been.

In 1958 Willie got a transatlantic telephone call from his mother, telling him that his father was dying. He borrowed money from the warden of Rhodes House to fly home: "Sixteen hours later I was in Mississippi, dislocated to the point of schizophrenia." Rae Morris was gaunt and wasted from cancer. This former church scofflaw had a surprise for his son: He had become a Christian. "When you got what I got, and know it, you do one of two things. You either blow your head off with a shotgun or you become a Christian." He also told Willie that "where ever he was" after death, he would always look out for him. Willie wanted to respond in a kind and healing manner, to tell his father that if he ever had a son he would name the boy after him, but the budding man of letters couldn't find the intimate words—a fact that bothered him forever after.

As soon as he decently could, Willie left his father's bedside to drive to Austin to ask Celia Buchan to marry him and accompany him back to England after his father's imminent death. This now seems an impulsive act, considering that Celia was not—it turns out—Willie's college sweetheart, as he long advertised. He both wrote and talked of his "sweetheart" who also was "the official Sweetheart of the University of Texas" (true) to whom hundreds sang "The Eyes of Texas" as she was presented an armload of roses. But by Celia's recollection, "We dated sporadically my junior year, when he was a senior. I certainly didn't date Willie exclusively, and I assume he went out with others. I've said and written that I fell in love with his prose style, and also his defiance, and I was very excited about his getting the Rhodes. With hindsight, I see that Willie and I were just *ideas* to one another. Good ideas, mind you . . . but that's not the stuff that anchors marriage." Celia recalls that even after Willie presented her an engagement ring, "I didn't say yes for several days and can only look back with sadness on that hesitation. Something in me knew I shouldn't do that. . . ."

Celia wrote in her memoir, *Finding Celia's Place,*

> Of course, marrying Willie gave me a precious chance to defy my father in ways that he could not object to openly. A man who thought drive and brains mattered could hardly complain about a Rhodes Scholar who had captured national press attention. And the prospect of living in Oxford among the most promising men of our generation was way beyond anything I had ever hoped for.
>
> So Willie was escape, defiance and adventure. And I expected us to go through life as crusaders together—he as a journalist, I as a college professor—and complementing each other; while he was actively fighting the most important social and political battles of our day, I would make sure we lived always in the presence of the "best that had been thought and written."

So Celia said "Yes."

Shortly after her commitment, Willie wrote a piece about their going to the courthouse in Houston to get their marriage license; it was published in *The Texas Observer* of August 29, 1958, under a headline obviously not written by a poet: "A Routine Ritual on a Rainy Morning"; it should have been headlined "Their Hearts Were Young and Gay." Willie's romantic streak was showing. He ended the piece with a reference to a marriage chapel lout who had been crassly hustling them, and all others in the marriage license line, and who approached them again grinning "obscenely" as they left the county clerk's office.

"Well, it won't be long now," he said. Celia smiled and winked at me with both eyes and took my hand and we walked outside. It was still pouring, and she laughed when she almost slipped down again. In the rain, her short black hair drenched, her dress wet and clinging close, little-girlish and alive, she was the most beautiful woman I had ever seen.

Celia now feels that she and Willie then felt a mutual sense of "hope and commitment." But—alas—she has recorded that she soon knew the match had not been made in heaven after all:

By the time we got to Oxford, some six weeks after our wedding, I had clues enough to predict how the marriage would end if I had known how to read them, but I didn't. Quite the contrary, I was so committed to the idea of marriage as a freely chosen partnership that it was unthinkable to me that our marriage could fail. . . . In time, Willie would write about our passionate honeymoon, but the passion was his . . . and though I hadn't acted implicitly on advice a formidable British Queen gave her daughters: I simply lay back and thought about England.

Beyond that, Willie was a loner. His father had died a few days after our wedding, and on the way over to England he spent a lot of time lying in his bunk with his face to the wall. I took this to be grieving, but it turned out that when he was troubled, confused, or just out of sorts, he would take to his bed and throw up an impenetrable barrier of silence. The tall tales and high spirits he saved for the most part for company and the pub.

NO ONE HAS EVER TOLD ME that Willie was more smitten than was Celia, but I would bet money on it. There was a misty, old-fashioned, impulsive romantic streak in Willie; he was in love, I think, with the *idea* of love. That was like him: for all his belief that racial integration was fair and just and simply *must be* for the U.S. Constitution to mean anything, for example, he still harbored gauzy notions of the Old Confederacy that probably had never been true—a Tara, noble,

Gone with the Wind Confederacy, one with dashing Rhett Butlers and brave young men dying for The Cause willingly and perhaps even bloodlessly. So, too, his violin-music-and-magnolia-moonlight vision of romantic love. He would learn in time—several times, in fact— that such a vision was difficult if not impossible to maintain unless one worked hard at holding two hearts and heads together; the record is clear that he didn't do much such work. Yet every time a new woman caught his fancy he mooned and sighed and for a time believed the old love songs all over again.

Celia was more practical; she examined "romance" with a keener and more demanding eye and is not known ever to have lost her heart to anyone sans prospects. Once Willie had attained a Rhodes Scholarship, "I began to look at Willie a little more attentively." Celia had had a purpose and never lost sight of it: "Since I wanted to live 'on the front lines,' and the world I lived in reserved its levers of power for men, the only way I knew to be 'where the action is' was to marry a man who might hold one of those levers."

Marriage to Celia likely would not have been easy for most men; she did not suffer fools gladly, she had a strong sense of her own worth in a time when many women did not (or, if they did, sup- pressed it), and she had an impatience with those who gave her short shrift that might have done credit to the angry Old Testament God. Her second marriage—which also ended in divorce—was to Texas Congressman Bob Eckhardt, an icon to liberals and who, like Willie Morris, was no slouch as a raconteur; he was also an essayist and cartoonist with a bite, and he long had been a political kinsman of Willie's as well as a personal friend. (Indeed, Willie wrote Eck- hardt an intimate letter when the latter married Celia, saying he could think of no one he would prefer over Eckhardt to be a stepfa- ther to David Rae.)

Certainly Eckhardt, named by *New Times* magazine as one of the "ten brightest" men in Congress and respected by his colleagues for his intellect and his mastery of House procedural rules, had his hands on one of those "levers of power" when Celia married him. Worst luck, however, Eckhardt soon lost his congressional seat in a district that had in a single decade moved from being a Democratic

to a Republican stronghold. Eventually, Celia found Eckhardt wanting in ways not dissimilar to her discontent with Willie Morris.

If Willie could not learn that romantic love of the hearts-and-flow-
ers kind was tough to sustain, Celia seemed strangely blind to the
truism that most ambitious men with their hands on power levers
are, at bottom, more concerned with themselves, their careers, and
their power than with anything—or anybody—else; that is why and
how they get to be so powerful in the first place. She was naïve, I believe—if ultra-confident in her own prowess—to presume that she
could turn her husbands against such old and proven drives and
compulsions to the extent that she would become a true partner in
their lives. Such men rarely seek true partners; what they want are
converts, followers, admirers who will do their bidding and/or
chant praises. So the exact qualities Celia sought in a husband—
power, prestige, status, a will to make the world turn—were the qualities that would, in the end, shut her out and frustrate her.

Celia and the young Willie Morris shared some traits in common,
yes. She was intelligent, socially and politically liberal for her time
and place; she loved good literature every bit as much as Willie did.
(And would go on to write several critically praised books.) Probably
she was the more intellectual, or at least more inclined toward *practicing* intellectualism. And certainly she doted on academia more
than did Willie, though both in their own ways had uses for it.
(Though Celia had stood in a spotlight while a band played "The
Eyes of Texas" when she was elected Sweetheart of the University,
when later elected President of Mortar Board, a National Honor Society, she said through tears that she was much more gratified than
when winning "that other" honor.)

But if Willie and Celia shared certain traits or outlooks, they had
been raised a great deal differently—and therefore shaped differently. Celia's early life in Houston was at once more urban and ur-
bane than Willie's; she grew up in a larger and grander house; her
parents were college graduates: mother an interior designer who
also drew up display ads for newspapers until—in the custom of the
day—she quit to become a full-time housewife; father an oil company chemical and petroleum engineer who could quote from

Chaucer's *Canterbury Tales* in Middle English, a talent that surely would have mystified Rae Morris. Both Celia and Willie had one parent who could be overbearing: although Celia stood up to her father in arguments and simply may have been tougher than Willie was, more determined to defend her turf.

Certainly Celia was more accepting of professional help when she was troubled, spending several years in analysis; Willie hated shrinks and blamed Celia's for her discontent. Celia ultimately recognized her alcohol problem and quit—after she and Willie divorced—though it was a battle that took years and was not without periodic setbacks; Willie never even admitted his alcoholism, conceding only, and rarely, "I'm not drinking anything but wine right now"—never mind that if one drinks enough wine he or she can become as grass-grabbing drunk as those staggeringly stoked on vodka, bourbon, gin, or whatever.

Celia was not as accepting of sub-par housing or a paucity of other worldly comforts, matters that did not much concern Willie. Oh, he liked the good things well enough, but if deprived of them he made do; it seemingly didn't bother Willie to sleep on a bare mattress or a pillow without a case—as he often did after he and Celia divorced—or to drink straight from the bottle as opposed to goblets or to wear wrinkled clothing perhaps stained by last night's supper.

Celia expected better and was accustomed to better; she had, I believe, a much stronger sense of entitlement than did the kid from modest circumstances in backwater Yazoo City. Only after Willie Morris became a "star" in the media world did he develop a sense of entitlement; it must be admitted, however, that once attained it grew like Topsy.

Perhaps it remains for Celia Morris herself to define a key factor in her marriage:

> Our everyday exchanges were usually pleasant enough, but neither of us had the slightest idea about how a man and a woman went about loving one another or managing intimacy. Since his parents, like mine, lived in a state of barely contained hostility that nobody

talked about, we had nothing, really, to go by; and for whatever deep psychological reasons, Willie wasn't about to risk trying.

WILLIE MAY HAVE SPENT much of the trip to England on the *Queen Mary* with his face turned to the bulkhead, brooding, but Celia had an absolute ball. Her new, and exciting, companions were the incoming Rhodes Scholars of 1958. A Houston friend had told the new boys, at the pier—Celia wrote—that Celia "was a red-blooded egghead's dream girl, [thus] I began that trip with a certain aura. Nothing, in fact, could have been more exhilaratingly safe: I was desirable and off limits. As a senior member of the Rhodes community, Willie was the source of precious knowledge about Oxford, so our table was always crowded. And since all these gifted men were showing off for each other, they were at the top of their form: funny, hopeful, sly." Celia danced with the young men into the wee hours, watched the sun come up over the ocean, "stood on deck in crisp fall weather watching whales on the horizon and fell into long disputes about the respective merits of Faulkner and Hemingway." And, she added, "Oxford itself was even better."

Celia's memoir goes on page after page enumerating the interesting people she met—scholars, dons, artists, a man who gave her a private recording of Casals playing Bach, others who read aloud the works of Tennyson, Hopkins, and Yeats; the films she saw by Ingmar Bergman and the early Fellini; on stage, there was Charles Laughton as King Lear, Michael Redgrave as Hamlet, Paul Robeson as Othello, Peter O'Toole as Shylock in *The Merchant of Venice,* and Vanessa Redgrave and Albert Finney as lovers in *A Midsummer Night's Dream.* There were ancient architectural marvels to explore, art galleries galore, libraries with valuable old tomes chained to the wall. It was, altogether, a cultural feast, and Celia Morris gorged on it; her enthusiasm shines through all these years later. A Rhodes friend even arranged for Celia to do tutorials with a New College don in her study of Greek tragedy. It just couldn't get much better than that.

"All this was breathtaking—no milder word for it—and I was profoundly grateful to Willie Morris, without whom none of it would have been possible." But, like the Lord, Celia giveth and Celia taketh away: "And my gratitude worked to muffle my deep unease with Willie, for when you live with someone who isn't really there, I soon discovered, it is much harder than living alone. That year I saw quite a lot of Willie's back, and nothing I could think to say or do bridged the distance between us. He wasn't interested in what I worked on, and when I asked about his own reading in British history, he said he didn't want to talk about it until he got it on paper. But somehow the right time never came. At the pubs—the King's Arms, the George, the Bear—and in company anywhere, he told good stories, but after a while I knew the repertory." And one day, Celia remembers, "Willie and I passed on opposite sides of the street while making belief we didn't see one another." In essence, in Celia's celebration of her years at Oxford, Willie is reduced to little more than a cameo role—a role, she obviously believed, Willie had already assigned to her in their relationship.

In New York in the mid-1960s, when I first met Celia Morris, she had sparkled in talking of her time at Oxford and once said she hoped one day to write about it. Willie, as I have said, talked little of Oxford and at that time had written absolutely nothing about it. One of my *Harper's* colleagues wondered aloud whether Celia had been "the star" at Oxford while Willie had failed to truly prosper there. In due erosion of time, I tried out that theory on Edwin Yoder, Jr., who had been a Rhodes Scholar with Willie, and before that—when he was editor of the college newspaper at the University of North Carolina, *The Daily Tar Heel*—had supported Willie Morris in Willie's battle against censorship of *The Daily Texan*.

"Not so," said Yoder, who had become a Pulitzer Prize–winning editorial writer, syndicated columnist, book author, and college professor; that was a cockeyed theory: Willie had done truly outstanding work at Oxford ("I can't think of anyone I knew who did more") and had become "one of the favorites of the great warden of Rhodes House, E. T. (Bill) Williams, whom we all admired and loved." Warden Williams had, in fact, arranged for Willie Morris to extend his stay at Oxford to a retroactive third year, with stipend, after he had earned a degree in modern history. He read American history, with Civil War and Reconstruction emphasis, under David Donald, Harmsworth professor of history.

As to why Willie never wrote much about Oxford, Yoder offered "informed speculation," saying: "Willie and I, and others among those who had a grain of sense and sensibility, held that place in awe; and Willie was haunted, in that special way of his, by the ghosts of all the great figures who had been there over the centuries. I think, probably, he yearned to write about the Oxford experience, but feared to be glib or superficial, and so shied from it. Few enough of us managed to compress that experience in prose or poetry." (In later years, Robert Penn Warren would tell Willie Morris that he himself didn't get so much as a poem out of his Oxford experience, although he considered his education there a valuable one.)

Yoder concluded, "I believe Willie shared my view that when you're walking in the footsteps and shadows of the likes of Shelley, Halley, Gibbon, Dr. Johnson, and innumerable others, some modesty is in order." Willie and Yoder knew each other well; Yoder for some years probably was Willie's best friend. Willie typically found a way to enjoy his pal Yoder's Oxford circumstance: Of Yoder, who was a member of Jesus College at Oxford, Willie often invoked the words of an old Protestant hymn, saying, "What a friend we have in Jesus!"

NEAR THE END OF WILLIE'S TIME AT OXFORD, he received a letter from Ronnie Dugger, founding editor of *The Texas Observer,* whom Willie had known and admired during his *Daily Texan* stint— and where Dugger, a few years older than Willie, had also been a campus editor-in-chief. He was tired and needed a break, Dugger wrote; he wanted Willie to join his *Observer* staff as associate editor and soon take over as top editor while Dugger went off to think, rest, and maybe write a book; he offered long hours and a salary of $110 per week, about the same money Willie had made as top man at *The Daily Texan* four or five years earlier.

Willie Morris found himself eager to again do journalistic battle. As he wrote in *North Toward Home,* "I accepted with alacrity, for I felt waterlogged with the past. I recognized then, with the same melodramatic seriousness as Jack Burden, abandoning his PhD dissertation in *All the King's Men* to enter the employ of Willie Stark, that I must 'go out of the house and go into the awful convulsions of the world, out of history into history and the awful responsibility of time.'"

When Willie and Celia sailed for America in June of 1960, there was a third member of the party: David Rae Morris, who had been born on November 1, 1959. Willie never tired of saying that under the British system of "socialized medicine" his son had cost the American equivalent of 82 cents, "and was worth every penny of it."

PART TWO

UPWARD AND ONWARD IN THE REAL WORLD

"I don't know if you're the man, but I have a hunch you are. You write pretty well and I notice you've put some humor into the Observer. You could try it up here for a while and see what you think. I'll do the same. It's premature now. I won't have an opening for three or four months. But get in touch with me . . ."

—JACK FISCHER

editor-in-chief of *Harper's* magazine,
stunning Willie Morris in early 1963 by writing
that he'd like to groom Willie as his successor

CHAPTER 4

WILLIE MORRIS AND RONNIE DUGGER had become fast friends long before Dugger asked Morris to join his *Texas Observer* staff. Willie looked up to the man, with whom he had a great deal in common and who, at that juncture, had accomplished more professionally. Indeed, Morris had written a front-page paean to Dugger in *The Daily Texan* issue of May 14, 1954, saying that even as an undergraduate Ronnie's "surname became synonymous hereabouts with vitality of thought and freedom of expression" and saying he had the potential to become an outstanding economist, teacher, or writer.

"I think we probably met in my second year at UT," Willie said years later. "I would almost bet it was over a pitcher of beer at the Scholtz Garden. Probably with Billie Lee Brammer or one of Dugger's legislative pals. When I recall Austin, it just seems Dugger was always there."

Dugger, political to the bone, had flown his liberal flag proudly while editor-in-chief of *The Daily Texan*. The lead story on the front page of Dugger's first *Daily Texan* issue was headlined "Three Negroes Approved for UT"; he spoke up for the civil rights of people of color, and he endorsed the university's affiliation with the liberal National Student Association. He wanted drunk drivers jailed in a time when most Texans seemed not to realize what dangers they posed to life and limb, and many thought their roadway madness somehow cute or humorous.

No consumer gouging was too small for Dugger's attention: He urged students to boycott barbers who had raised the price of a haircut from 85 cents to a dollar; sometimes he got so worked up about almost everything—not enough pencil sharpeners for students, not enough telephones in the dorms, the rolls weren't hot enough in the cafeteria—that one might have wondered if he could sustain enough outrage to go around. He poked his nose into city politics as well as campus politics, backing this candidate and opposing that one.

Dugger did not know what "compromise" meant. LBJ, who as a U.S. senator had felt Dugger's lash, attempted to court him but gave up when Dugger wrote a critical article about *specifically how* Johnson had been heavy-handed in his courtship, making it abundantly clear he found the heralded senator a crass opportunist not above selective ass-kissing. Thereafter, LBJ branded Dugger a "kamikaze liberal" or a "red hot"—liberals who insisted on the whole loaf where a practical, working politician would accept the half loaf rather than get no bread at all. Ultimately, LBJ grew so weary of Dugger's barbs he growled to a staff member, "If you investigate that boy's bloodline, you'll find a dwarf in there somewhere."

Dugger received his B.A. degree in government in the summer of 1950—two years before Willie Morris entered UT—with minors in economics and journalism. He did graduate work at UT in economics for a year, then won a Rotary Foundation fellowship to study at Oxford (again, economics being his main course) and after a year in England he returned, at the beginning of 1954, to UT for more graduate work. But in late 1954—at age twenty-four—he took over as founding editor of *The Texas Observer,* and for years thereafter had eyes or time for little else.

The "new" *Observer*—one that Ronnie Dugger largely shaped and defined before he agreed to be its editor—was the successor of a rather erratic publication called *The State Observer;* its first issue, on December 13, 1954—carrying as its slogan *An Independent Liberal Weekly Newspaper*—was further defined by Dugger: "We will serve no group or party but will hew hard to the truth as we find it and the right as we see it." Not long afterwards, he added the line *"A Journal of Free Voices."* Most of the money to begin the new *Observer* had been put up by Mrs. Frankie Randolph, of Houston, who was a rare combination for a Texan of that period or perhaps any other period—personally wealthy and politically liberal.

Dugger dug his talons into Governor Allan Shivers, conservative state legislators, uncaring corporations, fat-cat lobbyists, the reactionary *Dallas Morning News,* LBJ, and any person or institution who failed his high standards of honesty and caring. One week, early on, he actually worked 120 hours; he drove all over Texas, goading, questioning, preaching, writing "red hot" stories and smash-mouth editorials, trying to sell *Texas Observer* subscriptions—his goal was 10,000 subscribers rather than the 6,000 he had—and hoping to awaken the masses to how shoddily they were being served by most of their alleged representatives.

Billie Lee Brammer, Dugger's associate editor for a bit over a year, thought Dugger nearly demented in his frantic efforts:

> . . . his sap was high and clearly rising in the early days . . . his drives and demon-lusts and continuous manic flights and forced landings were clearly the offshoot of some whale-sized egomania. . . . He was never guilty of cozying his resources, of rat-holing on a human need; he was never covetous or grasping or even very thrifty with himself when it came to squandering emotion or imagination or any part of his ransacked warehouse of vitality on another. . . . I couldn't see why one should feel so all-fired obligated to any group, or crusade, however exalted and nobly motivated. . . .
>
> There's no point in dwelling on the abuses, the staggering corruptions, that so many of us news people knew about or suspected but couldn't print or wouldn't discuss in print. Ronnie got us off our dead centers by simply poking into things and talking to people and, most astounding, actually writing stories about what he had learned. Soon there were wounded hoots and wild cries and a crazy circus of exposures, copped pleas and even one or two indictments. . . . I don't claim that the *Observer,* all by itself, cleaned up the state of Texas or that the state of Texas is now, by any wishful stretch of the imagination, even reasonably responsive to the

public needs and public ethic. . . . But the *Observer* did outdistance the competition . . . and did it so dramatically that the very concept and thrust of political reportage in Texas underwent a general overhaul and reorientation. The *Observer* made this little miracle, and I seriously doubt whether the paper would have lasted out its first year without Ronnie, without his total commitment, all his resources and crackling nervous vitality. . . . From the day he took over the editorship . . . it was clearly obvious that if Dugger wasn't the *Observer,* the *Observer* was Dugger.

But even miracle men can run themselves ragged. Dugger after six years had done that; he said, later, that for about the last eighteen months of his stewardship he had lacked energy and was pleased with only one story he developed in that time. For a man as dedicated to his calling as was Dugger, that knowledge was both painful and intolerable. So he called on his friend Willie Morris to come give him much-needed respite.

Though Dugger had indicated he almost desperately needed to escape the *Observer* to recharge his batteries, he did not immediately surrender the editor's job to Willie Morris when Willie joined the staff in July of 1960. Probably there were two reasons for this: Willie, who had never in his Texas sojourn spent any appreciable amount of time outside of Austin—save for one summer when he worked for Dugger a few weeks between school terms—felt that he needed to travel widely in Texas; he knew that nothing would familiarize him with it quicker, or better, than to observe its local mores, rituals, and habits: everything from high school football—where stores closed on Fridays in mid-afternoon at the latest in Kermit, say, so locals could garb themselves in Yellowjacket maroon-and-gold to invade the lair of the red-and-black clad Colorado City Wolves some 140 miles to the east, jangling cowbells and singing fight songs as the noisy caravan moved rapidly down Highway 80, the old Bankhead Highway, for war under the Friday night lights—to local political pie suppers where the slyer candidates took pains to buy for top- dollar the pies or cookies allegedly baked by the wife or daughter of a particularly influential citizen, an act entitling him to eat the goodies with that family and smack his lips in ecstasy at the culinary heaven the womenfolk had made, to the usually secret and often brutal machinations of courthouse political machines, to beer joints where a quick understanding of the reigning protocol might save one from embarrassments that—given rotten luck—could include a broken jaw. "We're arbiters of manners down here," Texas club owner Eddie Wilson of Armadillo World Quarters in Austin once explained. "See, an ol' boy might call another one a chickenshit motherfuckin' cocksucker or some such and the second ol' boy will think that's ill-mannered and break the other fellow's jaw."

Willie took it all in: the lonesome and baked, flat, desert Trans-Pecos country; the scenic Big Bend and Davis Mountains; the Texas Gulf Coast with its palm trees and pelicans; the stark Panhandle with its limitless cattle ranges and sudden winter blizzards visiting from the North Pole; the East Texas piney woods with its thick accents and yah-hooing segregationists that must have reminded Willie of his native state; Midland, a management and Republican stronghold, only twenty miles from a blue-collar working man's town, Odessa, both of them sitting atop and prospering from the rich, vast Permian Basin oil pool; the good-old-boy informality of Fort Worth; the up-tight and tie-choked denizens of Dallas; the sprawl and early, whizzing freeways of Houston; San Antonio's meandering downtown river and the historic old Alamo pressed God-close now by hotels and smart shops not far away from abject slums populated by poor Mexicans.

The other reason that Willie did not immediately assume the top job at the *Observer*, perhaps, was Dugger's natural reluctance to relinquish the reins, despite his weariness. He had the strongest of proprietary instincts for the publication that he had, after all, brought into the world and he didn't really want anyone else to raise his love child. Several times, over the years, Dugger took long leaves of absence to write books or teach—living on the East Coast in Washington, New York City, or Massachusetts—but almost always, no matter who the editor replacing him might be, Ronnie seemed incapable of keeping his hands off the *Observer*. A year before Willie Morris died, in fact, he told his old friend Malcolm McGregor of El

Paso—"almost bitterly"—that Dugger would neither assume true control of the *Observer* nor permit anyone else a free hand to run it. He was also miffed that Dugger was flirting with becoming a Green Party candidate while maintaining an *Observer* connection. This, Willie thought, did the publication a disservice and flew in the face of its long-time printed pledge "to serve no group or party." Morris told McGregor that he and old friend Dugger had exchanged "harsh words."

But when the bloom was on the rose, Willie—who said that Dugger had taught him more about writing than anyone else ever did and who took control as editor and general manager with the issue of March 4, 1961—ran the *Observer* very little differently than had Ronnie Dugger, except for not being wound quite as tight.

Willie probably worked as hard as Dugger had—if that's possible—but on him it didn't show as much; he was quieter, more relaxed, he found more time to quaff a few beers with legislators and such writers and artists as a much smaller Austin then had; many of these became his best sources for finding out who was doing what to whom, and for what purpose, inside the state government.

Though Willie most enjoyed the company of liberals—State Representatives Eckhardt, McGregor, Maverick, and "Whiskey Bob" Wheeler, scion of a wealthy family who enjoyed saying that, like FDR, he was a "traitor to his class"—he also cultivated conservatives who visited Austin's most popular beer garden and its downtown hotel bars; he knew that some drinkers, tight-mouthed when sober, would, after a few hits of the residue of the grape that pleases, babble like a brook.

If there was one big change in Willie's *Observer* it probably was that the copy was brighter and humor was more prevalent. I once wrote of Dugger that he had "a sense of humor on a par with that of a firing squad" but now admit that may have been a slight exaggeration.

Robert Sherrill, an *Observer* associate editor who claimed to be a native of Frog Leap, Georgia, and who, Willie once said, stayed around to cover the legislature "because he found so much to laugh at," provided some humor in the *Observer's* pages, usually through sarcasm.*

Billie Lee Brammer chipped in with his barbed parodies, sometimes in the form of short plays. Non-staff contributor Dan Strawn occasionally sent in straight-faced country boy reports on political events in his hometown of Kenedy, Texas, that provided a few belly laughs and many wide grins. Not until Molly Ivins joined the staff years later, however, did the *Observer* find the biting in-house humorist it long had needed.

Willie Morris in the main limited his *Observer* humor to tongue-in-cheek sallies. He once called a press conference to lecture with a straight face on the new punctuation policies of the *Observer,* leaving many of the attending reporters thoroughly puzzled. He took a page from Bob Sherrill's book in allegedly "defending" legislators—who had adjourned without acting on numerous major public needs or problems—for passing bills lauding constituent birthdays and Boy Scout Troops in encampment and for "boldly" endorsing United Way or Red Cross drives and other such meaningless fluff designed to ass-kiss voters at no risk to the puckerer. He delighted in reporting the response of Jack Crain, a House member from Nocona and an early-1940s UT All-American running back, who said—on being asked why he had been the only House member to vote against a bill requiring trucks hauling migratory workers to provide good brakes and tarps against bad weather—"Aw hail, Willie, you start passin' stuff like that and there's no tellin' whur it'll all end."

*Sherrill could be personally committed, too, as he proved when working for a legislative committee headed by State Senator Don Kennard, who was investigating the plight of migratory workers and their families. An ex-football coach just promoted to school principal in the Panhandle area, whom Sherrill was interviewing, said naw, he *didn't* give a damn about the children of migratory workers—mostly Mexican—and didn't want them dirty little boogers in *his* school and for that matter did not want *Sherrill* there either so git on outta here.

Sherrill responded by driving a few blocks before deciding he had too easily retreated, so he wheeled about, re-entered the school, and whipped the mouthy fellow's ass satisfyingly enough that he was jailed. Senator Kennard had to send a lawyer from Austin to bail him out. Sherrill went on to write a number of books, including a bare-knuckle hit on LBJ as *The Accidental President.*

Politically, Morris deviated not a discernible whit from Dugger's endorsements of the leftward-most candidates available in statewide or legislative races—with one notable and, I think, notorious exception. Against the howls of many who called themselves liberals—myself included—Willie's *Observer* in a special election in 1961 endorsed Republican John Tower for the U.S. Senate seat that had been held by LBJ until he became vice president, rather than the conservative Democrat, Bill Blakley, who had been appointed as interim senator by conservative Governor Price Daniel. Dugger's—and Willie's—position was that "Dollar Bill" Blakley was no Democrat at all, but the tool of special interests; they could beat Tower, they said, when he ran for a full six-year term at the expiration of his interim term against a *good* Democrat running for the seat. They miscalculated by almost thirty years, which is how long the ultra-conservative John Tower held onto the Senate seat he captured with, ironically, help from those "kamikaze liberals" LBJ so despised.

Years later, I asked Willie why and how he could have made such a terrible decision in the Tower-Blakley race. "I followed Ronnie on that one," he said, "but I'll admit I thought he was right. I've had a lot of time to rue that decision."

Willie Morris kept hammering at Dugger's favorite targets in his remaining time at *The Texas Observer:* the shameful $67.50 per-month maximum that any individual in a rapidly growing old-folks population could draw in state assistance; continued segregation in campus housing and in sports programs at the University of Texas; the need for better wages and living-working conditions for migratory workers and their children. He urged mandatory health benefits and retirement benefits for working Texans in the private sector, many businesses—newspapers included—providing exactly none; protested unsanitary conditions in nursing homes that were regulated hardly at all; stressed the futility of the death penalty as a deterrent to future murders; decried illiteracy, especially among children of the poor.

Routine *Observer* fare, yes, but in a time when Texas daily newspapers did a rotten job of reporting political and legislative actions (or inactions), that fare was valuable. The problem was that not enough "plain folks" read the *Observer;* its readership seemed largely comprised of savvy political activists and influential liberals in Texas and elsewhere—meaning that, all too often, the *Observer* was preaching solely to the choir—except for some few conservative politicians who subscribed so as to keep tabs on the enemy. Some headway was made in placing the *Observer* in Texas libraries, but one must wonder how many people on the street knew of its availability, or cared. Willie Morris for a time tried an even larger circulation drive than had Dugger—he aimed for 12,500 customers rather than the old goal of 10,000—but, in reality, not many new subscribers were gained. (The only way the *Observer* has survived through the years has been by periodic fund-raisers among its die-hard supporters. Though *Observer* editors, and Ronnie Dugger, have several times publicly "hoped" each new rattling of their cups would be their last, money appeals to long-time subscribers and supporters were still going out at this writing.)

Willie kept up a torrid pace, chasing about the state with U.S. Senator Ralph Yarborough, Governor Price Daniel, then State Senator (and soon to become the first Mexican-American from Texas in Congress) Henry Gonzalez. He covered President-elect Kennedy's only visit to LBJ's ranch on the banks of the Pedernales, noting JFK's reluctance to put on a cowboy hat or shoot a deer as recommended by his vice president–elect. Willie wrote thousands of words per week, edited copy, laid out the paper's makeup, trucked it to the printer, stood by to make corrections, then trucked the product back to the *Observer's* hole-in-the-wall office to make it ready for distribution. Nobody could fault the job he did: Celia Morris recalls that after reading Willie's descriptions of the state legislators at work, no less than Norman Mailer said that "neither he nor anybody else need bother with the subject further."

But the job soon took its toll. Ronnie Dugger required six years before calling for help; Willie Morris, "worn out," threw in his cards after only twenty months. Much later he would say that running the *Observer* was the hardest job he'd ever had: "It was a lot harder than running *Harper's* because at *Harper's* I had good people working with me and it was a monthly. And you had the great writers contributing." Probably there was an unspoken reason why Willie didn't last as long as Dugger: The *Observer* represented to its founding editor something of a life's work, a dream, a love child he had sired. It held no such fascination for Willie Morris: The special place in his heart would prove to be reserved for *Harper's* magazine. Nor did Willie Morris ever feel a special affinity for Texas, to the extent that he loved Mississippi: Mississippi was his heart's country, and always would remain so, no matter where he wandered. And although Willie remained fond of numerous Texans he kept in touch with and saw when he could—Ronnie Dugger, Malcolm McGregor, Bud Shrake, Billie Lee Brammer—he went back to Texas largely to make speeches, sign and promote his books, or accept honors. In my opinion, it never became a place he missed. (JoAnne Prichard Morris disagrees, especially as applied to Austin. "I had never been to Austin until Willie took me. We went three or four times and he loved showing me everything and *remembering*. I think he knew that Texas had done for him what no other place could have, and he appreciated it.")

In December, his car packed and ready for the long drive from Austin to Palo Alto, California, where Celia—the recipient of a Woodrow Wilson Fellowship—was seeking her master's degree in English at Stanford, Willie joined Ronnie Dugger and a couple of mutual friends for farewell drinks at a spot aptly named The Tavern. The old chums talked about politics, writing, books, and the *Observer.* Willie Morris slipped out of the booth to go to the men's room. Within moments the waitress approached and extended a folded note toward Dugger. "He's gone," Dugger said. He then opened the note and read aloud, "Goodbye, Old Friends. Willie."

CHAPTER 5

WILLIE ARRIVED IN PALO ALTO just before Christmas, but it was not a particularly festive holiday. Celia was none too happy in California; she had for some months debated whether to leave Willie for an Englishman "with a bawdy laugh" whom she had met in Austin, one John Sullivan, a rakish adventurer with—in Celia's words—"merry brown eyes with fine lines that fanned out at the sides and crinkled when he was happy and an easy-going disposition that made the crinkles permanent."

Celia and Sullivan had been having an affair for about a year before she left Austin for Stanford, a coupling that Willie did not appear to know about, or, if he did, he kept his peace. Celia wrote that when she told Willie that John Sullivan was teaching her Latin and she was teaching him to drive, that's all, her lie "helped Willie believe the line he really wanted" to believe. Willie was "sleeping around," too, according to Celia, and on *Observer* assignments "whizzed in and out of town, absorbed in what he was learning about Texas and dismissed my worries about David"—their son, who was slow to talk and had other problems he eventually outgrew—"as though they were the detritus of an idle brain."

While Willie was learning about Texas, Celia had been learning about passion from John Sullivan. A working-class lad from Liverpool, Sullivan eventually had attended Cambridge on scholarship and had been persuaded by an admiring friend to come to the University of Texas to edit a literary magazine. Sullivan was an intellectual

59

whom Celia almost immediately found attractive: He actually talked and listened to her, made her laugh, and "took my work seriously before I did." Sullivan taught Celia "to appreciate good wine and read Yeats." Eventually, he wrote poems for her "so that in no very long time I learned why people die for love." The attentions John Sullivan showered upon Celia Morris were precisely the kind she had so long craved but never had experienced.

This "wonderful lover" who had awakened Celia Morris to the joys of sex ultimately asked her to marry him. Whether to do that occupied much of Celia's time and mind at Stanford; her quandary seemed "hopeless" and without end; she repeatedly drove in the hills above Stanford hoping to sort out and order her mind but making lists of pros and cons "seemed a bloodless exercise."

Shortly before Willie arrived after quitting *The Texas Observer,* Celia decided to stay with him: Willie "was David's father, and I thought he needed me, where John did not. . . . Still there *was* a trigger" prompting Celia's decision: her sudden understanding that John Sullivan had taken up with another woman (not his first such wandering during his affair with Celia); she was "furious" that John hadn't even waited until she left Austin to take another bedmate. Knowing that Sullivan "could never be faithful" Celia wrote a "painful" letter breaking off their affair. Celia seems to think her relationship with Willie improved at Palo Alto, recalling him as "genial" and good with David Rae.

One must wonder, however, whether Willie was at all content once he had rested his bones from their *Observer* punishments. Little at Stanford broke his way. He sat in on a few random classes for a couple of months and then applied for a fellowship to get a doctorate in history. He was admitted but was denied the fellowship—and, without it, didn't have the money to press on. So Willie jangled around quite without purpose; he became increasingly restive. It was, obviously, a bad time in his career: He knew virtually no one in the whole of California and, worse, nobody knew him or of the young glories he had won. And Willie never had been of a mind to accept anonymity, to be faceless in the crowd.

It is clear from a few paragraphs in *North Toward Home* that Willie grew miserable in

> the suburban nightmare called Palo Alto. . . . The campus itself, set down in that sprawling suburbia, always reminded me of a high-class prison with its grim architecture—"Late Southern Pacific"—its broad gray quadrangles, its bedraggled tower. . . .
>
> Nearby ran a road, from San Jose to San Francisco, less a road to me than a reminder of what we had become in this country in the 1960s; its name was El Camino Real, mile after mile of chrome and asphalt horror, slicing through the debris of this American age: the used-car lots, the hot-dog stands, the drive-in movies, the jumbled up shopping centers, the motels owned by movie stars and lesser entrepreneurs—streamlined abominations that looked as if they would be lucky to last twenty years. Ten miles to the west the land ran out; at the shores of the Pacific the game was up. Among the few compensations for these surroundings, and for the pinched, in-grown life of the graduate students, were the lectures of the critic and teacher Irving Howe. In those classes filled with fraternity boys, automobile heiresses, and a handful of tense and deadly earnest Ph.D. candidates, he spoke brilliantly of the nineteenth century, which deserved no place in Palo Alto, of Mark Twain and Howells and James, of those sleepy unencumbered mornings on Huck and Jim's raft on the Mississippi, of Manhattan replacing Boston as the cultural center three-quarters of a century ago. At lunch at some outdoor roadside hamburger stand, squeezed in between a motel and a used-car lot, we talked with Howe about New York, where he belonged; one sensed it by the way he glanced out at El Camino Real, a tentative glance, suggesting some private obliteration.

Willie wrote in *New York Days* that only three things had pleased him at Stanford: "My two-and-a-half-year-old son running the olympian literary critic Yvor Winters off a campus sidewalk with his tricycle. Sitting in the centerfield bleachers at Candlestick Park watching Willie Mays of the San Francisco Giants and talking with him two or three times between innings of one-sided games. And the Garden of the Palo Alto Public library."

Willie had begun going to the Palo Alto library to peruse back issues of *Harper's* magazine, there being the best of reasons for this. Months earlier, as Willie was winding down his stint at *The Texas Observer,* he had received a stunning confidential letter from Jack Fischer, editor-in-chief of *Harper's.* Fischer had been editing that magazine for ten years, he said in his letter, but now he wanted more time for his own writing and was looking for his eventual successor: "I don't know if you're the man, but I have a hunch you are. You write pretty well and I notice you've put some humor into the *Observer.* You could try it up here for a while and see what you think. I'll do the same. It's premature now. I won't have an opening for three or four months. But get in touch with me in a couple of weeks."

Willie called Fischer in New York to say he was leaving the *Observer* to join Celia at Stanford, and he was at the moment weary to the bone but, yes, he certainly was interested in an editing job at *Harper's.* John Fischer told Willie to go on to California, to read, rest, and reflect and that they would talk later. In May of that year—1963—Willie rode a Greyhound bus from coast to coast to talk to Jack Fischer and, shortly, to go to work as an associate editor of *Harper's.* He was twenty-eight years old.

"I came to the city and it changed my life," Willie Morris wrote some thirty years later in *New York Days.* "I was exalted by it, exulted in it. I was a young man at a great personal threshold at a place and a moment throbbing with possibilities, observing America from here in its extravagant peaks and turmoils, giving myself to the town and it to me: a most American covenant."

Lord knows he did not take the job for the money. Mr. Fischer paid Willie only $125 per week for starters, slightly more than he had made at *The Texas Observer* when he quit there; even in 1963 that paltry sum barely kept the legendary wolf from the door, especially in Manhattan where costs were shocking to an outlander from Yazoo City or Austin. Still, Willie and Celia made do, with a little help from the "expense money" he drew from *Harper's,* though it was coin-purse sums compared to the "expenses" drawn by writers for such richer magazines as *Life, Sports Illustrated,* and numerous others. "The Luce magazines rarely questioned our expense accounts," novelist and screenwriter Edwin (Bud) Shrake, long a *Sports Illustrated* staffer recalls. "We wouldn't have thought of spending our *own* money for booze and laughs." Jack Fischer, however, went over *Harper's* expense accounts with a bookkeeper's eye and a miser's suspicions.

Celia wrote:

Willie had taken a railroad flat a few blocks from *Harper's:* a third-floor walk-up on East 28th Street between Park Avenue and Lexington. On the ground floor were the Gibson Girl Bar and the Delmore Cafeteria, which drew the taxis and the cops, so we never had to worry either about safety or cabs in a pinch. And though the windows apparently had not been washed on the outside for decades, you could make out the Empire State Building from David's room. The kitchen was in our bedroom, which you had to go through to get to the toilet, and despite or perhaps because of its obvious shortcomings, it was a sporting place. People who made it up the stairs invariably gasped when they walked into a cheerful, inviting space, and for awhile their expressions were worth the price of admission.

She clearly recalls the monthly rental was $125—or a week's pay before deductions.

Celia's "nesting instincts came into play." With friends she gave her weekends to flea markets in upstate New York and Connecticut and picked up Victorian chests, spool beds, a dry sink; with tiles she had bought in Europe she had carpenters make "a bewitching coffee table of wormy chestnut." Celia also cooked lunch for colleagues that Willie sometimes brought home: Jack Fischer, the historian C. Vann Woodward, the academic John Silber, Roger Baldwin, who had co-founded the American Civil Liberties Union. The men ate, usually thought to compliment Celia on her culinary skills but—

men-like—then rushed back to their offices and left the clean-up chores to the hostess alone, not that Celia expected them to do otherwise.

These and other inattentions, and inconveniences, begat new discontent. The charming walk-up apartment became somehow less so as Celia struggled up three flights of stairs, her arms loaded with grocery sacks while pausing to wait for her four-year-old son as he scrabbled up behind her. She walked three blocks to the do-it-yourself laundry, often had long, tedious waits to get a machine, then walked back home and up the stairs with her burden. Five days per week she took David by subway to the Bank Street School in the mornings and fetched him home in the afternoons. (David Rae, however, recalls "riding the subway alone to school by the time I was seven.") With no decent playgrounds in the neighborhood—and the barren, marginal ones attracting dirty old men swigging from pints of rotgut booze or cheap wine—Celia spent many hours arranging for David to have other children come to his home to play or go to theirs.

"In Willie's account of our time together in New York"—she wrote in *Finding Celia's Place*—"I am struck by the absence of dailiness. There are various ways to explain this, but the simplest is that his life and mine were very different then. And this was true for most men and women of our generation. Willie was absorbed in his thrilling new job, for which David and I were the backdrop. As he wrote in *New York Days, Harper's* magazine was the heart of his existence."

There's no quarreling with that. Willie's original assault on his new job was as determined as that of a soldier bent on capturing an enemy island. His reading of old *Harper's* issues dating back to its 1850 origins, accomplished in seven- or eight-hour daily sessions in the Palo Alto Public Library, gave him a great sense of the prominent role the magazine had played in an older America, and of its changes and its history, and made the young man from Yazoo City ache to become an important part of its future. "In its early years," Willie wrote, its distinction largely lay as a showpiece of English fiction: Dickens, Thackeray, Hardy, Trollope, the Brontës, George Eliot. From this transatlantic emphasis it gradually began to transform itself into an American journal on wide-ranging topics, both articles and fiction for an authentic national audience. . . . It published portions of Melville's *Moby Dick*. Henry James's *Washington Square* ran serially beginning in 1881. William Dean Howells, Bret Harte, William Gilmore Simms, Stephen Crane, even Horatio Alger. And, of course, Mark Twain. And did anyone know, as I was to learn in that library out on the Western littoral, that on that fateful morning in 1892 in Fall River, Massachusetts, Lizzie Borden was actually reading a *Harper's* before Mr. and Mrs. Borden fell to the axe?

Willie searched out the issue published the month and year of his birth—November 1934—to see what had concerned the editors of *Harper's* then: "It included pieces on the dangers of federal crime control, the Russian economy, population increases and racism in America." And "The grand centennial number of 1950 included Thomas Mann, William Faulkner, W. H. Auden, Eleanor Roosevelt, and Katherine Anne Porter, and even had a congratulatory essay by the President of the United States. This was heady stuff indeed!"

It almost seems superfluous to add Willie's declaration of love and intent: "I loved the faint musty smell of those worn volumes in the dappled sunlight. How I wanted to be its editor someday!" He lost no time in heading in that direction.

CHAPTER 6

WILLIE MORRIS HAD SPENT relatively little time in New York City before arriving to work for *Harper's;* he and Celia, en route to England for a new term at Oxford, once had visited the Austin writer Billie Lee Brammer in Manhattan during Brammer's stint at *Time* magazine, and there had been other brief stops while Willie was a Rhodes Scholar. But he had no more than a nodding acquaintance with the metropolis that he came to call "The Big Cave." He nicknamed it that because he found Manhattan's "canyons of stone to be quite claustrophobic." He wrote, "In a metaphorical sense the city always seemed so dark and the mist coming out of sewers along the avenues—well, I don't know, it just seemed cave-like to me."

That sounds as if young Willie Morris didn't really take to the city. Quite the contrary: He embraced it like a lover and roamed Manhattan Island from tip to tip, downtown to midtown to uptown; he later wrote of especially loving New York on rainy nights, or snowy nights when the city's grime lay under a sparkling winter wonderland and he struck up conversations with street-corner Santa Clauses, "some of them a little tipsy."

Much of what Willie Morris saw he regarded in wide-eyed wonder, as perhaps befitted a lad from Yazoo City, though Willie knew—from reading—much more of the history of the ground he trod than did the average gawking newcomer. Indeed, he often marked passages in books by Fitzgerald, Wolfe, Faulkner, Sinclair Lewis,

Hemingway, and many others, passages recounting their recollections of and descriptions of their early impressions of the city, and then did his best to follow in their tracks, "stalking the ghosts of my literary heroes."

Harper's in 1963 was housed in a narrow, six-story red-brick building at 49 East 33rd Street, squatting behind the lofty Vanderbilt Hotel, which fronted Park Avenue. Willie Morris could not have been impressed with his first office there: "minuscule, approximating the size of a good-sized dining room table." This he shared with a young woman fresh from college—part secretary, part reader— typical of the liberal arts graduates who flocked to low-paying jobs on Manhattan's publishing totem poles, hoping to rise higher than they ever would, most of them eventually disappearing as quickly and completely as puffs of smoke.

Manuscripts were stacked so high on the common desk Willie and the young woman worked across that, if either wanted to see the other, they had to stand; manuscripts also were stacked on top of the lone filing cabinet, on a spare chair, and in ragged piles on the floor. These were unsolicited manuscripts, disjointed works for the most part, that came in "over the transom"—unloved, sans sponsors—and were unflatteringly referred to in the aggregate as "the slush pile." Hardly any proved useable, though a dogged attempt was made to comb through them and read just enough to officially disqualify them from *Harper's* pages. (Most magazines and publishing houses now discourage "over-the-transom" entries, some even refusing to accept them; among those that do, much less time and attention are awarded than was the case in that earlier time.)

New contributions to the slush pile always out-raced the pace at which Willie and his young assistant could read the mountain of accumulated works, and so it grew and grew until, in desperation, Willie would set aside two or three days in which he and the young woman would speed through the slush pile—eschewing correspondence, phone calls, and all other duties, even lunch—discarding the misshapen, sending printed form letters of rejection to authors they knew would be disappointed, heart- broken, or angry, and probably not for the first time—nor the last. But amazingly quickly the small office would grow a new paper mountain, there being no shortage of would-be Shakespeares.

"This was the beginning of a long period when manuscripts dominated my life," Willie wrote in *New York Days*, "manuscripts stacked man-high on tables, crammed in my old black briefcase, spilling off bookcases. Manuscripts from every humble corner of the Great Republic. Immaculate manuscripts, greasy manuscripts. Literate and semi-literate and illiterate manuscripts . . . words, words, words: words that mattered, words that half-mattered, words that did not matter at all."

Unlike most young associate editors, however, Willie Morris was not abandoned to a long apprenticeship among slush pile words. Jack Fischer having larger plans for him, Willie soon was assigned new and more rewarding duties. He edited manuscripts that the magazine actually intended to use, working to hone the prose of former CIA Director Allen Dulles, David Lilienthal—the first director of FDR's TVA—and lesser-knowns, including a monsignor driven to reveal church improprieties, a soldier from the 82nd Airborne who had served at Ole Miss during the riot attending James Meredith's admission there, a congressman who pledged to reveal scandalous "pork barrel" tales, and several others who had birthed ill-formed manuscripts. Willie shaped and saved a few of these, but most failed for one reason or another: The monsignor grew frightened and clammed up, the congressman refused to let a word of his deathless prose be cut even though he had trouble with simple declarative sentences, and Allen Dulles, as befitted a former head of the CIA, simply had trouble revealing secrets—without which his recollections were not all that hot.

Still, Jack Fischer turned to Willie Morris again and again: When the old muckraker Upton Sinclair, who once had almost been elected governor of California, turned up unannounced, Mr. Fischer steered him to Willie Morris; he did the same with other visitors of note. Willie was also encouraged to travel to the nation's capital in search of *Harper's* material or authors new to its pages, and it was Willie and Willie alone among staffers that Jack Fischer invited to join him for lunch at the staid old Century Club. At the weekly or twice-weekly staff meetings on which Mr. Fischer doted— and which Willie secretly despised—more often than not Willie was the editor most frequently asked for suggestions or opinions. "I can't fault Jack Fischer's conduct," Willie said in later years after their relations had cooled. "He groomed me for the job he had promised me. I can't think of a thing he left undone." The obvious "grooming" clearly signaled to senior staff members that plots were afoot that several of them could not have felt good about or been comfortable with.

The old hand who probably felt the most neglected (or threat-ened) was Russell Lynes, the managing editor—number two behind Jack Fischer—a pipe-puffing gentlemanly New Englander who also was the most prominent among *Harper's* staffers. He had authored two books that caused something of a stir—*The Tastemakers* and, par-ticularly, *Highbrow, Lowbrow, Middlebrow;* the latter caused him to be-come at least a minor celebrity in cultural circles. He had long written "After Hours," a monthly featured column in *Harper's,* and likely had reasons to expect he might rise to the top job. Instead, Jack Fischer was brought in from an editorship at Harper Brothers, the book publishing house allied with the magazine. Russell Lynes had to be surprised—apparently not having been given the courtesy of a private audience to gently inform him he was about to be passed over. He and Fischer existed only one door away from each other in the magazine office and conferred from time to time, but never enjoyed a warm or special relationship.

It had to pain Lynes to watch Jack Fischer train Willie Morris for the top job, and that is what anyone experienced in office politics, as Lynes was, knew was going on—though it was never voiced. When, four years after he arrived at *Harper's,* thirty-two-year-old Willie Morris became editor-in-chief, the twice-burned Russell Lynes was the first among the old hands to grab his hat and leave.

I first met Willie Morris in the early fall of 1963, during what I be-lieve was his first foray to Washington on behalf of *Harper's.* At the time I was administrative assistant to Congressman Jim Wright of Texas, who in later years became Speaker of the United States

House of Representatives. I had been a congressional aide for almost a decade and had become restive and bored in a job that once
had excited me and had given me a good political education: restive
because I had too long postponed my goal of becoming a "real
writer"—not just a ghost for others—and bored because I seemed to
be repeating myself in my daily duties; nothing seemed new under
the sun. I had no way of knowing it at the time, but I soon would
leave Capitol Hill: The assassination of John F. Kennedy shocked me
into the near-instant realization that I had not accomplished any of
the goals I had aspired to since childhood, and would die a failure
and unfulfilled should I, like JFK, go unexpectedly even if much less
publicly.

But that decision lay down the pike the mid-morning that Willie
Morris came to Congressman Wright's office and introduced himself. I had, of course, read his stuff in *The Texas Observer* and had
heard good things about him from such mutual friends as Billie Lee
Brammer and Texas legislators such as Malcolm McGregor and Don
Kennard. Likewise, I had been touted to Willie Morris as a generally
genial companion, one who did not shirk drink and also one who
probably knew where a few political bodies were buried.

After we exchanged pleasantries, I offered Willie a cup of our admittedly rank office coffee. He asked whether we might go out for a
cup. "Sure," I said, and started for the house cafeteria. "Ah," Willie
said, after a few steps, "is there some place we might get something
stronger than coffee? Maybe a Bloody Mary?"

"Right across the street," I said, and led him to the Congressional
Hotel's Filibuster Room, the cutesy name for its public bar. Mr.
Johnston, the black man who presided over the Filibuster Room as
if it might be his personal property, and who *insisted* that one use
"Mister" in addressing him, scowled at me—a regular—and said,
"It's too early and you know it. We don't serve drinks for another
half hour." I said, "But there's no law against it, Mr. Johnston. Mr.
Morris here has come down from New York at the request of the
Speaker, and needs a libation or two before meeting with Mister
Sam. So that he'll be oiled for action, so to speak." Mr. Johnson hes-
itated: It would not do to cross someone Speaker Sam Rayburn had

summoned; Capitol Hill employees—and not just those on the government payroll, but all who worked for private establishments dependent on Congressional patronage and favor—existed only for the convenience of, and at the pleasure of, The Powerful. At least that's how The Powerful and their haughty minions saw it and, believe me, no truly Powerful Person is half as haughty and demanding as those who work for him or her, when dealing with *their* presumed inferiors.

I soothed Mr. Johnston's unease with a couple of bucks he expertly palmed, and very soon Willie Morris and I lifted our glasses to each other in a first toast. We laughed, chattered like back-fence neighbors, told political stories—his about the Texas legislature, mine about the Congress and its most colorful denizen, Senate Majority Leader Lyndon B. Johnson. Soon Willie Morris said words I heard for the first time, though I would hear him say them to me, and to others, countless times in the future: "Now one day soon you simply must *write* that for me!"

By the time we left the Filibuster Room—in, I must admit, mid-afternoon—Willie Morris was in no condition for his fictitious appointment with Speaker Rayburn, and I may have lacked a bit in timing and balance myself. But I felt as if I had met a life-long friend, one very close to being my brother. And I know, now, I was not the first to feel those emotions after an initial encounter with Willie Morris. He was, I would discover, a true expert at winning one over in a very short time, and I don't mean to imply any ulterior motives on Willie's part or that he was simply using a convenient "technique": He was, as David Halberstam has noted, a "reader of people" and he asked many questions of new acquaintances to learn more about them and the way their minds worked. He did this in such a genteel and interested manner that few failed to be impressed or flattered.

Jack Fischer knew few literary types and had no use for parties. So for years he had ignored or politely declined the many social invitations extended to him because he was editor-in-chief of *Harper's*. "He did not know or care much about the major American writers of the day," Willie wrote in retrospect. "I believe he considered the

American novel more or less dead and most of its best practitioners wanton and destructive."

For all of that, Fischer decided it might be good for Willie Morris, and for the magazine, should Willie attend the literary lunches, parties, and other social events that Fischer himself eschewed. Willie, the born raconteur, was, of course, delighted. And, of course, Willie was personally eager to meet writers, editors, publishers, and agents he knew only as names or from their pictures. As his connection with *Harper's* became known to more and more of the literati, Willie knew, he would be made even more welcome among them.

Of course, Willie-like, he later would say, and write, that at any minute he had expected some noted person to sing out, *Willie Morris, what are you doing in here? Get out of this room!* Don't you believe it. Willie soon became the center of attention at many such gatherings and he damn well knew it. Word began to circulate that he was a real comer, a player, a man to watch and perhaps to court. And, without question, Willie reveled in his newfound acceptance. For the rest of his life he seemed to need to pinch himself to be certain the "Yazoo Kid" was, indeed, in the laughing presence of "Betty" Bacall or exchanging friendly barbs with Norman Mailer or sharing drinks with Mickey Mantle or shooting basketballs with the New York Knicks' Bill Bradley—people he had only seen in the movies, or on television, or had read about before his New York days.

Willie took pains to court writers he had never met; he simply picked up the telephone, called them, and invited them for lunch or after-work libations. Most met with him, editors being sources of work and money, but not many established writers initially rushed to heed his call. Jack Fischer's paltry pay scale put them off, or they waited to see if *Harper's* would truly become the lively, progressive publication that Willie promised them it was on the way to becoming.

Another problem was Mr. Fischer himself: He knew little about most of the writers Willie urged him to recruit and several, whom Willie arranged for him to meet, did not impress him, nor did he impress them with his quick handshake, perfunctory comments, and even, sometimes, frequent peeks at his watch.

Willie several times asked Norman Mailer to write for him, but Mailer declined because of the *Harper's* pay scale and because, he said forthrightly, the magazine was so "arid" it would not take anything of his anyway. Hoping to interest Jack Fischer in Mailer, Willie remarked that he had been seeing a great deal of him and had talked with Mailer about appearing in the magazine. Mr. Fischer expressed little interest beyond asking how crazy was Mailer and did he drink as much as reputed?

Ultimately, as Willie persisted, Mailer sent him a small portion of his book-in-progress, *Cannibals and Christians*. Willie gave Jack Fischer and his senior colleagues a hard pitch at a staff meeting. Mailer, he said, had a big audience, he was a major writer, perhaps the best-known living American writer because he appeared on television frequently and performed well there; people paid attention to him even when they disagreed with him. Mailer's appearing in *Harper's* for the first time was bound to attract attention and be widely remarked. "I virtually begged," Willie said.

The senior staffers read Mailer's piece and vetoed it unanimously. Jack Fischer returned it to Willie with "little more than a shrug." When Mailer got the news, he said, "Didn't I tell you?" and vowed never again to submit anything to *Harper's*. Willie was frustrated beyond any singing of it; it was his low point at the magazine until his resignation.

"That casual rejection of Norman Mailer—and of me, as I saw it— made it harder to field all those telephone calls that drove me nuts, or to sit through those tedious staff meetings," he said. "I soon arranged to be called out of meetings by 'important' long-distance calls or other ruses." Likely he repaired to the Empire Chinese Restaurant, on Madison Avenue near 34th street, and enjoyed a couple of drinks while perusing a manuscript or passing a few words with the proprietor, Mr. Suey, who Willie privately nicknamed "Chop."

There is no doubt in my mind that the Mailer incident caused Willie Morris to privately vow that if and when he got the captain's chair at *Harper's* he would sweep the decks clean both fore and aft.

In late September I was somewhat astonished when editor Robert Gutwillig of McGraw-Hill—on the basis of one thirty-six-page chapter and an outline—bought my political-novel-barely-in-progress, *The One-Eyed Man*. True, the advance money was modest—only $1,500—but it was my first chance, since working at three small newspapers more than a decade earlier, to break into print in my own name. I was elated and would have taken $1.98 had that been the sum Bob Gutwillig offered.

Willie Morris whooped and hollered with me when I telephoned him with the good news; the next time he came to Washington we toasted my novel's success almost until our tongues bled. "If your novel makes money," Willie said, "maybe you can quit politics and write some of your marvelous political tales for me."

Within days of that meeting, John F. Kennedy made his fatal trip to Dallas. Almost from the moment he died, my interest in remaining in politics—and in a stagnant marriage—also died. Before January of 1964 I had left home and taken up residence in a series of boarding houses and second-rate hostels, one of which I dubbed Heartbreak Hotel for the number of failed husbands who lived in it, one moment glorying in their newfound "freedom" and in the next haunted by the many problems attendant to a marriage gone kaput: debts, property disputes, lawyer's fees, harsh judgments by friends and even some relatives. Perhaps the worst was weekend custody outings with confused and unhappy children, the outings somehow causing more tensions rather than being the intended curative. In May of that year, I woke at dawn and said aloud to my small portion of Heartbreak Hotel's ceiling, "Fuck it, I'm out of here. Today."

I called Bob Gutwillig and Willie Morris to break the news of my imminent defection from Washington; I would, I said, retreat to Austin, Texas, and stay for a while at the home of my cousin Lanvil Gilbert and his wife, Glenda, and work on my book in the daytime while they were at their jobs. And I would write some magazine articles to pay my child-support obligations and provide beer and cigarette money. After that . . . who knew? Nothing in my world seemed certain anymore after JFK's brutal public murder.

Gutwillig flat told me I was crazy. "How is a writer who has never published a book *or* a magazine article, a writer no one ever has even *heard of*, gonna make a living? You've got to be crazy! Don't quit your job! Keep it and work on *The One-Eyed Man* at nights and on weekends. I really think you'll make some money off that novel if you'll settle down and get to work!"

Willie Morris was almost as astonished as Gutwillig, but a great deal more encouraging. "Start working on a piece about what it's like to be a faceless, nameless force behind the throne in Congress, and all the frustrations. Write it just like you've told me about it. Make it real and make it funny. I'll see if I can get you $500. If it's good, and if Jack Fischer likes it, then write another one about lobbyists in Washington. Their influences, their modus operandi. Again, it's stuff we've discussed. I'll talk you up with other magazine editors if what you write for me is good as I think it will be." Willie was true to his word in every instance—excepting the money: Mr. Fischer would sail for only $400, not $500, for my first *Harper's* article, "Washington's Second-Banana Politicians." It got me my first fan letter, from no less than John Kenneth Galbraith, and made my cup runneth over. Within the next year I appeared in *Harper's* three times; because my work there drew attention—and because Willie Morris did, indeed, tout me to other editors—I soon published in *The Progressive, The Nation, The Saturday Evening Post, Sports Illustrated, The Texas Observer, Cosmopolitan, Life, Playboy,* and, well, eventually in more than one hundred periodicals. Such exposure caused publishing houses to sign me to book contracts; the writing of TV documentaries, lecture dates, teaching jobs, and finally writing for the stage and screen followed.

If ever one editor made one writer's career, Willie Morris made mine.

Two years into his *Harper's* job, in 1965, Willie Morris was named executive editor. In terms of day-to-day duties he almost was editor-in-chief. Jack Fischer hung onto the title and the bigger office and presided over his cherished staff meetings, but in many ways he turned over the daily operation to Willie. A weariness, health concerns, his wife's insistence that he slow down, and his own wish to write a book or two led to Mr. Fischer's decision to give Willie at least a loose grip on the reins.

This was not an easy time for Willie: He thought perhaps Jack

Fischer was testing whether he had the stuff to actually become edi-tor-in-chief. If that should be the case, Willie felt he would be work-ing under a handicap in that he had the responsibility of getting the magazine out but not the necessary authority. He could not, for ex-ample, stray from Jack Fischer's pay scale for contributors to the magazine, nor could he publish certain articles or stories without gaining Fischer's approval. An example of the latter: I was working on a short story I thought to turn into a novella, the premise being that a small detachment of American soldiers—about twenty-four, say, or two squads—were sent on a hush-hush combat mission; they expected to be air-lifted out, after completing their mission. In truth, they were unknowingly on a suicide mission: Their superiors wanted them to be discovered by the enemy and for the enemy to draw the erroneous conclusion that their reconnaissance mission was a preface to a larger attack to come. The enemy then would re-inforce its battlements, rushing in large reserve units, and concen-trating on defending their turf—while, in truth, the larger attack would be launched at the site from which, logically, the enemy would have drawn its reserves. This, of course, would have weak-ened resistance where the military brass really intended to attack. Eventually, the leader of the suicide mission would recognize it for what it was and be forced to deal with having been betrayed by his own.

Willie asked to see the story when it was done and mentioned it to Mr. Fischer. "It really made him angry," Willie told me. "He said, 'That is a false premise! The American military would *never* sacrifice its own! I do *not* want to see a story like that in my magazine!'" I did not share Mr. Fischer's belief in the purity of those who make war from the comfort of their soft chairs and gleaming planning tables; one might recall that U.S. troops were exposed to fallout from atomic tests in the late 1940s and early 1950s and also were used as unknowing guinea pigs in the testing of mind-altering drugs; in the 1960s, and early 1970s, almost six thousand American troops— most of them not informed—were deployed in tests of more than fifty chemical and biological agents, causing an investigation by the Pentagon in later years so as to preclude such folly in the future.

And a quarter million young Grunts, we have known for more than twenty years, were exposed to the poisons of Agent Orange in Vietnam. War is never nearly as fastidious as Mr. Fischer apparently thought it. He did continue to hold the big whip at *Harper's* when it counted, however, so Willie said no more.

"I walked a fine line," Willie remembered. "I couldn't get the writers I wanted, as quickly as I wanted, or significantly steer the magazine in a direction I thought would improve it. I had to be careful to avoid even the appearance of grabbing power. And I didn't dare tell *anybody* that things would change when I got the top job because I had been cautioned never to let that information go public."

Willie did soon put together a *Harper's* issue of which he was extraordinarily proud, the first of several times that he would devote almost the entire magazine to one theme. *The South Today: 100 Years After Appomattox* caused much favorable comment and shortly was published by Harper & Row as a book, for which Willie Morris wrote a short foreword. He also wrote in the dust-jacket copy, "The dominant theme of this collection as a whole . . . is the need for more humane leadership and the acceptance of the fact that the problem of the South is the problem of the North, the tragedy of the Negro, the tragedy of the white, the shame of the South, the shame of the nation."

The contributors constituted a distinguished group: historians, editors, novelists, academicians, and a political scientist. Three blacks were included—Arna Bontemps, Louis Lomax, and Whitney M. Young, Jr., executive director of the National Urban League. D. W. Brogan, a professor at Cambridge, was the only non-American. The other contributors were Jonathan Daniels, James J. Kilpatrick, Walker Percy, Philip M. Stern, William Styron, C. Vann Woodward, and Edwin M. Yoder, Jr. Kilpatrick, the only avowed Southern hardliner in the group, then editor of the *Richmond News Leader,* was the author of a book titled *The Southern Case for School Segregation.* With the exception of the muckraking Phil Stern, all of the Americans were native Southerners, and even he had founded and published *The Northern Virginia Sun.* These years later, the omission of women writers or black militants leaps out, but such obvious omissions were little remarked in 1965—which is stunning considering that public outrages already had been committed against blacks in the South (and a rare few whites) who sat in at segregated lunch counters, tried to register to vote, or to enter all-white schools, or marched for freedom and their citizen's rights. These outrages included pressurized fire hoses turned on peaceful dissenters, police dogs that bit, cops who bashed people, kidnappings, and murders most foul: bombings, lynchings, and shootings. Eventually, Willie Morris would begin to deal with such outrages in *Harper's* but the time—or the opportunity—was not quite yet. Not with Jack Fischer still calling the shots.

CHAPTER 7

WILLIE MORRIS MADE FRIENDS IN ALL FIELDS, from every section of the country and abroad, among celebrities and just plain folks, people of many religious persuasions and those who professed none, people of all colors and shapes and sizes. But he had, I think, a special place in his heart for two kinds of people: writers and Southerners.

Perhaps the person Willie was closest to over a large span of his lifetime—with the possible exception of his dear friend James Jones—was William Styron, from the Tidewater Country of Virginia, and one of America's premier novelists. Morris had literally memorized lengthy sections of Styron's first novel, published in 1954, and later said he had vowed that if he ever became an editor, "I want the man who wrote *Lie Down in Darkness* to write for me."

They met at Yale, in the office of historian C. Vann Woodward—an Arkansas native—though even earlier Willie had solicited from Styron an article called "This Quiet Dust" that was published in *The South Today*. Styron's article traced a bloody afternoon of murder and violence in Southampton County, Virginia, during a slave uprising led by Nat Turner, in 1831; it was a revolt briefly dismissed in most history textbooks—including those used in Virginia—and amazingly had been virtually ignored in American letters. Styron as a teenager became curious about the slave revolt he never had heard of until it was mentioned briefly in his textbook. Years later he decided to write a novel about it.

"This Quiet Dust" came from Styron's personal research, including the tracking of Turner's footsteps during the carnage of the uprising, as nearly as they could be established, and cued the literary world that Styron was working on *The Confessions of Nat Turner.* That novel would be published, in 1967, to rave reviews, before blacks among the literati, and activists outside it, launched counter-attacks, some of them vicious, causing a few namby-pamby critics to "re-evaluate" downward their earlier reactions to *Nat Turner.* Many of the attacks questioned whether Styron as a white man had "the right" to speak in the voice of, or relate the thoughts of, a black slave. Well, as a novelist *of course he did.* Novels are works of the imagination, and what person—no matter his or her color—is commissioned to censor the imagination of another? Only James Baldwin among black writers defended Styron—and very few white writers were willing to wade into the swift tides and treacherous currents of passions, then attendant to the civil rights movement, to defend him. Willie thought the attacks on Styron to be extreme, mean, and unfair; they probably bound the two Southern writers even closer.

Not that the two of them didn't blend like hot dogs and mustard from that very first meeting at Yale. "That afternoon"—Styron has remembered—"I drove Willie into New York City and we got so passionately engrossed in conversation, as southerners often do when they first meet, about places and historical events and ancestral connections . . . we got so *hypnotically* involved in such talk that I missed the correct toll booth at the Triborough Bridge and drove far into Long Island before the error dawned." Neither of them minded the accidental detour.

In due course, Willie would persuade Styron—or his publisher—to sell him 45,000 words of the Nat Turner novel itself, at a time when "it meant a lot to me and to *Harper's.*" By that Willie meant that the *Nat Turner* excerpt was helpful in signaling that *Harper's* was, indeed, serious about counting for something in the court of public opinion, and thus influencing events.*

*It's hard to realize now, when many get their news and views from the old established television networks and ever-sprouting cable networks, to say nothing of the uneven-but-ubiquitous Internet sources, that—in the words of David Halberstam—

Styron wrote a number of pieces for Willie's magazine, including one on masturbation that caused a flurry of protests and a few canceled subscriptions, but certainly he did *Harper's* far more favors than harm. Here was an established, even celebrated, writer working at his peak, one who really did not need *Harper's*, who not only published there but, on trips to Manhattan from his Connecticut home, dropped by the office to talk with Willie, sometimes to give his younger friend advice, and always to bestow his good will. Willie Morris never forgot that, frankly, he and *Harper's* needed Styron more than Styron needed either of them. It showed in his near-worshipful regard for Styron. When one of the several writers Willie had brought aboard as "contributing editors" couldn't find Willie and asked where he might be, one of us was likely to respond, "He's somewhere talking about the South, the soil and Styron." There may have a been a little envy in that; we were, after all, in our early-to-late thirties for the most part and still scrambling for rungs on the big career ladder.

Willie began spending some evenings or weekends at "Styron's Acres" near Roxbury—in Connecticut—a wooded retreat where he enjoyed shaking off his city dust, and where James Baldwin had repaired to an adjacent visitor's cottage near the main house, to finish his novel *Another Country*. Neighbors included playwright Arthur Miller, novelist Philip Roth, and movie tough guy Richard Widmark. "As at Elaine's [restaurant] or George Plimpton's or Jean Stein's in the city one was able to conduct his magazine solicitations there," Willie wrote in *New York Days*. "You never knew whom you would meet next in that domicile, and it was an editor's paradise."

Sometimes Bill Styron and his wife, Rose—a poet and children's author—were guests at a great old farmhouse Willie and Celia had bought in Putnam County, New York, in the Hudson Valley. Willie and Styron there liked to sing the old Protestant hymns from their

"We knew a time when *Esquire* may have been, culturally, one of the nation's most influential sources and *Harper's* held that distinction politically." The sad fact now is that very few magazines amount to diddly-squat in the big picture, being directed at specialized audiences or fawning over celebrities or treating gossip about celebrities as if it actually is worthwhile news.

childhood days, usually with drinks in their hands. Every now and again the Morrises invited a collection of writers and their spouses to the old farmhouse for a weekend of . . . well, the only honest word is "carousing." I was there for what was supposed to have been a celebration of the blooming of a dogwood tree that Willie claimed was "the northmost dogwood in America." Alas, a Yankee cool spell lingered and of dogwood blooms we had none. (The party was billed—by Willie, and reported in an article by me—as The Old Southern Boys Party, a designation that irked Celia because, she said—rightly—that it ignored the very real accomplishments of the wives of The Old Southern Boys: Eleanor Clark, married to Robert Penn Warren, was an accomplished novelist, Rose Styron had published poems and children's books, Celia—who would go on to write books on serious subjects, some of which won awards—also edited the first draft of Willie's *North Toward Home*.)

The evening's entertainment, however, obviously had been planned only by male chauvinists: After a certain amount of wet goods had been consumed, bogus literary prizes were awarded, the presenters making exaggerated oratorical declamations full of southern rococo and rhythms, quoting from Huey Long's "Evangeline Tree" speech, Faulkner, the Old Testament, and the combined works of those Old Southern Boys assembled. Styron, winning the Bull Connor Award for the best dog story (named after the segregationist Commissioner of Public Safety of Birmingham, Alabama, a cad who sicced German shepherd dogs on civil rights demonstrators) or some other imaginary honor, was presented with a pair of Boss Walloper work gloves, a tin of snuff, and a Spanish-language fuck book. The survivors gulped Bloody Marys at a Sunday brunch and closed with their favorite fundamentalist hymns; mine always was "Jesus on the Five-Yard Line."

Styron was a moody fellow. None of us knew, then, of his bouts of chronic depression, revealed in the 1990s in his short but powerful nonfiction book, *Darkness Visible*. I therefore was less understanding than I should have been when, in early 1970, Styron went into a deep funk and collapsed at my apartment, requiring overnight hospitalization, while I was a Nieman Fellow at Harvard. His collapse had been occasioned—I thought—solely by attacks made on his *Confessions of Nat Turner,* though possibly assisted by applications of scotch and exposure to clouds of Mexican Boo Smoke. At any rate, my basic position was that Styron simply should have been "tougher." So much for my keen perceptive abilities.

All the more remarkable, therefore, that Willie Morris made Bill Styron laugh, or at least smile, so often; Styron otherwise struck me as a man constantly on edge, a little apprehensive even when working at having fun. He *wanted* to have fun, I thought, but somehow appeared to fear that fun might not be appropriate, or was afraid to trust it. With Willie Morris, however, Styron even reached the point where he could retaliate in the kind of practical jokes Willie loved pulling.

Not long after Willie telephoned Styron in Connecticut late one night to read him the hot-off-the-press *New York Times* rave review of one of Styron's novels—throwing in, to Styron's puzzlement and consternation, bogus quotes such as, "One of Mr. Styron's faults is that he does not know the meaning of many of the big words that he uses" and "His main weakness is that he cannot describe landscape and weather"—Styron found a way to retaliate. Let Willie tell it: "When Richard Nixon, shortly after being elected President in '68, announced that he was soliciting nominations for important Federal posts in the new administration and the White House widely circulated long and intricate nominating forms, Bill Styron nominated me for the post of Warden of the Women's Federal Reformatory in Alderson, West Virginia and mailed the form to Washington. It must have taken him the better part of two days to fill out the document, but I never did hear from Nixon about that job."

Willie believed that Styron and Norman Mailer, hands down, were the two prominent writers who were most helpful of the many talents he lured to the pages of *Harper's.* He admired not only their great writing skills but also their professionalism. "They taught me," he said, "that the better writers give editors less trouble than lesser writers. They don't quibble or quarrel over minor matters, and they generally turn in work so complete and finished that little editing is required."

I was not yet one of Willie's four contributing editors—or staff writers, more accurately—that he hired on becoming editor-in-chief, so I recall little about the purchase of *Harper's* by the publishing Cowles family, of Minneapolis, less than two years before Willie succeeded Jack Fischer. Scrabbling to make a living as a magazine freelancer, and working on the novel I had sold, I knew little of the day-to-day operation of *Harper's* and so did not view the sale as portending any great changes at the magazine, nor in my life. *(Hoo Boy! Let that be a lesson to you!)*

Willie originally was made a bit nervous. Would this change affect the succession agreement he had with Jack Fischer? Would the Cowles family—stolid Midwesterners known to be Republicans from the cradle, and whose newspapers(the *Minneapolis Star-Tribune* and *Des Moines Register*) were Republican to a fault—be in sympathy with the kind of freewheeling political and cultural magazine Willie intended to make *Harper's?* Would *Harper's* be just another link in a chain of publishing properties the Cowles family owned in a half-dozen states and Puerto Rico? Would John Cowles, Sr., the hands-on patriarch of the publishing empire, have anything like the appreciation for *Harper's* that long had been evinced by the Groton-and-Harvard types who headed Harper's Brothers publishing house, later known as Harper & Row? *Harper's* magazine then had a circulation of about 260,000 and ran an annual deficit—in Willie's words—"of $125,000 to $150,00, depending on what book-keeping method one looked at, which each year the [book] publishing house had satisfied." But would the Cowles family be willing to so subsidize the magazine, and if so for how long? Or would they insist on *Harper's* soon turning a profit, something Willie Morris knew would be difficult, if not impossible? Willie said nothing of his worrisome ruminations to me at the time, but later confessed they made him highly uncertain about his future.

John Cowles, Jr., then only thirty-eight years old—to Willie's thirty years—became president of the corporation formed by the new owners. He was a tall, slim, not unattractive man, one who caused me the first time I saw him to mentally sum him up thusly: *rich boy, preppie clothes, right schools, tennis, old money.* Willie took heart that

Junior Cowles was an Exeter and Harvard man, assuming a certain sophistication. There seemed to be a nervous energy in him that Willie could not define either as to cause or purpose, and though he had a generally serious mien he also "had a good smile" and "moved about at an invigorating patrician pace from one task to another."

Willie soon was much encouraged: Young Cowles seemed to enjoy his trips from the Midwest to New York and meeting a few writers Willie introduced, some of them "eccentric," according to Willie, who included me in that description. Cowles talked with enthusiasm of improving the magazine, of making it livelier and less "arid." One evening after a certain amount of wine, Cowles confessed that once he had hoped to become "a writer like Fitzgerald" but, realizing he could not, "aspired to become at least a medium and agent for publishing others who might have such promise. Hence *Harper's*." Think that didn't warm Willie's heart?

"Often we were joined in these sessions by one of his ranking financial lieutenants from the Minneapolis headquarters, Philip von Blon, a cultured Amherst man, to whom I took an instant trust and liking," Willie wrote in *New York Days*. "In such moments of rapport a histrionic ripple of the brain would seize me: '*Achtung!* Cowles and I are going to change America!' There were the first happy indications. Cowles agreed with me that we had to increase payments for writers. We were to pay William Styron $7,500 for the forty-five-thousand-word excerpt from *The Confessions of Nat Turner.* 'Pay him ten thousand', Cowles said. 'It will sound better when word gets around in the trade.'" After suffering disadvantages in corralling good writers due to Jack Fischer's native parsimony, Willie suddenly felt he had died and gone to Heaven.

Still . . . there were some moments causing doubts. When Jack Fischer brought Cowles to a staff meeting, allegedly to have him suggest ideas for *Harper's* articles, "He suggested one on the finer points of bridge." Robert Kotlowitz, then an associate editor, came into Willie's office afterwards "a little grim and unnerved." Cowles reminded him, he said, of another rich publisher he once had worked for and who made asinine suggestions as to articles. "We're in for trouble," he told Willie. Willie asked what kind of trouble. "Troubles of a rich and dim-witted nature," Bob Kotlowitz replied.

David Halberstam had reasons to wonder about young John Cowles, too. In 1963, when Halberstam was covering the war in Vietnam for *The New York Times,* John Jr. visited Saigon and, one evening, had dinner with Halberstam and other correspondents. "We were very tough on how the war was going," Halberstam recalled in later years. "Cowles didn't like it, or for that matter, I suspect he also didn't like me very much. When he cited the wisdom of the senior people in the American embassy, we scoffed. And later on, when I won the Pulitzer, a friend of mine—Chuck Bailey, who'd worked for Cowles in Washington—said to him that I had been right after all. And Cowles said yes, but I had been *precipitous* in thinking and writing as I had! A perfect Cowles story, I think; it provides a great insight into him: it isn't whether you're right or wrong that matters, it's that you might be out ahead of the curve by too much."

Apparently signs that a John-and-Willie team never could work together in harness were more visible than I knew: Years later, von Blon—a gentlemanly sort with a dry wit and an innate sense of fairness—would say that, in retrospect, it was easy to see that Willie and young Cowles never were a match: "John was meticulous. He was a list maker. And when he had accomplished an item on his things-to-do list, he neatly drew a line through it. Willie, well, Willie had many talents but he was far from a list-maker! His casual approach to what John considered serious matters drove John up the wall."

There was a "caste" distinction in young Cowles's appraisals of others, I came to believe in time. If you were a bit out of the mainstream, if you questioned the conventional wisdom, if you were critical of those who made policy, if your personal habits were a little loose, if you did not *fit in*—well, then, could you really amount to much? Were you to be trusted?

Willie Morris appeared, originally, to be "safe": a Rhodes Scholar, a well-spoken Southerner and raconteur who gave no indications of being a bomb thrower, one who might be at home in the Century Club and would surely understand the need for leaders to stand together. But hold on here: What's *this?* It's become apparent the fella doesn't like *meetings!* He doesn't make *lists!* He not a *team* player so much as an *individualist!* He drinks more than *wine!* How did we go so wrong in our appraisal?

Young Cowles was not accustomed to appraisals going wrong: The Cowles family had been influential among gentlemanly moderates in seizing the Republican Party apparatus away from the old know-nothing hard-liners in 1940, dispossessing those who had willingly followed Herbert Hoover to a catastrophic defeat in 1932 and Alf Landon of Kansas in 1936; the moderates rallied to Wendell Willkie in 1940. They were also instrumental in grabbing the Republican nomination away from the Old Guard again in 1952, and this time their choice—Dwight D. Eisenhower—did what Wendell Willkie couldn't do: He won. The Cowleses were white-hot for Nelson Rockefeller during the Nixon years, too, and though Rocky talked a pretty good liberal game he never deviated far from moderate Republicanism: He was staunchly for business, and a strong defense; hadn't he urged backyard bomb shelters, and when those scumbag prisoners rioted at Attica, didn't he come down on them strong?

Not long after the Cowles family bought *Harper's,* the poet Robert Lowell, who had just been featured on the cover of *Time* magazine— if you can imagine that today—came to dinner at Willie's and Celia's weekend farmhouse in the Hudson Valley. Lowell complimented Willie on improvements he had made in *Harper's* and said he largely liked the poems being published there. Encouraged, Willie began to enumerate his plans for making the magazine better still, "almost babbling," Willie later said. Lowell listened, nodding. Finally he said Willie's goals were admirable but—forgive him, please—"You won't be able to have or sustain the kind of magazine you want. Your people won't allow it." Puzzled, Willie asked *what* people. "Your owners," Lowell said. "I know a great deal about people like that. . . . I'm sorry to say it, but in the end they will never allow it."

Early each year, Jack Fischer indulged in a ritual that, over time, began to worry Willie. Mr. Fischer wrote an undated letter of resignation, listing the reasons he would soon be leaving, and then called Willie in. Handing it across his desk, Fischer said, "Read this," or words to that effect. Willie always did, hardly knowing what to say or what reaction Mr. Fischer might want or expect. When Willie had read the letter, Jack Fischer reclaimed it and stuck it in his middle desk drawer. Sometimes he said nothing, sometimes he made a terse comment about needing to get to his own writing soon. "I was in an awkward situation," Willie later told me. "After Jack showed me the letter, he'd not say another one word about quitting until the *next* January or February when we'd go through that ritual anew."

I, of course, knew nothing of all that, Willie still holding close the secret that he was the anointed top-dog-in-waiting. My first small clue came after Willie called me following a call my agent, Sterling Lord, had made to Willie at my request. Sterling's message was that I no longer could continue to write for *Harper's* at the rate I was paid—$750, I believe, being the top price Willie had been able to extract from Jack Fischer—when other magazines were paying me much more. My agent dressed it up in diplomatic language and sang hymns of praise about Willie's kindness to me, and my love for Willie being greater than my love for life or Jesus, or some such, but inside the tender valentine was a demand for more money. Willie said only that he would "do what he could," asked Lord for "a little time" to work on the problem, then immediately called me.

"Look," he said, "some things likely will change here before too much longer. That's all I can say right now, and you can't even tell Sterling Lord or anybody else I said *that* much. It might really mess up a delicate situation. Just trust me, and when I can take care of you, I will. I guarantee you won't regret it."

Somehow it never occurred to me that Willie, at age thirty-two, might soon be named to succeed Jack Fischer. My guess was that Willie was negotiating with Mr. Fischer for the authority to pay writers a little more money and thought he was on the verge of being granted that. Within a few weeks, Willie telephoned to say he needed me to come to New York as quickly as possible. "What's up?" I asked. "I'll tell you when you get here," he said. "And get here *sober.* Can you be here by noon tomorrow? It's important."

Willie shut the door to his office when I arrived and spoke almost in a whisper. My excitement mounted as I learned he was to succeed

Mr. Fischer and that John Cowles, Jr., wanted it done soon. He told me of Mr. Fischer's "annual" letter of non-resignation, as it were, and said, "I told John Cowles that you were in big-time politics for years and maybe you'd have a solution." I said, "Jesus Christ, Willie, did you tell him that after I solve his problem we'll stroll over to the East River and I'll walk on water?" Willie sharply said I should keep a civil tongue in my head around Cowles, "not make a bunch of wise-cracks," and have no more than two drinks: "This is a serious matter for both of us, Larry!" I had never seen Willie Morris anywhere near as tense.

At lunch, I proposed a simple solution: "The next time Mr. Fischer pulls the resignation-letter bit—and that shouldn't be long, this being November—then you, John, must call him and then go see him and say you're *so sorry* he's leaving, but you understand. Wish him well. Shake his hand. Tell him you want to give him a granddaddy of a going-away party and you'll need his guest list. If he doesn't respond quickly, call him again and talk about the retirement party. Keep nudging him. He can't ignore you for long if you persist."

"That might just work," Cowles said with a small smile. The smile was not of long duration. He frowned, "But, I don't know. What you suggest seems a little . . . pushy."

"Well, hell," I said. "You *will* be pushing him. How else can you get him out the door?" Cowles said it seemed there should be a better way. I said if I knew of one I would have recommended it. Perhaps, I said, he might soften the blow by asking Jack Fischer's recommendations on a thing or two or by saying he would be soliciting his advice from time to time, or maybe even suggest he write an occasional guest column. But if the man needs nudging, I said, "John, *you've* gotta nudge him. *Willie* can't."

Cowles looked uncomfortable but said he would take it "under advisement." I shrugged and said, "The decision is yours, but I know no other way. There's not any magic: you just *do it* if you really want him to move on, and I thought such was the case." Willie gave me an almost imperceptible shake of the head as if to say I had pushed it far enough.

When Cowles left us with a quick handshake and perfunctory leave-taking words, I said, "Okay, Willie. Now let's drink some whiskey!" We did, though Willie restlessly twisted and turned, second-guessing whether he should have called me into play, wondering if I had pushed Cowles too hard—all of which pissed me off. "You and Cowles want it to be painless," I said. "It won't be. You're trying to oust a man who's not yet ready to let go." Willie said yeah, and he felt a little guilty about that: Jack Fischer had been his patron; on the whole he'd been good to him.

I said, "Goddammit, Willie, you and John Junior are agreed you want Fischer's ass *gone,* but you both want to feel good about it. That's not a package that I, or anybody else, can deliver. If you guys don't have the nerve to follow through, then we've just been beating our gums to no good purpose." Willie said little more, drinking with his eyes downcast and minus his usual bar-room sparkle; I could see there would be no more fun on the day's program. For the first and only time I ever flew to New York on *Harper's* business I took a shuttle back home the same day.

Flying back, I worked up righteous indignation against both Willie and Cowles. Goddammit, I hadn't asked Willie to make me the strategist; hell, he hadn't even consulted me before doing it. I also resented how he'd reacted when Cowles had not warmed to my advice. And I thought Cowles next to rude when he left us with only a few perfunctory words, not one of which was "thanks." Unlike Willie, I felt no guilt in conspiring to dump Jack Fischer, who had never truly been friendly to me: He complained each time Willie asked for a few bucks more for me, more than once he had wanted to change language I had used that neither Willie nor I saw the need to change, he refused to pay one small expense account I had turned in after he asked me to come to New York to discuss an assignment—an assignment I had turned down after Mr. Fischer said he would pay me $400 for the piece plus $100 toward my airfare to Texas for interviews. "Christ, Mr. Fischer," I had said. "That won't even pay for my round-trip ticket! And what am I supposed to do when I get there: Live in an open field and eat bush berries?" Mr. Fischer pursed his lips as if he had just sampled a green persimmon and said, shortly, that was his final offer. I had disliked the stingy old fart from that moment on. (I wrote ten pieces *Harper's* published while he was editor-in-chief, but they were for Willie Morris, not Jack Fischer, as I saw it.)

For a couple of days I had the glooms about the way the meeting with Cowles had turned out, and they might have lingered had not Willie Morris called with glee in his voice: "HE'LL DO IT," Willie almost shouted. "Cowles said he will do it!" Then he fell to profusely thanking me for my help. I felt vastly relieved, not so much because I had not struck out in my first time at bat with the new *Harper's* owner, but rather because the unusual tensions I had felt with Willie flew away like a wild goose that had been shot at. And that meant more to me than all other considerations.

PART THREE

RIDING HIGH: THE TOAST OF NEW YORK

"There were eight million telephone numbers in the Manhattan directory, and every one of them would have returned my calls."

— WILLIE MORRIS

in his 1993 book, *New York Days*

CHAPTER 8

"ON A BURNISHED MORNING of New York springtime, 1967, I had moved my things into the editor-in-chief's rooms of *Harper's*," Willie Morris wrote a quarter century later in *New York Days*. "The editorship of this venerable national institution mattered to me greatly. . . ." Willie Morris that day became the youngest editor in *Harper's* 117-year history, only the eighth man to hold the job.

The magazine by then had moved to more commodious quarters at Two Park Avenue. "[T]he editor's office occupied a considerable corner suite," Willie recalled, "with a precipitous view of Park and the animated Murray Hill neighborhood, and if you peered long enough between the skyscrapers across the way, you might catch a hasty little finger of the East River, somnolent and tawny in the early sun." Willie sat in his new tall chair, behind a polished oaken desk cleaner than it would ever be again during the time that he occupied it, regarding walls that hosted century-old framed covers of the magazine, a portrait of one of Willie's predecessors, William Dean Howells, and "wonderfully illustrated posters of Mark Twain's *Personal Recollections of Joan of Arc*, which had been serialized in *Harper's* in 1896"; he recalled a vow Twain had made about the big time: "If I ever get up there, I'll stick if I can," an obvious clue to his own state of mind in the moment that meant so much to him.

His ruminations were interrupted when Jack Fischer, looking "thin and tired," suddenly appeared. Willie sprang to his feet, not quite knowing what to say. Fischer said, referring to a financial meeting they'd had with the owners a couple of days earlier—which had revealed the latest annual deficit to be about $150,000—"I feel badly about leaving you with that situation." "I'll take it ten years, Jack," Willie said. "Five's enough," Fischer replied. "I did it too long. Well, I'll be going."

"I thanked him. We shook hands, then in a skittish haste he was away," Willie wrote. "Now, from the pinnacle of the years, I wish I had said more in that moment, that I would not have so much as been there had it not been for him—as with my own father on his deathbed in the Kings Daughters' Hospital back home long before, when I had wanted to tell him that if I ever had a son I would name him after him, but could not say it. Perhaps it had something to do with being young and not knowing much about such things, and thinking you will live forever."

Jack Fischer's widow in mid-2003 produced for Celia Morris a letter Willie had written to his old boss on December 23, 1966—a few months before Willie actually would take over the top job at *Harper's* but soon after, obviously, that arrangement had been made.

In the "Dear Jack" letter, Willie Morris wrote:

> I've not had time to sit down and properly tell you how honored I am over the choice of me as your successor. I deeply appreciate this expression of faith and I hope I don't disappoint you. You are going to be a difficult fellow to follow. From all I've heard, you took over this magazine when it was in an extremely shaky condition, and we all have you to thank for its strength and its important role in America. I am touched to be considered worthy of your standards. It is crucial to all of us that your relationship with the magazine remain a close one.
>
> On a personal note I want to say that I'll never be able to repay you for all the help and encouragement you have given me. I still have a great deal to learn, but you have taught me more about the magazine business in four years than I could

have learned under lesser men in twenty. Very few young men have had the opportunities you have given me.

I've learned from you not only as one of the truly great editors of our day but also from your profound human kindness. And all I ask is that your friendship and loyalty remain undiminished. They are very important to me.

You and John [Cowles] will be turning over to me a great institution in American journalism. I intend to do everything within my power to keep it that way.

Celia and I love you for the human being you are, and we are grateful to you.

Willie

Mrs. Fischer told Celia that, apparently, was the last time, ever, that Willie Morris initiated contact with Jack Fischer. David Rae Morris put that little matter in perspective: "How many times did Jack Fischer contact Willie after *he* left?" Good question. I'm not certain of the answer, but if Jack Fischer did initiate contact I never knew of it.

VERY SHORTLY WILLIE HIRED FOUR OF US—myself, Pulitzer Prize–winner David Halberstam of *The New York Times,* John Corry of the same newspaper, and Marshall Frady, a freelancer living in Atlanta—as "contributing editors." As I have said before, we really were staff writers; I do not know the name of the institutional disease causing us to be erroneously designated, though it might have been "pretention-itis."

Halberstam was the most "serious" one—though not without fun—a man of utmost integrity whose bullshit detector was infallible. He had irked John F. Kennedy with his critical early dispatches about the conduct of the war in Vietnam, to the extent that JFK had complained to Halberstam's superiors at the *Times;* he had been expelled from Poland by a communist government angry at the blunt and revealing articles he had written about it. In short, he wore no man's collar. He was as intent as a Super Bowl linebacker and just as likely to tackle anybody who intruded on his territory. He may be the most fearless man I have ever met. Willie Morris described him thus: "I had never known a man, and never would, with such a blend of belligerence and sweetness, nor one who so loved the possibilities of America." None of us worked harder than Halberstam. Articles he produced for Willie's magazine were the starting points for two of Halberstam's best-selling big books, *The Best and the Brightest* and *The Powers That Be.* At this writing he has a string of fourteen consecutive *New York Times* best sellers—the latest being a small book about four members of the Boston Red Sox (Ted Williams, Dom DiMaggio, Bobby Doerr, and Johnny Pesky) called *The Teammates.* Three of Halberstam's books have risen to No. 1 on the *New York Times* bestseller lists; they also have received excellent or good-or-better reviews, not always the kind fate awaiting best sellers, many critics seeming to get their jollies by gleefully attacking successful books from ambush.

Halberstam's father was a small-town boy who became a medic in World War I and so impressed several physicians that they encouraged him to go to college and medical school when that war ended, and he did. When World War II began, he was a forty-five-year-old surgeon who volunteered to go back into the military for the duration. His family followed him to El Paso, Austin, and Rochester, Minnesota, before he went overseas to France and Germany. So young David lived in a number of states, often changing schools, though the family called Connecticut home.

Halberstam was a Harvard graduate, one who did not distinguish himself academically but who did become a mainstay at *The Harvard Crimson.* As such, he probably could have had an entry-level job at *The New York Times* had he sought it, but he made an unusual, and far-sighted, youthful decision: "I didn't want to write stories about breaks in the 57th Street water main," he has said. In truth, he wanted to work for a small-town newspaper so as to "be able to cover everything" and he wanted it to be in the South because he thought, accurately, a racial revolution was in the making there. (This was in the late 1950s.) "Probably," he says, "my having lived in different towns and sections of the country, due to my father's assignments, made it easier for me to go to Mississippi."

Halberstam's stay in West Point, Mississippi, was of only a year's duration because his publisher got nervous about Halberstam's dispatches to New York's *The Reporter* magazine about the politics of race in Mississippi; what he was writing had no more chance of being published in Mississippi than front-page porn, but what worried Halberstam's publisher was that someone in Mississippi might *read* it—and connect the writer to his newspaper. "Can't you just write for something like *Field & Stream*?" he asked plaintively. Halberstam moved on to the *Nashville Tennessean,* the town's liberal newspaper, the *Nashville Banner* being so conservative that when it editorialized against Daylight Saving Time it referred to Standard Time as "God's time." Halberstam became friendly with a *Tennessean* colleague, John Seigenthaler, then an underling editor, who in 1962 would become the top editor, and who would become Attorney General Robert Kennedy's top aide in the South during the civil rights wars. Seigenthaler was, indeed, knocked unconscious by a brick-throwing mob of Alabama rednecks while trying to get a busload of largely white "Freedom Riders" through the South undamaged, and lay in the street unattended for about forty-five minutes although Birmingham city cops and state troopers were nearby.

Halberstam never regretted his time on the small daily in West Point: "I learned that city hall and the courthouse crowd would tell the same sort of lies I later would hear from the Pentagon and the White House." Nor did his *Tennessean* years go to waste: He made friends, and sources, of many young blacks who became leaders in the civil rights wars and in the late 1990s he would write of them and their ground-breaking actions in another big book, *The Children.* I met Halberstam in 1961, when he was a new member of the Washington bureau of *The New York Times*, and I worked in Congress; we soon became fast friends.

Frady, the youngest of us at twenty-eight, originally a Georgian, a graduate of Furman University and the son of a Baptist preacher, did not require much time to yearn to escape the series of small, dusty South Carolina and Georgia towns where his father ministered; he was an impractical romantic who fled home at age fifteen vainly hoping to join Fidel Castro's revolutionaries in the mountains of Cuba, an attempt he made three times without once setting foot on Cuban soil. Frady also was our institutional Lothario—darkly handsome, bent on adventure, falling in love at the drop of a skirt, though true-in-his-fashion: At least once he divorced a wife to marry his latest mistress. His writing talent was prodigious and he talked like he wrote: in the poetic rhythms and rolling cadences of the Old Testament, his exotic vocabulary and run-on sentences often being dead-on Faulknerian. There was a wild streak in Frady that might produce great humor and laughter—or, almost as likely—sudden anger and invitations to fisticuffs. There was no shortage of passion in Marshall Frady.

Willie had become interested in Frady after reading his articles in *Newsweek* and *The Saturday Evening Post;* he made it a point to meet him and came away persuaded that if given free rein to write, he would deliver astonishing copy. That proved to be true. Willie sent Frady to Israel and Egypt, Frady going on military patrols with units from both sides, and he turned his long article into a perceptive book, *Across a Darkling Plain.* He also wrote an excellent book, *Wallace,* about the segregationist governor of Alabama who stood in the schoolhouse door to preserve "segregation forever" and who later was permanently crippled by an assassin's bullet while running for president, a book that Willie Morris thought brought to life "in the living flesh" the fictional governor, Willie Stark, of Robert Penn Warren's *All The King's Men.**

Corry came from Irish Protestants who had arrived from Ireland in steerage. He was a native of a lower-middle-class neighborhood in Brooklyn—which he grew to dislike—and he suffered more than any writer I knew then or later; always he had trouble meeting his deadlines, sleeping on couches in the *Harper's* office and increasingly looking desperately haunted as due dates relentlessly stalked

---

*Frady died of cancer in March of 2004, at age sixty-four. This was a shock, as none of his old *Harper's* comrades had known of his illness. He had last been in contact when he attended Willie Morris's funeral in August of 1999. Frady was working on a biography of Fidel Castro, his youthful idol, when he died.

him, sometimes despairing of being able to complete his project of the moment, occasionally upchucking from tension, frequently shoving his manuscript at Willie at the last moment, as if ridding himself of a dead rat, and saying, "It's not any good" or words to that effect. He was consistently wrong about that, whether writing of the fascist colonels who had grabbed power in Greece, Castro's Cuba a decade after the revolution, or the back-bench congressman who had been Corry's roomie at a small Dutch Reformed college (Hope) in Michigan; his prose may not have stirred me as did Frady's fascinating rococo, but it was clear, to the point, and often contained flashes of insight I had not known John to harbor. Something about Corry, however, held him back from many passions shared by the rest of us; he was not all that keen about the upheavals and excitements of the 1960s, which I believe most of us reveled in not only because they made good copy but also seemed to portend exciting social changes. We shared bar-stool confidences many times, yet I never felt the close camaraderie for Corry that I did for my other *Harper's* colleagues. He was, I believe, at once more conservative and more wearily cynical than the rest of us. I could never rhyme Corry's façade of not truly caring about much with the agonies attending his writing—about which, obviously, he cared greatly. (For all of that, he has produced but two slim books, one about William Manchester's problems with the Kennedy family while writing *The Death of a President* and *My Times,* a memoir subtitled *Adventures in the News Trade.*)

I was the group "Elder" at thirty-eight and the first Willie brought aboard, though Halberstam soon followed. I also had, by far, the skimpiest curriculum vitae of the group, as a high school dropout who had but briefly sniffed the intellectual gases on deposit at Texas Tech. I had grown up in hardscrabble circumstances, the son of a dirt farmer and one-time village blacksmith and I became, at a husky if apple-cheeked age fourteen, a World War II oil-field worker in West Texas and New Mexico; so long as I wore my hard hat, brogans, and greasy oil patch coveralls, I could buy any drink sold in any bar or beer joint I entered, the unwritten law running, "If you're old enough to do a man's work you're old enough to buy a drink." I became all too adept at drinking all too quickly and was known for being apt to do damn near anything outrageous when properly oiled.

After military service, I worked for a little over five years for newspapers in Hobbs, New Mexico, and Midland and Odessa in Texas, before going to Washington as administrative assistant to a newly elected Texas congressman, J. T. (Slick) Rutherford, a Democrat representing the sprawling 16th Congressional District stretching from Midland on the east to El Paso 300 miles to the west, then meandering for hundreds of miles along the Mexican border; indeed, that district was bigger than the states of Ohio and Tennessee, encompassing 42,067 square miles; we sometimes campaigned in small airplanes.

When Rutherford lost in the election of November 1962, I was quickly hired by future Speaker Jim Wright, from Fort Worth. It was not long until I met Willie Morris. Perhaps because on that day I got him drinks when he sorely needed them, I became one of Willie's favored drinking companions. "He has staying power," Willie said of me, "and puts on a good show." Of Halberstam I mock-complained that he "drank barely enough to stay alive." Frady and Corry I gave much better marks for their belly-up-to-the-bar techniques. I was not yet aware of the ravages that drink can afflict on the careless or unwary, though in time I would learn the hard way.

WILLIE SOON BROUGHT JOHN HOLLANDER ABOARD as poetry editor, a man I never knew well because he was not required to spend much time at the office. I did get to know, and admire, Robert Kotlowitz, whom Willie had promoted from associate editor to managing editor, and Midge Decter, who joined the staff as Willie's executive editor. This insured that he had truly talented people around him, people who could put out the magazine should Willie be busy in his role as public spokesman, off lecturing at colleges, courting writers he wanted, or occasionally taken ill with whiskey vapors. And certainly either Kotlowitz or Decter could outshine Willie in routine administrative abilities, duties he had little talent for and even less patience with.

Kotlowitz, forty-two, who had joined *Harper's* two years earlier, was solid bedrock: bright, hard-working, not only an excellent editor but also a fine writer of matters cultural, having grown up in a Baltimore family that appreciated good music, good books, and good theater; in time, he became an accomplished novelist. He had graduated from Peabody Conservatory Prep and Johns Hopkins University. I did not know—until Willie persuaded him to write of it in *Harper's*—that Kotlowitz, as an eighteen-year-old infantryman, had fought in desperate battles in the European theater, being one of a very few survivors when his platoon had been ambushed "in one of those wasteful engagements that litter the landscape of war and benefit no one but the enemy." Perhaps that is why he was capable of weathering any office flap with the greatest equanimity. Bob Kotlowitz valued excellence and honor above all else; discovering a new writer of unusual talent, or a manuscript he prized, he spoke in excited superlatives. His choice accolade was that someone was "a noble man"—not a bad description of Kotlowitz himself. It is hard to think of a better person among all those I have known.

Midge Decter was—and is—married to Norman Podhoretz, longtime editor of *Commentary* magazine, and by her husband's testimony "has always been a better editor than I am." At forty-one, she was "the earth mother" to the staff writers Willie brought aboard: wise, kind, unflappable, and professional to the bone. Before joining *Harper's* she had edited at numerous small magazines and was also a good writer. She published in *Harper's* commentary about the excesses of the sixties and early seventies, but did not lash out at liberals until she and Podhoretz in later years became neoconservatives; Norman in particular turned on numerous of his old friends, including Willie Morris, and seemed somehow to enjoy writing about how old friends had dropped *him;* it was a theme at the center of two of his books. I was astonished at how Podhoretz seemed to view himself as one who once—and mistakenly—had manned liberal barricades because, frankly, I am willing to bet serious money that he has yet to even walk in a picket line. Perhaps "Pod," as we called him in friendlier times, indeed did move from Left to Right but the movement did not cover miles so much as inches, as seen by my naked eye.

The last staffer Willie Morris brought aboard, Herman Gollob, came from Atheneum Publishers to become the founding—and only—editor of Harper's Magazine Press. He was an exotic mix: a Jewish intellectual from Houston who had proudly marched in the military cadet corps at Texas A&M and who bled Aggie maroon. He was great fun in those days. Once, joining Herman Gollob and Willie Morris for lunch, Bill Moyers—an ordained Baptist minister—pointed at Gollob's glass and said, "I didn't know Aggies drank wine." Quick as a flash Herman responded, "It was water until you got here, Reverend."

Unfortunately, at a low point in Willie's life, Gollob felt constrained to turn down Willie's novel, *Taps*. He was amazed to later learn that Willie had considered his act a betrayal. "I wrote as nice a letter as possible," Gollob said. "We wanted a novel with a narrative flow, but Willie wrote an episodic novel without much plot. It wasn't what we had contracted for. I explained that to Willie and asked him a number of times to make changes. There came a day when I knew he would never deliver what we wanted. So what the hell was I supposed to do?"

But that incident was far in the distant future when Willie Morris hired Herman Gollob, and it's just as well that none of us could see a number of unhappy events lurking down the line.

SHORTLY AFTER I BECAME a *Harper's* staffer, Willie asked me to fly to New York to discuss pieces I might soon write. To my surprise, I found myself closeted in Willie's big corner office not only with him but with four staff elders—three holdover ladies and one gentleman from the Jack Fischer regime, none of whom I really knew. I tried to fix Willie with a glare: I hated meetings as much as he professed to, and now he had trapped me in one. Willie was serene, however, and ignored my staring at him. I was astonished to hear him say, "Our new contributing editor, Mr. King, has asked to open this meeting with his favorite song. Go ahead, Sir."

My God, could he mean "Jesus on the Five-Yard Line"? Yes, Willie had asked me to rise and sing it in bars, at a few restaurants, and at private parties, and I always had done so without visible reluctance, shame, or talent. But *here?* Well, what the hell, I'd had a couple of drinks, so I thought, *Okay, Willie, you wanna play hardball? Here's my pitch coming at you!* So I rose and loudly sang, giving cheerleader gestures at the proper places:

> *Oh the game was played on Sunday*
> *In Heaven's own back yard*
> *Jesus played right halfback*
> *And Moses played right guard.*
> *The Angels on the sideline*
> *Christ how they did yell*
> *When Jesus scored a touchdown*
> *Against that team from Hell!*
> *Stay with Christ!*
> *Stay with Christ!*
> *Jesus on the five-yard line*
> *Moses blockin' goddern fine!*
> *Stay with Christ!*
> *Stay With Christ!*
> *HOKE 'EM POKE 'EM*
> *JESUS SOAK 'EM*
> *Staaaaay with Christ!*

Well, sir, the aftermath probably set a new record for thunder-struck silence. In all the years I had performed my semi-bawdy little specialty song, I had been cheered, jeered, threatened, asked for encores, and stood to drinks by strangers—but never had my performance reaped such a deafening silence. "Thank you, Larry," Willie said, and went on for a few minutes talking business with the elders as if nothing untoward had happened, while I sat there feeling like the fifth-place jackass at the county fair, certain that the elders were shooting me scathing looks of disgusted disapproval—though I feared to look up from my twiddling thumbs.

When the elders departed, Willie doubled over in glee: "Did you see their faces?" I had not of course, having fixed my eyes on the middle distance while singing and then on my thumbs when received in such a stifling silence. "Goddammit, Willie," I said. "What was that all about?" He just continued to snicker. Then: "I'll buy you a drink. I owe you that much." We repaired to the Empire Chinese restaurant, and Willie periodically chuckled while we drank but changed the subject every time I tried to ask why he'd embarrassed me. Not for some time did I realize that Willie wanted to ease those elders out the door and replace them with his own people, and having me sing "Jesus on the Five-Yard Line"—in a *staff meeting*, which most of them revered—sent the certain message that the Morris Administration might not be their cup of tea. Soon enough, they all left *Harper's*.

"THERE WERE EIGHT MILLION TELEPHONE NUMBERS in the Manhattan directory"—Willie wrote late in life—"and every one of them would have returned my calls." If that was not precisely true, it was true in spirit. Willie was "good copy"; his youth, his Southern roots and drawl, his yarn-telling ability, his job and his oft-stated ambition for his magazine, his astonishing contacts—well, all these attracted reporters with pens and pads or microphones in their hands. *The New York Times, Newsweek, Time, Publisher's Weekly, The Saturday Review of Literature,* and many other sources gave almost Second Coming headlines or space or air time to his taking over *Harper's* and also took note as he hired several of us for his staff. "Every thing I do or say gets coverage," Willie said—not, I thought, without pleasure—"whether or not it's really news."

At least once, Willie truly "made" news, of a sort, though truth would have been much better served had he not. Having looked up the date, I now know it was the night of August 10, 1970, that Willie appeared on *The David Frost Show*—only four nights before he would be a guest on *The Dick Cavett Show,* so great was Willie's popularity and so ubiquitous his presence at the time.

I settled back in my easy chair to watch *The David Frost Show* that night, and Willie—great raconteur and entertainer that he was—had both Frost and the audience doing his bidding as if they were puppets dancing on his strings: laughing, applauding, enjoying him. Willie told one of his old stories, about a black man from Mississippi—Ben McGee—who died and went to Heaven where the Lord, looking up his record in the Book of Good Deeds, was so impressed he wanted to send Ben McGee back to earth to continue his good works.

"Oh Lord," said Ben McGee, "please don't send me back. You've never been to Mississippi! You don't know what it's like!"

"Well, Ben," the Lord said—perhaps a bit sternly—"I think you should go back and continue your good work among your people. I would hate to put that in the form of an order, but I will if necessary."

Ben McGee sighed and said, "Well, Lord, if I agree to go back to Mississippi, will you go with me?"

Willie gave the Lord the perfect long pause before having Him say, "Well . . . . I'll go as far as Memphis."

That got the biggest applause and laughter of the night—a reaction noted in the official transcript of that program—and the mention of Mississippi probably led to David Frost's next question: "Looking back over the years . . . who's the favorite Mississippian you met?"

For a moment I thought I had misheard Willie when he said, "I guess the favorite Mississippi character I met, and it was in unusual circumstances, was William Faulkner."

I bolted up from my chair, spilling precious Scotch all over myself and the floor, and screamed at the television set, "God*dammit,* Willie! You never met William Faulkner!"

But Willie smoothly continued, "He's a great hero of mine. And I was just a kid. But I'd started reading his work."

"You had *not!*" I yelled.

"And I think Faulkner was writing things in his great catastrophic fiction fifteen or twenty years ago that have become prophetic in human terms today. And I went out on Sardis Lake with him, outside of Oxford, Mississippi, and we went around in a sailboat!"

"*Bullshit, Willie! Bullshit!*"

"He didn't say anything for two hours. So it really wasn't a conversation. He was smoking on his pipe. And finally after two hours he turned to me, and he said, 'Well, Morris, anybody tossed any dead cats on your front porch lately?'" Willie laughed at that non sequitur, Frost laughed, the audience laughed, and Willie quickly segued into a story about his favorite *Texan,* Bob Eckhardt, while I took the Lord's name in vain.

Knowing the Frost show had been taped earlier, I sprang for the telephone. I didn't think Willie would be at home to answer it, or— if he should be home—I very much doubted that he would answer. To my surprise, he *did* answer, though in a clipped British "Hello" unlike his normal voice.

"God*dammit,* Willie!" I shouted. "Have you lost your fuckin' mind?"

"Well now, Larry," he said—obviously embarrassed—"he caught me by surprise and I said 'Faulkner' before it really sunk in that he'd said 'someone you've met,' see, and so I didn't quite know what to do and I just had to make up stuff as I went along."

"Jesus Christ, Willie," I said. "Whatta you gonna do if some reporter from *The New York Times*—or some Mississippi paper or, hell, from *anywhere*—calls and asks you about it?"

"I don't know," he said.

"Well, you better damn sure *think* about it!" I advised.

Willie said, "I'll hang up and start right now!" I next heard the dial tone growling. I couldn't help but chuckle at how quickly he'd turned my advice into an escape hatch. Willie, Willie, Willie: You were, indeed, one of a kind!

MAYBE WILLIE MORRIS NEVER MET William Faulkner, but he soon popped up everywhere with everybody else, it seemed: at a

New York Knicks basketball practice where, after the team drill, star player Bill Bradley might linger to shoot a few baskets with Willie and his young son David Rae; at the home of billionaire politico Averell Harriman to join historian Arthur Schlesinger, Jr., Harper & Row's Cass Canfield, professor-economist-writer and former ambassador to India John Kenneth Galbraith, and other Eastern Establishment Democrats hoping to agree on one or another candidate or cause; at his favorite Chinese restaurant, having a few pops with whatever visiting writer might be in town: James Dickey, Frank Conroy, Edwin (Bud) Shrake, who had persuaded *Sports Illustrated* moguls to permit him to work out of Austin rather than Manhattan.

And surely Willie might often be found at Elaine's—"my nighttime office"—the East Side watering hole of the literati, where he might preside over a table including, say, Norman Mailer and his then-wife, the actress Beverly Bentley, *Sports Illustrated* staffer and novelist Dan Jenkins and his lovely wife, June, playwright Jack Richardson, a visiting fireman such as El Paso lawyer-politico Malcolm McGregor—"One of only two Texas legislators who reads books," Willie might introduce him—and Elaine Kaufman, the owner of the place.

Any number of familiar faces might pause at Willie's table to say hello: Mayor John Lindsay; former Miss America Phyllis George; actress Lauren Bacall and her escort; Congressman and New York Governor-to-be Hugh Carey, as well as common-garden-variety agents, editors, and writers. Willie trolled Elaine's for writers for his magazine and while some late-night deals didn't work out, many more did. A few, admittedly, carried comic overtones: illegible "contracts" scrawled at 3 A.M. on soiled napkins, a manuscript or two lost in a cab, Willie recalling after a night's hard drinking that he had contracted for an article about something with somebody but recalling no specifics. "That could be the worst thing," he confessed to me some years later. "Waiting for the other shoe to drop."

One such "forgotten" assignment involved Joe Goulden, managing editor of *The Daily Texan* when Willie was editor-in-chief, and Willie's sometimes antagonist. (Goulden said often of those early days, "I appeared to be more of a mossback than I truly was, just to agitate Willie.") At any rate, Goulden had written one article for *Harper's* about those Spiro Agnew had called America's "silent majority"; Willie liked it. And published it.

Sometime later, Goulden sought Morris out at Elaine's and proposed doing a piece on conscientious objectors—young men who, for religious or moral reasons, refused to serve in the military during the Vietnam War. "Many are in prison"—Goulden told Willie—"and I'll seek them out, and their girlfriends or wives and their weeping mothers." Willie said it sounded good to him, according to Goulden, and authorized him to write the piece for *Harper's*.

"I traveled and interviewed for about six weeks," Goulden says. "Then I wrote the piece, and sent it to Willie. By then I had a couple of months invested, to say nothing of the money I'd spent. And a day or so later Midge Decter called me and said, 'Joe, what's going on about this conscientious objector piece?' I told Midge Willie approved the assignment at Elaine's one night and she said, 'Don't *ever* act on an assignment Willie gave you when he was drinking, without checking with him—or me—the next day. Willie says he didn't make the assignment, that you must have sent the piece in on your own, and he doesn't want it.'" Goulden was stunned. "Midge did get me my expense money and doubled the magazine's usual kill fee," Goulden recalls. "But that broke me of doing business with Willie."

But there were successes when Willie trolled Elaine's; I recall these off the top of my head: Pete Axthelm's "The City Game," illustrating how playground basketball eventually provided an escape from the ghetto for many young black men, appeared in the magazine and then was expanded into a book for Harper's Magazine Press; Jack Richardson's much-remarked piece on the Ali–Quarry fight in Atlanta, and another essay, on gambling—which was the love of Richardson's life and which became a book; Norman Mailer's slant on the women's movement, "The Prisoner of Sex"; Bud Shrake's "In the Land of the Permanent Wave," treating the cultural mores and prejudices of deep East Texas, a work of which Willie Morris said, "Few finer magazine essays have ever been written"; my own *Confessions of a White Racist* began as a *Harper's* article following a discussion with Willie at Elaine's in the wee hours when he said, "Write that for me." My article, the theme of which was that most whites were racists to one degree or another. turned into a book that was a finalist for the National Book Award.

PERHAPS ONE THING SET WILLIE MORRIS APART from all other editors, in the eyes of writers: Far more than others, he was prone to permit whatever space a writer needed for a given work. That does not mean that he encouraged, or accepted, careless spewings. So long as a writer used the space he needed wisely and well, however, the sky was the limit. Willie did not believe, as virtually all magazine editors do today, that readers' attention spans were no wider than butterfly wings.

This was most dramatically illustrated in a piece Norman Mailer wrote about an anti–Vietnam War march he participated in, as one of the leaders who led thousands of protesters in a march on the Pentagon. The moment Willie Morris heard that Norman Mailer had been arrested and jailed for his civil disobedience, he knew that Mailer could no more resist writing about it than a glutton could push away from the dinner table. He made frantic attempts to reach Mailer by phone, but learned he was ostensibly in hiding; Willie did reach Mailer's "big money" agent, Scott Meredith, who refused to put Morris in touch but said he would pass messages; after a bit of to-and-fro they began negotiations. Mailer wanted $10,000 for as many words from *Harper's,* but that wasn't all he demanded: The magazine would also be responsible for finding a book publisher willing to pay $25,000 for a short book. Without that—no deal.

John Cowles, Jr. came up with the $10,000, but Willie knew that finding a book publisher to shell out $25,000 was on his head; he took along Midge Decter, a close friend of Mailer, to help. Several editors flatly turned Morris-Decter-Mailer down; one said he was not in the market for an expensive "pamphlet." Robert Gutwillig, who had bought and edited my 1966 novel, *The One-Eyed Man,* when I was unknown to everyone except bill collectors, again proved bolder than others and grabbed the opportunity on behalf of New American Library.

Willie went for celebratory drinks and then, on the way to catch the subway home, literally bumped into Norman Mailer at the corner of Seventh Avenue and 44th Street. "We just closed the deal!" Willie happily announced. "I know! I know!" Mailer said, spryly dancing and peppering Willie with light jabs—inspired, perhaps, by the company of a companion, light-heavyweight champion Jose Torres. Throwing punches at the air, Mailer said he would be off the following day to his house in Provincetown, on Cape Cod, to commence work, and "This one could be kind of good."

Two weeks into the writing, Mailer called to say his piece had expanded beyond the agreed-upon 10,000 words; he required another month, perhaps five weeks, to finish the job. Without hesitating, Willie Morris pushed publication back from the issue of February 1968, to the March issue, and that meant a new printer's deadline of January 10. Mailer went back to work; he did not communicate except for terse messages passed through Scott Meredith.

With the printer's deadline a week away, Willie and Midge Decter flew by chartered airplane to Provincetown, high winds buffeting the small craft, and snow blowing across the ground; the wind-aided waves of Cape Cod crashed onto the shore near Mailer's home. Mailer was still writing the end of the piece, scrawling in longhand on a yellow legal tablet. In another room his secretary decoded his penmanship, the longhand pages replete with cross-outs and inserts running crazily uphill and down like a drunk jogger's path. In a third room, Willie Morris sat down to get his first glimpse of Mailer's manuscript, handing pages to Midge Decter as he finished them. Fifteen minutes into the reading, Willie looked at Midge and said, "It's marvelous!" She agreed that they had something extraordinary.

Willie called Bob Kotlowitz, waiting for word in his *Harper's* office.

"How is it?" Kotlowitz asked. He was delighted when Willie said, "Marvelous."

"Great! How long!"

"Ninety thousand words.

Kotlowitz was temporarily speechless. "Uh . . . should we run it in two installments or three?"

"I think we should run it all at once."

Silence. Then: "Well, why the hell not?"

They did, of course, run it all in a single issue, under the title "On the Steps of the Pentagon." As a book, published as *The Armies of the Night,* Mailer's work won both the Pulitzer Prize and the National Book Award. Only later did Willie Morris learn that he had published the longest article in the history of magazines, Mailer's piece eclipsing John Hersey's "Hiroshima," published in 1946 in *The New Yorker.*

Within months, Mailer again got almost a full issue to expound on the two national political conventions of 1968, "Miami and the Siege of Chicago." It, too, became a book, won several awards, and was a National Book Award finalist. Three years later Mailer had another near-full issue with "The Prisoner of Sex."

Willie's experience with long pieces began with the 45,000-word excerpt he took from Bill Styron's *The Confessions of Nat Turner.* Halberstam, Frady, and I were given unusual space for several articles, mine being "Confessions of a White Racist," a long piece about my father after his death ("The Old Man")—and my last article for the magazine, as it turned out, "The Road to Power in Congress," about a relative newcomer, Rep. Morris (Mo) Udall, who believed reform was needed in the national legislative body, and made a serious challenge to the leadership by running for House majority leader. (And learning the hard lesson that no matter what one's colleagues may say to one's face, they are not above a little lying, horse-trading, and backbiting in order to retain the comfort of the status quo; only minutes after losing the secret ballot vote in the Democratic Caucus to Hale Boggs of Louisiana, 140 to 88—with Bernie Sisk of California getting 17—Udall, who thought he had at least 108 votes going in, asked a small group of his consoling supporters, "Do you know the difference between a cactus and a caucus? Well, a cactus has all its pricks on the *outside!*")

Bill Moyers, who had been on LBJ's staff as both a Senate and vice presidential aide before becoming his White House press secretary, and who also had been Sargent Shriver's top aide at the Peace Corps, was assigned to travel around and about America by bus and car, to go where his instinct or impulses carried him, to talk to people of all walks of life about anything and everything. The notion was Willie's, but Moyers executed it to perfection. His "Listening to America" ran 45,000 words long in the magazine, then became the first best-seller published by Harper's Magazine Press. (This occurred after Moyers had been relieved of his editorship at *Newsday.* Moyers has said that the book he wrote for Willie led to his job with PBS, and, so, in effect, Willie Morris had a large hand in Moyers's career in television.)

Another big project—one of the best Willie bought—almost fell in his lap, but at least he had the judgment and skill to catch it. It began when Gay Talese, a former *New York Times* reporter and a free-lance journalist who published fine work in *Esquire* and elsewhere, got his friend David Halberstam to introduce him to Willie Morris. Talese brought along his book-in-progress, eventually to be published as the award-winning best seller *The Kingdom and the Power,* which was a marvelous, detailed look at the history of *The New York Times,* profiles of many of its editors and reporters and how they operated. In short and in sum, it was the first of the big "media" books—and that is precisely what originally caused Talese so much grief.

Nobody—editors at publishing houses kept telling Talese—wants to read about journalists. It's a boring subject. One editor, fascinated by *The New York Times,* ultimately gave Talese a modest advance. Talese was a deliberate writer rather than a rapid one and also a patient writer in that he spent far more time than most hanging out with his subjects; he stayed with them until he thought he had his story. That technique served Talese well—nobody was writing better stuff than Gay Talese then wrote for *Esquire;* he was a true star—but he spent so much time on magazine pieces he could not finish his *New York Times* book unless he could get more front money. But the one editor interested in his book refused to put more money into it; without more money—essentially, to buy time—Talese thought his goose was cooked, though he sensed he was writing a work that might financially free him.

That's when Talese went to see Willie Morris, hoping against hope to sell him an excerpt of his manuscript. Willie Morris bought a $10,000 chunk and published it in two issues. Not only did Willie recognize it as brilliant work, he knew that having Talese in his magazine would be another strong signal that he was, indeed, dead serious about making *Harper's* second to none.

"I don't know what might have happened to my writing career," Talese has said, "if Willie Morris hadn't bought those excerpts. His buying them gave me a shot at having the kind of career I wanted, and it all worked out."

After Willie's death, Gay Talese wrote a tribute in which he told that story, adding that, years later, he encountered Willie Morris at a journalists' symposium being conducted by former newspaperman and novelist Winston Groom, and called Willie aside to let him know how important his decision had been to Talese's career, and how grateful he had been and still was. I'm particularly delighted those flowers were delivered to the living.

CHAPTER 9

THE 1960S AND 1970S were decades in which political activists seemed to sprout like wildflowers. Journalists, for the first time in large lots, became partisans who often took to the stump for their favorite candidates. I was guilty of that sin—if it is one—campaigning for, among others, Eugene McCarthy and Mo Udall for president, and for Norman Mailer as mayor of New York City. None of my candidates won, though I don't know that I deserve full blame.

Willie Morris didn't believe that I should be any candidate's "man"; he thus advised me to turn down Governor Nelson Rockefeller's attempt to hire me as a speechwriter for his aborted presidential campaign in 1968, though "Rocky" had offered me enough money to burn a wet mule.

That does not mean, however, that Willie Morris was without political friends or political influences. Bill Moyers, when he was LBJ's press secretary, gave him a midnight tour of the Oval Office and spoke of Willie's perhaps contributing to the president's speeches, but that never happened. Willie did set up a meeting in Washington and escorted the New York Knicks basketball star Bill Bradley to the home of Congressman Mo Udall (D-Ariz.) where Udall and Senator William Fulbright (D-Ark.) persuaded Bradley not to return to his home state, Missouri, to run for state treasurer. "It's a nothing job and a stepping-stone to nowhere," Udall bluntly told him; they convinced him he should run for the U.S. Senate, either in New York or New Jersey, due to his fame as a former Princeton All-American and

Knicks star; in due course, Bradley served as senator from New Jersey and—as had Udall before him—later tried unsuccessfully for the Democrats' presidential nomination. In his glory years, Willie Morris could call on any number of powerful politicians—from future Speaker Jim Wright of Texas to Vice President Hubert Humphrey to Senator Ted Kennedy—fully confident they would make time for him.

Willie enjoyed telling how he had come to be friendly with Senator Kennedy. It had occurred at the Manhattan home of Jean Stein on a hot summer's night when the air-conditioning went on the fritz during the party where Willie first met the writer James Jones. Willie took off his coat and tie and turned back the cuffs of his shirt, because of the heat, and was standing by the bar—waiting, indeed, for the bartender, who had stepped away from his duty station—when suddenly Senator Kennedy handed Willie his glass and said, "That's Scotch and water, please." Willie realized that Kennedy had taken him for the bartender; Willie smiled to himself—because he had met the senator and exchanged small talk on a couple of occasions, including earlier that very night. Willie moved behind the bar and mixed the senator's drink. When Senator Kennedy departed with it, Willie saw Jim Jones leaning against a wall, laughing his ass off. Jones then said to the senator, "Did you know you just mistook the editor-in-chief of *Harper's* for the bartender?" Kennedy rushed to Willie to make amends and even insisted on mixing *him* a drink. Thereafter, Willie could pretty much call his shots with Ted Kennedy.

The incident also helped along a quick friendship between Jim Jones, who was visiting from Paris, and Willie Morris. A few days later, Willie took Jones to his favorite Chinese restaurant near the *Harper's* office and maneuvered matters so that when the novelist who wrote so graphically about war opened his fortune cookie, it read, *You made your wad off the misery of others.*

Soon there was another reason for Willie Morris to be celebrated: publication of his "autobiography in mid-passage," *North Toward Home.* I worried about the book on first hearing Willie was writing it: Might not he be slammed for having the audacity to write his *memoir* at age thirty-two? I needn't have worried; Willie's first book was warmly received, to say the least; I never saw a bad review of that book. The London *Sunday Times* called *North Toward Home* "the best evocation of American boyhood since Mark Twain." It won the Houghton-Mifflin Company's in-house $5,000 prize as its best liter-ary offering of the year, and the $1,000 Carr P. Collins Award for the best book of nonfiction, given by the Texas Institute of Letters. (Celia Morris would, fifteen years later, win the Carr P. Collins Award for her *Fanny Wright: Rebel in America*.)

Willie was more relieved than exhilarated: He had many mo-ments of doubt during the writing. "I got time off from Jack Fischer to finish the book," he said. "About three months, I think. He said *Harper's* couldn't pay me, however, so I borrowed money from a bank to live on. Every time I'd bog down or have a bad day—and you know that happens on *any* writing project—I'd be in a panic. If I failed . . . Well, I could not afford even to *think* about failure."

Ironically, the only real criticisms of *North Toward Home* came from Willie's mother and a few disgruntled townspeople in Yazoo City. That worried Willie, but finally a Yazoo friend spoke helpful words: "The only people knocking your book are the ones pissed off because they aren't in it!"

SOON WILLIE HAD ANOTHER TRIUMPH, though for a time it seemed to him a torture. The good news was that Max Ascoli, the owner and editor of *The Reporter*, a long-respected liberal publica-tion of politics and ideas—about to fold the magazine because of its deficit and debts—approached the Cowles family about buying its subscription list. *Harper's* would pay a fee—Willie never was told how much by the money men—and, additionally, it would send *Harper's* to *The Reporter*'s subscribers so that, when the latter folded, Ascoli would not have to refund money they had paid for their subscrip-tions; *Harper's*, once such obligation had passed, presumably would manage to get most *Reporter* readers to subscribe to *Harper's*.

The bad news—as Willie quickly came to view it—was that Max Ascoli would join *Harper's* as a "consulting editor"; his articles and columns would be published in *Harper's* and some few of *The Reporter's* editorial features included. Additionally, several of Ascoli's writers and editors—Meg Greenfeld and Claire Sterling come to mind—would join the *Harper's* staff. Willie had not been consulted by the money men though, obviously, his magazine's content would be changed; he had doubts as to whether so many changes in his domain might be for the best, both for the magazine and for himself personally. John Cowles, Jr., however, insisted on the deal going down: "We need those subscribers."

During the early negotiations, the seventy-year-old Ascoli, who had fled his native Italy when Mussolini and his fascists came to power—seemed to Willie to be "a paradigm of charm, of solicitude, and intimate camaraderie." When Willie said as much, a veteran *Reporter* editor laughed without mirth. "He'll love you for two months," the old editor said to the young editor. "Then he'll turn on you so bad you won't know what's happening. Believe me, your arrangement [with him] won't work. Take the damned subscriptions and run." Willie began to make inquiries and found that "Max Ascoli was infamous in New York for his tyrannies and impetuosities. He had left in his wake over the years a trail of shattered relationships, personal and professional, nearly transcontinental in its smoky breadth and sweep." Not good. And it would get worse.

Ascoli quickly began acting as if the editor-in-chief of *Harper's* might be little more than his office boy. He told Willie the many things wrong with his magazine, knocked many *Harper's* writers, and made it known that he looked forward—once the deal had been signed for *The Reporter's* subscription list—to advising and consulting Willie Morris on a daily basis. "I'm sure he stalled the signing of that subscription list deal to gain more leverage over me and over *Harper's*," Willie later said.

Almost daily, Ascoli in his chauffeured limousine picked Willie up at the corner of Park Avenue and 33rd, near the *Harper's* office, and took him to the kind of pricey, fancy restaurants Willie despised. In addition to lecturing him about the shortcomings of *Harper's,* the old man also instructed him as to haute cuisine and fine wines—this torture inflicted on one who enjoyed telling some puzzled, if haughty, maître d' in a celebrated French restaurant, "Bring me a slab of cornbread and a glass of clabber." (The only food I ever heard Willie Morris rave about was the catfish in a country café about a half-hour drive from Oxford, Mississippi.)

If Willie begged off lunch, Ascoli without prior notice dispatched his liveried chauffeur to drive Willie to his grand mansion across from Gramercy Park, the only private park in Manhattan: Property owners surrounding the fenced park had keys to unlock the gates, and others were unwelcome. Only after the limo had been dispatched did Ascoli telephone Willie to tell him it was en route— whether at 9 A.M. or 4 P.M. Should Willie's secretary say he was not in, or was unavailable, Ascoli would scold her and order her to find him and send him to the corner to await his carriage. Willie, of course, hated those drills even when they took place in the grand mansion on the park among fine paintings, great books, and with Puccini resonating from the stereo. Several times he called John Cowles, Jr. to say he just couldn't put up with Ascoli's bullshit another day. Always, he was told that he must: that the new subscriptions *Harper's* would reap were vital.

This was a dubious plan, frankly: *The Reporter* had slipped greatly in influence and readership, not being nearly what it had been a decade earlier. And *good* magazines, *serious* magazines—*Atlantic Monthly, Esquire, Harper's* itself—were having trouble retaining subscribers while once-popular periodicals such as *The Saturday Evening Post, Collier's, Liberty,* and *Life* had folded or soon would. Television, which took up time, had a great deal to do with America's rather sudden change in its reading habits, as did book clubs; many newspapers were being written brighter and better, columnists, op-ed pages, and even some news stories offering more opinion and analysis than long had been the case. But, strangely, nobody in Minneapolis seemed aware of that reality. Or perhaps it wasn't so strange: I do not recall our *Harper's* group, or other writers, being preoccupied with the changes already beginning to reveal themselves in the "information" business. We all seem, in retrospect, to have been myopic.

At long last came the great day. John Cowles, Jr. and his top money men flew to New York from Minneapolis to sign the subscription list deal at Ascoli's mansion. Ascoli demanded several amendments to the deal earlier agreed upon, almost all of them having to do with how much money he would be paid not only for his subscription list but for his varied services. At each such impasse, young Cowles and his money men stepped into another room to make decisions—leaving Willie Morris in the dark. Willie was so eager to have his Ascoli tortures over with, however, that he took no umbrage over being excluded from the proceedings, though that really was an insensitive and unforgivable outrage; an insult almost the equal of a slap in the face.

When, at long last, the papers were signed, "Outside, in the cool night air of regal Gramercy"—Willie wrote—"we slapped hands like cornerbacks after an opportune interception, and ventured out into the city to celebrate. I felt fine, and as close to them in that moment as I ever would. . . ."

WITHIN A FEW DAYS, Willie felt even better. What eventually proved to be a blessing began when Ascoli threw a hissy fit, claiming that Willie Morris had booked the historian Arthur Schlesinger, Jr. to write an article *he* had intended soon to write for *Harper's,* on violence in America; it was, Ascoli said, a deliberate betrayal by Willie. Not so, Willie said: Schlesinger's speech on that subject at a university commencement had impressed him, so he had asked him to recast the speech as a magazine article; he had not been aware of Ascoli's intent to write on the same subject. Ascoli would not believe him, and insisted on John Cowles, Jr. coming to New York to see him about Willie's "betrayal." Though feeling a bit of trepidation, Willie arranged for Cowles and a couple of his top business associates to fly to New York. There, Ascoli bluntly said he would have nothing more to do with *Harper's:* He could do nothing about the subscription list, that was a done deal, unfortunately, but by God he would not write a line for *Harper's,* nor permit any of the defunct *Reporter's* features to appear in it, and he would urge his former employees not to write for *Harper's* either. Then he turned away from Willie Morris and in a last defiant gesture refused to shake his hand. Apparently Ascoli was persuaded he was punishing all within the sound of his voice, *Harper's* itself, and all of its readers—new or old. In truth, Willie Morris had to bite his lip to hide a grin. Once the *Harper's* contingent left Ascoli, however, Willie didn't have to hide his satisfaction. "You did it!" one of the Minnesota Mafia members said to Willie. "You won't have to put up with that old bastard ever again!" That thought inspired Willie Morris to release a long and loud *Yeeee-Haaaaw.*

Yessir, Ol' Willie was drinking wine as fine and heady as any Max Ascoli had urged upon him . . . until the bottle broke.

THERE HAD BEEN AMPLE SIGNS—had we paid close attention—that all was not perfect in Paradise. David Halberstam's keen nose got the first whiff of trouble, sometime in 1970, when he talked with me about Willie's being harder than usual to reach and becoming much more casual about his office hours. We knew that Bob Kotlowitz and Midge Decter were perfectly capable of putting out the magazine, but we found it a bit disconcerting that our leader wasn't around to lead us as much as formerly. "We began to have to cover for Willie maybe forty percent of the time, rather than the usual twenty percent of the time, when he couldn't be found or reached during office hours," Halberstam later recalled.

When he was around, Willie Morris increasingly and resentfully complained of being "harassed" by the Cowles family and their retainers on his periodic business trips to Minneapolis. When we tried to pin him down as to *specifics,* however, Willie would neither name nor define them beyond generalized statements that he wasn't being adequately "appreciated" and he would close the subject by saying something like "Don't worry about it, I'm taking care of it, everything's under control." Well, that simply wasn't true. Willie's personal life had spiraled out of control by late 1968; he and Celia got a far-from-amicable divorce in May of 1969, Celia getting the degree in Juárez, Mexico, after a battle she won over Willie requiring that the profits from the sale of their country house in the Hudson Valley be placed in a trust fund for David Rae. For years after the divorce Willie and Celia rarely spoke except through lawyers or by letters that read like grand jury indictments.

Who knows what goes wrong in a marriage? Many malfunctions, misunderstandings, grudges, and hostilities—generally accrued over the years—contribute to any divorce, and almost always each party feels somehow victimized. Willie claimed the main problem was Celia's "slavery to goddamned shrinks." He told me, "She can be in a fine, good humor, we'll be getting along perfectly well. Then she goes to the goddamned shrink and comes home crying and trying to pick fights with me. And after awhile, it makes me avoid going home."

Celia saw it quite differently: Willie had rarely rushed home no matter the circumstances. And as for analysis, "the long process saved my life . . . and the stronger I got, the worse the marriage became." Willie couldn't understand why Celia wasn't happy "being a part" of his *Harper's* life, while Celia felt that she was not a part of Willie's professional life so much as a distant and ignored spectator; it frustrated and angered her that Willie showed no interest in her ambition to have a professional life of her own, that when she might be reading authors Willie liked—Twain, Fitzgerald, Wolfe, whomever—he wouldn't join in her efforts to talk about them. He simply gave his wife very little of himself.

Drinking—by both of them—fueled their quarrels and sometimes aided tumultuous conduct; they exchanged slaps and curses. Willie, in his cups, a couple of times actually followed Celia's analyst, whom he blamed for "undue influence" on his wife, and even considered attacking him physically. Fortunately, he pulled back from such madness. Bob Kotlowitz recalls Willie coming in to *Harper's* one midday with an entire arm bandaged "from shoulder to thumb" and recalls now that Willie's terse explanation did get across the notion he had cut himself on broken glass during a domestic dispute. *This is incurable,* flashed in Kotlowitz's mind.

(Celia Morris said, after reading the above, in the first draft I sent to about a dozen of my sources to invite their comments, that I needed to examine "more positive moments.")

At least a paragraph or two about the upside of our marriage. As it is, it's all downside and hard stuff. But Willie wouldn't have tried so desperately to keep that marriage together if he hadn't wanted it. And he wanted it for a whole bunch of reasons including, frankly, that he was proud of me. Most of his friends quickly became my friends too—and a good many of them, at least before the *Harper's* period, more mine, in the end, than Willie's. And I brought lots of friends into the marriage and kept them there. The passages in *my* book in which I talk about the thrill of Oxford, the excitement of the [Texas] *Observer* period, the dynamite of New York—Willie was an integral part of New York, and we were together in it. I finally gave up on Willie, as I said, for reasons you now understand so well. But I wouldn't have stayed so long if a lot of it hadn't been vital and full of adventure. When Willie left he said, in tears, "But we grew up together. . . ." I think you need to get some of that in your book.

ALCOHOL WAS BECOMING an increasing problem for Willie Morris—and, unknown to us at the time, he also became dependent on Valium, taking "a dozen or more" pills daily—potentially, and literally, a deadly combination.

David Halberstam tried to talk to Willie about drinking but Willie froze him out. Old Texas friend Malcolm McGregor chastised him: "Willie, you don't have to go through this 'tortured writer' routine just because you're in the same trade Scott Fitzgerald was in. Drinking ruined his talent and killed him young." I didn't try even try to talk to Willie about heavy drinking: It would have been a case of the pot calling the kettle black.

Joseph Epstein, who wrote a sometimes acerbic, sometimes whimsical column for *American Scholar* magazine, who has taught English at Northwestern University for years, and who later became a neoconservative, sold Willie an article in which he voiced his fear that gays might somehow pose a threat to his two young sons; this was a year after the 1969 Stonewall Riots in Greenwich Village, which gave rise to the gay rights movement. Charles Kaiser, later to become a *Newsweek* editor and the author of a book about gays in New York, *The Gay Metropolis,* called Epstein's 1970 article "one of the most disgusting pieces ever printed" on the subject of gays; he was particularly incensed by Epstein's having written, "If I had the power to do so, I would wish homosexuality off the face of the earth." David Halberstam has said, "Change 'homosexuality' to Jews to understand just how terrible that statement was."

Hardly had that issue of *Harper's* hit the newsstands than a large delegation of angry gays marched into the offices at 2 Park Avenue. They spilled into the halls, the small waiting room, even the working offices of all *Harper's* employees, and demanded to see the editor-in-chief—bold actions for the time. Bob Kotlowitz managed to contact Willie by telephone about mid-day to apprise him of the growing anger of the visitors. "You handle it," Willie said, claiming he had an appointment he couldn't miss. "Willie, *you're* the editor," Kotlowitz said. "It's you they want to see." But Willie was adamant: He could not and would not come in. And he didn't.

Periodically, Willie would blossom anew: keeping longer office hours, hustling writers, spending more time with the staff, putting more into an issue-in-progress. "Even at reduced speed," David Halberstam has said,

Willie Morris was far better than ninety-nine out of a hundred magazine editors. He may not have been laced as tightly as John Cowles, Jr. would have liked, and he may have been too far ahead of the curve to please either John Jr. or his father, but he was just about irreplaceable as an editor with the right instincts. What Willie *liked* to do he did very well right to the end. What he didn't like to do, he didn't do very well. And the more success you have, the more responsibilities are thrust on you and this means many of them are things you don't like to do. Willie let those distasteful chores—answering mail, returning phone calls, responding to complaints, attending meetings—pile up, unattended. And the more they pile up, the more you have to hide from later on because you've let those things get away from you.

Willie sometimes confided that old John Cowles often complained to his son that *Harper's* was much more trouble than was *The Minneapolis Tribune,* that John Jr. was giving too much time to the magazine and too free a rein to those who practiced the "New Journalism"; it was a kind of journalism the elder Cowles disapproved of, being too opinionated, too judgmental, grinding axes, attacking established institutions or long-time social or cultural practices newly fallen from favor; its practitioners resented publishers and claimed they were being "hobbled." The old patriarch liked none of that. Willie told us that though Cowles-the-Younger was disturbed by his father's litany of complaints, "nothing will come of it."

David Halberstam wasn't so sure. He had felt a backlash when he wrote critically in *Harper's* of McGeorge Bundy, Robert McNamara, and other high muckety-mucks who frequently war-whooped of a sure and certain victory in Vietnam, at that bright "light at the end of the tunnel." His targets' friends in the Establishment—among them Archibald MacLeish and, yes, ex-*Harper's* top dog and one-time Willie Morris mentor Jack Fischer—had sent letters of protest to the Cowles family or to Harper & Row Publisher Cass Canfield. Canfield passed on Fischer's letter without comment, but even that was enough to disturb Junior Cowles who was, after all, himself of the Establishment, having been born to it; he coveted the Establishment's good will, and surely didn't wish to be seated below the salt when he next dined at the staid old Century Club where—Willie Morris once privately joked—the attendants carried little mirrors to give covert breath tests to any inert old form suspiciously too long still in a distant cracked-leather chair. So John Cowles, Jr. reflexively agreed with those who were his social pals and business friends.

Eventually, Halberstam got word of that. He wrote Cowles-the-Younger a blunt letter: If you have questions or problems about my work, then come to the source; writers have the right to expect their publishers to deal with them openly and to back them up when the facts warrant it, rather than siding with their complaining friends. Junior knew the ring of honest anger when he heard it; he wrote Halberstam a contrite apology, offering to fly to New York to make personal amends. Not necessary—Halberstam responded—just don't *ever* do it again. One must wonder—in light of future events— if being upbraided by one of his own writers, as Cowles saw it, didn't leave a lingering bitter taste in his mouth.

WILLIE'S PERSONAL LIFE continued to be a roller-coaster ride. In mid-1969, the ink hardly dry on his divorce decree, Willie got engaged to be married. The bride was to be Taddy McAllister, twenty-three, a tall, lithe young woman whose grandfather was the long-time mayor of San Antonio and whose father and brother were prominent there in the savings and loan business.

A graduate of the University of Texas, Miss McAllister aspired to write and at the time she visited New York—and called Willie Morris, whom she never had met—she had written a novel with the fetching title of "Sweet Pussy." She invoked my name, and that of Ronnie Dugger, among other of Willie's friends, and Willie received her in his office. They began to keep company. In just a few months, they made plans to marry. Before long Willie visited the big house on the hill in one of San Antonio's better precincts, to meet the McAllister clan. A wedding date was set—for October 25, 1969— and Willie was introduced to Taddy's friends in San Antonio, where the wedding was to be held.

Taddy and her younger sister, Eloise, planned to travel around Europe that summer, but with her wedding pending "I almost didn't go to Europe," Taddy McAllister said in later years. "But Willie said, 'Oh no, go ahead, and enjoy your vacation. I'll be here when you get back.'"

Except that he wasn't, really. Though the couple had exchanged sweet words over the telephone "from almost every stop in Europe," Taddy realized on reaching New York that Willie was a bit distant and preoccupied—not at all the eager lover she had expected to welcome her home. On Taddy's second day back, Willie broke the bad news: He had met someone else, someone he was certain he loved; he felt wretched about it but—where Taddy was concerned—it was over. Sorry. The young lady was devastated, but left New York immediately and never called Willie again, returning to the curative waters of the family's Gulf Coast retreat on Mustang Island and to the therapeutic attentions of her family. Say for Miss McAllister that she recovered quickly and thereafter suffered no shortage of suitors.

Willie Morris had been introduced by Bill Styron one evening at Elaine's to a wealthy divorcee, Muriel Oxenberg Murphy. And Willie was smitten on the spot. Listen to how he described her in *New York Days:*

> She had light brown hair, blue-green eyes, a narrow-bridged nose, her slender face in profile uplifted in an odd, almost haughty gaze, and then, contradistinctively, a riotous grin and giggling laughter, a slouch of the shoulder, a long gliding gait, and slight toss of the head, a Manhattanite of the deepest core, irreverently bright, educated at Barnard, a founder of the American painting and sculpture department at the Metropolitan. . . . On a wall she had a picture of herself when she was twelve years old, taken at her brother's *bar mitzvah,* a picture that haunted me so with her dark brooding gaze and an air of repose of such vulnerability and expectancy and gentleness that I told her I would write a little story one day about her called "The Girl in the Bar Mitzvah Photograph. . . ."

She had serious money, too, if you're keeping a tote sheet: Her factory-owning father had made a fortune in sardines, and her ex-husband another fortune in lumber; apparently, both her inheritance and her divorce settlement had been as far from miserly as can be calculated either in miles or millions. Muriel Oxenberg Murphy owned a four-story townhouse in the East 60s high-rent district and a big duplex in the Hamptons with a private "pond" that a desert rat such as myself might have called a lake. More amazing than anything else, Willie Morris seemed to willingly accompany Ms. Murphy to an endless parade of art-gallery openings, to the American Opera Society's events, to artsy charity auctions and other cultural traps that his friends might have expected him to flee from, screaming. I half-wondered whether Muriel Oxenberg Murphy had hypnotized Willie, or maybe laid a voodoo spell on him. Nothing else seemed to explain the influence she had over him, or his willingness to do her every bidding. Unless, of course, he was seriously in love—and I think that, for a pretty long time, he was in love with Ms. Murphy.

Not all of us at *Harper's* were as delighted with her as was Willie Morris. We thought she treated Willie's proud staffers like "the help"; when we visited her "salon"—at *Willie's* invitation, you may be sure—she usually spoke only French to her cosmopolitan guests, many visiting from abroad, even knowing that we understood no French beyond "Chevrolet coupe." One night, in our cups, Willie and I retaliated by loudly talking to each other in Pig Latin. Ms. Murphy was not amused.

And I was not amused to see Willie pick up large tabs in posh restaurants for friends or guests of Muriel Murphy, even though by our standards she had more money than God and Willie's salary was but $37,500 annually. Willie charged such evenings to his expense account, but very early saw the sums would not look good on the *Harper's* balance sheet. He tricked me into coming along one interminably endless evening—not telling me that Muriel and her entourage would be joining us. When I several times tried to leave, Willie almost desperately signaled that I must stay. When I stood to go to the rest room, Willie quickly followed as if fearing I might sneak away. "Goddammit, Willie!" I said. "How much more of their phony-baloney horse shit do you expect me to tolerate?" Willie said he was sorry, but I had to stay to put the bill on my credit card because he couldn't load any more on his; I was to turn in an expense account equal to the evening's cost; he would see that I got promptly reimbursed. I said, "Willie, I won't do this again. Get the goddamned check when we get back to the table, I'll pay it and then I'm gone!" Not long after, Willie cut up his credit cards so he couldn't use them, then tried the impossible task of gluing them back together the next day.

The thing I found most troubling—as did David Halberstam—was that Muriel Murphy often told Willie, in effect, that he *was* *Harper's* magazine, that no one could edit and promote the magazine with the ability that he did, that he was indispensable; she said that to me, and others, one night in Willie's presence and I got the notion it was not the first time Willie had heard that message. Willie had by then received accolades enough to turn the heads of a den full of Hydras, but had managed—I thought–not to take his publicity, or himself, too seriously. But, somehow, he seemed to begin to believe himself "not appreciated" by the Cowles family, to say that he was not given credit in Minneapolis for the prestige and acclaim he had brought to the magazine; maybe he should threaten to quit; maybe that would by God show 'em. That's when I told him, "Willie, remember this: Unless you own the mill, you ain't nothing but a mill hand. And you don't own the mill."

IN EARLY 1969 one William S. Blair had suddenly appeared as business manager at *Harper's*. I did not see much of the man or know much about him; cancer, which had been discovered in my wife, Rosemarie, only nine months after we were married in early 1965, had again attacked her and she was despondent; I spent most of my time with her—at home or in the National Institutes of Health cancer ward—when not on the road interviewing or gathering material for various magazine articles. And later that year, when Rosemarie's cancer again was in remission, I became a Nieman Fellow at Harvard and during that academic year only occasionally visited the *Harper's* office in New York.

Willie told me that Blair was an advertising man, married to a rich woman, and that he lived in commodious quarters near Gramercy Park, close to Max Ascoli's mansion. When Willie and Celia were getting divorced, Blair pressed Willie to use a spare bedroom in his home until he could make permanent arrangements. Willie did so, though he expressed reluctance. "Why?" I asked. Willie said he didn't trust Bill Blair; that he thought John Cowles, Jr. had sent him to spy on Willie, to be "the plantation overseer with a whip in his hand." Willie said he could not discern what Blair's duties were: "He spent a small fortune redecorating his office, money we damn well could have used to pay writers for articles, and yet Blair just sits on his butt for the most part except when he's nosing around me."

On the other hand, Willie thought Blair did too much in terms of trying to set the editorial agenda. "All those damned surveys, asking our readers picky questions about which article they read first in the last issue, which one they read last, did they like this thing or that thing, what would they *like* to read in *Harper's?* Asking our readers about their hobbies, what sports they liked, where do they vacation, all manner of rot." Willie had called Minneapolis to complain that he thought such surveys were worthless—though terribly costly—and asked if they were designed to take control of the magazine's content away from the editor? Oh no, Cowles assured him: just routine. Willie didn't live in Blair's house long, feeling that stay would give the "spy" more time to observe him. Probably, he feared that Blair would learn too much of his drinking and late-night carousing.

I never learned at what point Cowles told Willie that he was changing Blair's title to president and chief executive officer of the corporation running *Harper's* and that he was to thereafter be considered Willie's superior. Willie didn't tell his staff. Indeed, he seemed to have a CIA "need to know" policy when it came to sharing with us just what occurred at all those high muckety-muck meetings in Minneapolis; we were told next to nothing. My best guess is that the change occurred in early 1970, because that's about when Blair referred to himself as "The Boss" when talking with me. Being a skilled diplomat I immediately said, "You're not *my* boss. I'm not a goddamned accountant. I'm a writer. Willie Morris is *my* boss." I number that incident among the several times I forgot that I was a mere mill hand, too.

Still, none of us realized the extent to which Willie and the Cowles people were on the outs—until the opening volley of shots of a very heavy caliber. We knew a little something was amiss, just didn't feel right, and at times we fretted a bit over Willie's erratic conduct. But he continued to produce; with each new *Harper's* issue came praise in the media, at dinner parties, from other writers and editors, on our travels, in the mail. Jay Milner, a writer teaching journalism at Texas Christian University, was typical: "I can't wait to get my hands on each new issue of your magazine. And my colleagues, students and friends feel the same way." We could compare what we were publishing with our competitors and feel confident that nobody was putting out a better magazine: not *Esquire,* not *The New Yorker,* not *New York,* not *Atlantic Monthly,* not *Life,* not *Playboy,* not *Commentary,* not *The New Republic,* just no-by-God-*body.* So how could that be faulted? We wrote our articles and our books, feeling maybe a bit smug, certain that any problems between Willie and Minneapolis were minor bumps on our smooth highway. And when the firing started, we were as startled and unprepared as American forces had been at Pearl Harbor.

PART FOUR

TROUBLES IN PARADISE

"This is the saddest day of my life."

—WILLIE MORRIS

to *The New York Times*, March 2, 1971

"Willie seemed interested only in chitchat. On the stereo, Morris played the same two records over and over again: an album of Mahalia Jackson spirituals, and someone reading Robert E. Lee's farewell address to the Confederate army."

—EDWIN YODER, JR.

a friend of Willie's since their days
together in England as Rhodes Scholars,
on visiting Willie in exile on Long Island,
shortly after the *Harper's* fiasco

CHAPTER 10

I SKIPPED INTO the *Harper's* offices on Monday, March 1, 1971, light of heart as always when visiting Gotham, anticipating fun and games with my writing pals.

Trips to Manhattan got me off the road, when I had been interviewing in lesser cities—Des Moines, Atlantic City, Baltimore, or such exotic garden spots as Burkburnett, Texas, or Hershey in Pennsylvania or Humboldt in Tennessee—or delivered me from long, exhausting bouts at the typewriter, or from the ever-present pressures and demands (including lengthy spirit-killing visits to the cancer ward at the National Institutes of Health) brought on by Rosemarie's declining health.

I would almost vibrate with energy, *shine* with it in my eagerness to reach *Harper's* and my colleagues and friends. I recall that on that March day I was toting my just-completed article "The Road to Power in Congress," little dreaming it would be my last ever to appear in my favorite magazine. And so I entered Two Park Avenue with a quip and a grin, only to find Bob Kotlowitz and Midge Decter sitting in a fog of gloom and looking as if their dogs had died.

"There was a big fight in Minneapolis," Kotlowitz said. "Willie has drafted a tough letter of resignation, with no room for compromise. I fear if he mails it, he's through." Of details, Willie's two top editors had very few. Kotlowitz did tell me that Willie was waiting for me in a small restaurant near the office, not one to which we normally repaired—but, as I would quickly learn, nothing about that day or my entire trip would be "normal."

Willie shoved a copy of his letter to John Cowles, Jr. at me. Dated that day—March 1—it got down to the nut-cutting without softening preliminaries: "After considerable thought, I have decided to resign from the editorship of *Harper's,* effective March 15th. Because of my feelings of loyalty and dedication to the Magazine, this has been an agonizing decision, but under the circumstances I feel I have no other choice."

It did not get any sweeter or prettier:

Speaking both professionally and personally, I will not continue to allow our hardest efforts to be undercut and denigrated by your Representative on the premises [meaning, obviously, William S. Blair]. From the very start, he was a cloud of doom and defeatism. Rather than being a source of strength and support . . . he has been an antagonist and a loser. While our editorial staff has been moving ahead and taking the inevitable risks, he has merely protected his flanks—suspicious, hostile, bereft of ideas. He has spoken badly of us and our efforts not merely within the office but outside it as well. . . . I am speaking of a calculated mood of destruction and defeat. . . .

Furthermore, I feel that in terms of our principal competitor, *The Atlantic Monthly,* the rug has been yanked from under our editorial efforts. This is a serious charge, and I make it as a serious professional. Officials on the *Atlantic* have been telling others, and not in an atmosphere of confidence, that *Harper's* will severely retrench, and that they welcome these developments. How could we conceivably continue as a viable and competitive editorial force under these sad circumstances?

We could live with reduced budgets and lower expenditures across the board, as I mentioned in my memorandum of February 17, and indeed our editorial expenditures relative to the business side of our operation gives me no cause for guilt, but I cannot continue to devote myself to a magazine already defeated and dead, with only the date of the funeral unresolved.

"Willie, Willie, *Willie!*" I said. "This is irrevocable. It leaves no wiggle room for anybody. You simply can't mail this! I'll work with you on a firm letter, one that doesn't grab Cowles and Blair by their throats. I know you've worked hard, that you're proud of what you've accomplished. And I believe that, because of it, you've got a little money in John Cowles' bank. But remember what I've mentioned to you before: he owns the mill, and you're just a mill hand. So if you *really* want to stay in your job—and I think in my heart you do—the letter you've written isn't gonna serve that cause. It is, in effect, a suicide note."

Willie flared at that: "You haven't been out in Minneapolis eating shit like I have! You have no goddamn *idea* the abuse they've heaped on me! Or what they have in mind."

I flared back at him: "No, I don't! Neither does anybody else in the office, because *you* haven't told us shit!"

"I won't be a figurehead editor," Willie said, heatedly. "And that's what they want! Those bastards are talking about making *Harper's* a damned specialty magazine. 'Like *Ski*,' Bill Blair said. Can you imagine? The oldest magazine in America, the one with the proudest history, and they want to scrap it without a backward glance."

"Well, you didn't call Cowles a 'chickenshit idiot,'" I said. "*That* might have helped bring matters to a quicker head, if you insist on self-destructing!" I immediately regretted those hot, harsh words, and apologized. Willie obviously was distraught: I needed to sooth and calm him, rather than ignite him. So I asked what, specifically, had triggered him in Minneapolis?

A lot of things, Willie said. He'd been "raked over the coals" for four hours by Cowles, Blair, and three other executives. "Nobody said a kind word, an encouraging word." They had criticized what Willie had published, blamed him for stagnant circulation, falling ad revenues, a lack of profits. They proposed firing the five contributing editors (Lewis Lapham had just come aboard) and complained that Willie paid us too much. They also wanted to fire either Midge Decter or Bob Kotlowitz, and fill the vacant chair with a "junior editor"—meaning one who would work cheaper, never mind he or she surely would lack the skills of either of Willie's veteran editors.

Had Willie kept his head he might have countered that circulation was slightly higher than when he became editor-in-chief; that an economic recession had affected ad revenues throughout the publishing industry; that the *Harper's* deficit had been worsened by an act of Congress removing postal subsidies magazines long had enjoyed; that John Cowles, Jr. had urged him to pay William Styron $10,000 for excerpting *The Confessions of Nat Turner* because "it will sound better when word gets around in the trade" (rather than the $7,500 Willie had agreed to pay); that contributing editors were paid more by other magazines than by *Harper's;* that the *entire* editorial budget at *Harper's* was far less than the annual salary of a single network TV anchorman (at that time around $250,000); that Bill Blair had spent $60,000 spiffing up his office while preaching economy to everyone else; that when Willie had suggested that he and Blair take pay cuts—in order to retain both Midge Decter and Bob Kotlowitz—Blair, who was being paid $55,000 annually to Willie's $37,500, had summarily refused.

But Willie had been so infuriated by Bill Blair's goadings ("Nobody's interested in your magazine other than a few Eastern communicators. Who are you editing it for, a bunch of hippies?") and by Junior Cowles "not once interrupting Blair's abusive tirades" that he couldn't gather himself for a counter-attack. What I did not then know—and would not learn for several days more—was that Willie had become so furious he had caught an airplane back to New York as soon as that meeting broke up. What was bad about that was this: Willie had been invited to join Cowles-the-Younger for dinner that night, and he simply stood him up.

MATTERS FESTERED OVERNIGHT. Bill Blair picked up the rumor that Willie Morris was resigning and—being a good lapdog —called Minneapolis to report it. Junior said, "We'll do nothing unless and until a letter of resignation comes in." I thought that foolish: Why not talk before matters dramatically worsened? I telephoned Cowles, to tell him the contributing editors would like a word with him; by noon the next day I had heard nothing from him, and groused about that to Willie at lunch.

Willie gave me a sly half-smile and said, "I guarantee he'll call before this day is over." Suddenly, I realized why Willie seemed so laidback compared to his tensions and anger of twenty-four hours earlier. I said, "Damn you, Willie! You mailed that tough letter didn't you?" Yes. Air Mail Special Delivery. "When?" Willie said he'd mailed it the day before, just a few moments before showing me a copy of it. Cowles should be getting it any minute now.

I should have been miffed that Willie had let me fume and holler at him the day before, while knowing it was already too late to change his course of action no matter what I advised. But I, too, suddenly felt a surge of calm. So I just sighed and said, "Well, Willie, we're screwed." Willie said he didn't think so. I told the waitress to make my next drink a double and to step lively with it, please. Just one double wouldn't do, it turned out. We lingered over our liquid lunch.

When we returned to the office, Bill Blair's secretary met us just across the threshold—as if she had been posted in ambush—and said, sweetly, "Oh, Mr. Morris! I'm so sorry you're leaving us!" Willie and I exchanged one quick, sharp glance before he virtually bolted toward his office; I scurried behind him, trying to catch up. "They've *accepted* my resignation!" he said, sounding shocked.

"Didn't you think they would?"

"No," Willie said, softly.

He asked to be alone for a few minutes. I wandered away, aimlessly walking the halls, but couldn't find anyone to commiserate with. Where they had all gone, I don't know to this day. When I judged that Willie's "few minutes alone" might be over, I went back to his office, but the door was still closed and I heard his voice raised in anger. I later learned that Cowles Jr. had called Willie to read a statement he was about to release announcing Willie's departure. Willie objected because, he said, the statement sounded as if he had been fired. After a few minutes of unsatisfactory back-and-forth, Cowles said—according to Willie's account later—"Well, issue whatever

statement *you* wish to make. I'm going with what I read to you."
Morris, angry, banged down the phone and fled the *Harper's* office,
brushing by me with a quick apology: "I'm sorry, I've got a matter to
take care of and it won't wait!" He went somewhere and wrote his
statement, which he released to *The New York Times* and the Associated Press. It read, in part:

> I am resigning because of severe disagreements with the
> business management over the purpose, the existence and the
> survival of *Harper's Magazine* as a vital institution in American life.
> My mandate as its 8th editor in 120 years has been to maintain
> its excellence and its courage. With the contribution of many of
> the country's finest writers, journalists, poets and critics, I think
> we have succeeded.
>
> It all boiled down to the money men and the literary men.
> And, as always, the money men won.
>
> The article in our current issue by Norman Mailer has deeply
> disturbed the magazine's owners. Mailer is a great writer. His
> work matters to our civilization.
>
> . . . My resignation grieves my heart, but I am leaving as a
> protest against the calculated destruction of *Harper's*.
>
> All writers, editors and journalists who care passionately about
> the condition of the written word in America should deplore
> with me the cavalier treatment by business management of
> America's oldest and most distinguished magazine. This is the
> saddest day of my life.

WITHIN AN HOUR of the statements released by Willie Morris and
Junior Cowles, a media war was on. The phones rang incessantly in
the *Harper's* offices, reporters seeking comments from the survivors
of the wreck and few of them were disappointed; all of us spoke
more in haste and anger than in thoughtful analysis, and soon "spin
doctors" were at work—though I don't believe that term was then in
the language.

We contributing editors shouted at Bill Blair, for neither he nor Cowles had advised us of the content of Cowles's statement—which we termed "inaccurate or misleading"—prior to its release. Blair professed not to understand: Cowles had accepted Willie's resignation, that's all, so what were we so worked up about? No, we said, the goddamned statement sounded as if Willie had been fired and that was bullshit and he knew it. He knew no such thing, Blair rejoined. Someone called him a lying shitass and we stomped out to regroup. By day's end we had reached no conclusion as to exactly what we should do, or how to do it, and agreed to meet the following morning.

I had accepted, days earlier, an invitation to a dinner party at the townhouse of Muriel Oxenberg Murphy. Norman Mailer was among the guests, as were Bill Moyers and Bill Bradley. Willie had me break the news of his resignation and its acceptance, and he then told Mailer that his long piece "The Prisoner of Sex"—just published— had been a big factor in bringing about the tumultuous events leading to his resignation. Mailer gave a long, low whistle and then turned to me—the only contributing editor present—to ask what we intended to do. I said we had not decided, but we wanted a meeting with John Cowles, Jr. Our first goal would be reinstatement of Willie as editor-in-chief; if that failed, we might ask for the managing editor, Bob Kotlowitz, to become editor-in-chief with Willie as a roving writer-editor. This might work, I said, because Willie would be relieved of administrative duties—which he hated anyway. And we would join in Willie's earlier complaints against Bill Blair, as one who contributed nothing but negative and inaccurate criticisms. Beyond that, we'd have to await Cowles's reactions before we knew what we'd do.

Mailer's eyes flashed and he said, "You guys owe Willie your loyalty. You've got to quit now." He, he said, would make an announcement in support of Willie Morris, and it would include his promise *never* to write for *Harper's* again.

I much admired Mailer as a writer, and liked him personally, but I resented his ordering us to quit when he had scant details—hell, *we* had only scant details—and when, I knew, he had much deeper pockets and a larger reputation than any of the contributing editors and thus would find it easier and less penalizing to make a dramatic protest. I also doubted—accurately—that Mailer's "Prisoner of Sex" piece had been the factor Willie claimed, and thus felt Mailer was asking us to resign in support of him as much as in support of Willie. Hotly I said, "Goddammit, Mailer . . ." And then I could say no more, commencing to sob in anger and frustration, my ire including Willie's sitting calmly as a spectator while leaving me to deal with Mailer's indignation. In an effort not to attack Mailer physically, I kicked an antique chair, which shattered into very expensive debris. Nobody mentioned that, however, because I was ranting like a wild man—sobbing and cursing—and it probably appeared not a good time to negotiate restitution. I stormed from Muriel Murphy's house before the sit-down dinner began but no longer have any recollection of where I went or what I did—other than to say the odds are great that liquor was my companion.

By the next night, when I saw Mailer at another party, he called me aside to apologize for his comments, in the absence of knowing all the facts, and I apologized to him for having gone crazy on short notice and for making him the object of my public wrath. No permanent damage was done except to the antique chair.

THE FOLLOWING MORNING, Bill Blair approached me in friendlier tones than formerly, asking whether I would be willing to talk to John Cowles, Jr. to see what might be salvaged from the chaos. I told him, Hell yes, that was why I had called Cowles two days earlier: that *all* of the contributing editors wanted to explore that possibility. Blair said he would get in touch with Cowles and urge him to return my earlier call. I felt an appreciation for Blair's sudden efforts to help sort through the debris. But soon Marshall Frady and John Corry came into the office I shared with David Halberstam, hardeyed and demanding to know why I had gone over to "the other side." *Whaaaat?*

Blair, it developed, had told them that I had agreed to stay on at the magazine and had a call in to John Cowles, Jr. to work out a deal for myself. I was furious; they could have heard me yelling curses in Minneapolis had they been listening closely. I grabbed Frady and Corry and propelled them into Blair's office, demanding that he admit he'd lied to them about me; the most he would admit was "a misunderstanding." I verbally abused him and promised physical harm should he even *speak* to me ever again, it being pluperfectly obvious he had deceived me in trying to use me and had damn well known what he was doing. I was convinced, by then, that Blair's limited familiarity with the truth wouldn't have permitted him to recognize it had it walked in the door wearing a neon nameplate and a red suit.

Soon thereafter David Halberstam cursed Blair and threatened an ass-whipping because Blair had told *The New York Times* the contributing editors were behind in the number of pieces they were contractually obligated to provide. Not true: Only Corry was guilty of such a shortfall, and then only by one article, as I recall. Halberstam and I had actually produced more pieces than required and Frady had exactly met his obligation. Such angers had been directed at Blair within the space of an hour that he soon disappeared from the office and thereafter made himself scarce. It was the wisest thing I ever knew Bill Blair to do.

On Friday—five full days after the chaos had started—John Cowles, Jr. agreed to meet with the contributing editors and Bob Kotlowitz that evening in a suite at the St. Regis Hotel. Keep the time and place of the meeting secret, he instructed: He did not want "the Press" nosing around asking questions. "That's what's wrong with the son-of-a-bitch," I raged to Halberstam. "We *are* 'the Press' but Cowles defines 'the Press' as the enemy."

We first met at David Halberstam's apartment and quickly agreed to act as a unit; it was the only way, we felt, that we might exert any pressure on management. Halberstam told Lewis Lapham that we would exempt him from the unit rule, since he had signed aboard only scant weeks before and could have had no notion he was joining the *Titanic* in a sea full of icebergs. Oh no, said Lapham, making a bold all-for-one-and-one-for-all declaration: He would go along with the rest of us, he would be a part of the team. We welcomed him to the brotherhood. Lapham would remain a member in good standing for roughly three hours.

Our "secret" meeting was advertised on a sign posted prominently in the St. Regis Hotel lobby: "Harper's Magazine staff meeting in Suite Such-and-So," giving us just about our last laugh of the night.

Cowles took from his coat pocket a 1,700-word statement he plowed through without raising his head while reading in a monotone. We got the message, however: He had not come to the city to negotiate with us but to dictate to us, mill owner to mill hands. The statement quickly established (1) that William Blair was being named publisher, effective immediately; (2) Blair would choose the new editor-in-chief and be that editor's superior; (3) *Harper's* editorially would go in unspecified "new directions"; and (4) Willie Morris was gone for good and all. We gaped at each other, stunned that there was not even a possibility of negotiations.

Halberstam, our designated spokesman, asked Cowles to specify what "new directions" *Harper's* would take. Cowles either could not or would not be specific. Halberstam tried another approach: To what did Cowles object in the magazine? Cowles said only: "A magazine can't live on press notices and dinner-party chit-chat." Halberstam further pressed Cowles as to what he personally objected to in Willie's version of the magazine. "Much of it bores me," Cowles snapped. Halberstam was a dog not willing to let go of the bone: "*What* bores you? I think we have a right to know!" Cowles said only that "readership surveys" indicated "we should go in a new direction"—but again, no specifics; he was in short, unresponsive to questions and never really added anything to the 1,700-word ultimatum he'd read to us.

At that point I made my one "contribution" to the discussion: "John, if you can find one self-respecting editor or writer willing for his life's work to be guided by goddamned reader surveys, I'll kiss your ass till my nose bleeds." That caused the only eruption of laughter of the night, with even Cowles managing a wintry smile, but my wisecrack changed things not one whit.

Halberstam reminded Cowles that he had promised us—first I'd heard of this—five years in which to turn the magazine around, and he thought we certainly had done so to a great extent—but now Cowles was pulling the rug from under us more than a year before his own deadline. Cowles, looking pained and impatient, said he couldn't give us any more time, that his father had urged him either to sell *Harper's* or to padlock it "because it simply isn't worth the trouble." His cavalier dismissal of a magazine that had an honored history and a tradition in American letters, a magazine we loved and had worked hard to serve, infuriated the brotherhood. We began to shout about management having wasted money redesigning the magazine's binding, establishing a posh over-sized office for Bill Blair, conducting readership surveys that apparently had not been helpful in defining the "new directions" *Harper's* should take, paying big money for *The Reporter's* subscribers and then doing nothing special in the way of promotion to keep them. So why was Willie Morris made the fall guy?: *He* had nothing to do with those goddamned decisions—and neither had we! Cowles crossed his arms in a classic defensive use of body language and it seemed the air in the St. Regis grew chillier.

Robert Kotlowitz, we said, had earned a right to have a shot at the top job, even if Willie Morris had become persona non grata; Kotlowitz had not made policy at the magazine, but no one had labored harder, more honorably nor more honestly. He was among the best editors in the business—and if you don't believe it, someone suggested a bit sarcastically, take a damned survey among those in the trade.

Cowles said it was "quite possible" that Kotlowitz was on the list from which Blair would make his choice, but he refused to give any commitment. I leaned over to Marshall Frady at that point and whispered something I had been thinking almost from the moment the meeting began: "The bastard wants us *all* to leave. Let's accommodate him!"

Just then John Corry said, "All right, John, are you telling us the magazine will change but you won't say in what direction, and that Bill Blair will remain in power or become even more powerful?"

Cowles said, "That's pretty much the case."

I knew my cue when I heard it. So I stood and said, "Then fuck it, there's no reason to stay here. I resign." I walked from the room without bidding Junior Cowles goodbye. One by one the other contributors followed me out: Halberstam, Corry. Frady. Cowles shouted, "Wait! Stay and talk!" I shouted back, "*Why?* You aren't *listening!*"

In the elevator we counted noses; only Lapham's nose was missing and from the way things developed we now have a good notion of where it was and what it was sniffing. Kotlowitz, honorable to the last, felt that he should stay and assure Cowles that he would remain to put out the next issue if wanted; we consented, though for once I wished Bob was not quite so noble a fellow.

WILLIE WAS WAITING at Elaine's to learn the results of our meeting and gave us all big wet cheek-kisses on learning we had resigned. He said he was "not surprised" by the high-handed attitude Cowles-the-Younger had displayed: "I have been through that drill in Minneapolis many times." We sat with Willie, remembering the good times as best we could, though as time passed we increasingly felt and acted more somber.

Lewis Lapham came into Elaine's perhaps an hour later and blithely announced that he was the new managing editor to replace Bob Kotlowitz. I was flabbergasted and furious, Lapham having made his "one-for-all" speech and then recanting at opportunity's first sniff; in the back-and-forth with Cowles, Lapham had several times sided with the publisher—the only one to agree with a word Cowles said. A rich boy—his father held a seat on the New York Stock Exchange—Lapham was hard up neither for money nor for a job; he had left *Life* to join *Harper's* and had also been a staffer at *The Saturday Evening Post*. One with his experience and connections surely would not have worries about raising the rent money.

"They will never say of you as they said of FDR, that you are a traitor to your class," I hissed to Lapham. "You saw the opportunity to cozy up to power and another rich man's spoiled son and zoomed in like a goddamned homing pigeon." Halberstam hotly told Lapham that he would never write a word for *Harper's* so long as "you, Cowles, or Bill Blair have any connection with that magazine." (It was a vow all of us who quit joined in; the next day Norman Mailer, Bill Styron, Gay Talese, Bill Moyers, and Tom Wicker made the same pledge; thirty-four years later, none has broken it.)

Midge Decter, for reasons best known to herself, did not participate in the meeting with Junior Cowles, but the day following the meeting she, too, resigned as did poetry editor John Hollander. Decter made it clear, however, that she was unhappy, telling the press, "I owed Willie one, and I paid my debt"—meaning, apparently, by resigning from the job Willie had hired her for. Years later in an oral history she sounded a plague-on-both-your-houses note:

> The story that "The Prisoner of Sex" was responsible is nonsense. That's the line Willie sent out—"the man of business against the man of literature"—and that's what [the press] wanted to hear and that's what they wrote. But it was all a lie. Willie was in trouble with the ownership over money. . . . A magazine like *Harper's* can never make big money, but the owner of the magazine was a dope who had this fantasy about large profits. Willie played his cards very foolishly by agreeing with him, and then he got into a fight with Blair over who was responsible for the bad balance sheet and went traipsing off to corporate headquarters in Minneapolis saying, "It's me or him."

Not a lot of feeling for Willie's dilemma in those chilly remarks, though until the *Harper's* blowup Midge Decter gave every indication of approving of Willie and the rest of us; indeed, as indicated earlier, she was our "house mother" and always appeared supportive. Either we badly misread her or she was adroitly faking it. And in any case, there is nothing to even hint that she ever talked to

Willie—or tried to—about how "foolishly" he was playing his cards with Cowles.

Frady later said that Lapham told him in Elaine's that he, too, should remain at *Harper's:* "There's no reason why we need to follow Willie over the side. . . ." Then said Frady, Lapham "began to retail an inventory of all of Willie's [alleged] gross delinquencies. Far from being depressed, he was filled with a kind of furtive glee and elation at the way events had gone." Frady added that he had been "surprised to find, that far north, in such an urbanized and civilized demeanor, a Snopes."

In 1993, the writer Michael Shnayerson wrote a long piece about Willie Morris for *Vanity Fair* in connection with the publication of *New York Days.* Lewis Lapham told Shnayerson so many fables that had they been yellow bricks laid end-to-end they might have reached Oz and then circled it. Lapham claimed that Halberstam and I told Junior Cowles at our St. Regis showdown that Willie was "a drunk. Willie's lousy. Willie's no good, to hell with Willie, we want Kotlowitz to be the editor." Only when Cowles wouldn't give us an immediate positive answer—Lapham claimed—did we quit. Then, Lapham added, he got to Elaine's before we did—never mind that he had stayed behind to talk with Cowles and Kotlowitz for at least a half hour and then shared a cab uptown with Kotlowitz, while the rest of us had gone directly to Elaine's. Lapham also claimed he told Willie Morris, "Your friends walked in and said you were no good, they were glad you were gone, and they wanted Kotlowitz to be editor. That didn't work and they quit." (Willie said he never talked to Lapham at all that night: "If anything, he avoided me, and I damn sure had no reason to seek *him* out.")

"Later," wrote Shnayerson, "I bounce this version off King, Halberstam, Frady, and Kotlowitz. 'That's almost a scandalous disremembering,' says Frady. 'Unimaginable,' says Kotlowitz. 'He's a fucking liar,' says King. 'He's a pathological liar,' says Halberstam, barely able to restrain himself. 'When you have misbehaved, and there are five or six witnesses, it takes a certain amount of hubris to lie like that.'"

The *Vanity Fair* writer then wrote: "Not long after the St. Regis meeting . . . Kotlowitz quit, leaving Lapham, the newest arrival, as the only remaining member of the Morris team. If he had hoped Cowles would appoint him editor, he was disappointed. . . . Cowles's choice was Robert Shnayerson, a *Time* senior editor and, as it happens, my father. Against his better instincts, Shnayerson kept Lapham on . . . but when another recession, in 1975, brought heavy losses, Shnayerson was fired. Lapham, the scrappy survivor, was chosen to replace him. My father felt strongly that Lapham had betrayed him, bad-mouthing him to Cowles's people and lobbying for the job."

Qui male agit odit lucem.

Or, in plain English, "He who acts badly hates the light."

CHAPTER 11

AFTER THE ADRENALINE RECEDED, after the blood cooled, after the *Harper's* shake-up faded from the headlines, after the phone quit ringing, reality hit Willie Morris a numbing blow.

"The Big Cave" suddenly became "large and hostile"; its rumbles and screeches set his teeth on edge; should he even *see* a copy of *Harper's* while passing a newsstand, Willie averted his eyes as if looking away from carnage or obscenity. He felt at loose ends: no job to attend, no writing or editing awaited him, no salary existed to pay his bills or his child support. And, yes, he missed . . . well, the perks and the power. Years later, he would say that power was like cotton candy, it tasted good but it didn't last. But that was after he had healed.

Not that Willie was totally ignored. Indeed, he was offered a number of jobs—editing at this or that publishing house, becoming writer-in-residence at Duke University, writing magazine articles or books, teaching writing courses—but he didn't bother to respond until weeks later, when he sent short form letters saying thanks but no thanks to all. I doubt that he could have responded earlier, being something of an emotional mess.

He was heartened by supportive letters from many: Robert Penn Warren, Alfred Knopf, Jr., Bill Bradley, Mo Udall, many writers and academicians. A young Southerner named Bill Clinton wrote, "I will never forget how good you were to take time out to see me twice in New York, when I was coming from and going to Oxford. . . . I hope you will find some purpose and peace of mind. Know that a lot of us who can't even scrawl an intelligent sentence are grateful for the work you have done at *Harper's*. And of course especially for *North Toward Home."* Robert Penn Warren wrote Willie, "I have just read the morning *Times* and rush to my typewriter. It is a real blow. I won't deny that it is a blow to me. I have felt very happy, very happy indeed in my association with *Harper's,* the sense that whatever was sent would be judged on its merits, and that is something hard to come by. I feel this is another door being closed on serious writing." The publisher Alfred Knopf, Jr. wrote Willie, "No news from the so-called book business has been more shocking to me than the story in this morning's *Times . . .* you have performed an absolutely exqui-site act of magic, and the magazine is far and away the best there is. I cannot conceive a vision so narrow that the course of the magazine will now be set by someone else. I think everyone in publishing will mourn this outrage." Literally hundreds of readers who had loved Willie's magazine or his book—strangers to him—wrote as if they might be his intimate friends.

There was balm, too, in the writers, columnists, and publications lamenting the loss of Willie Morris: *The Saturday Review of Literature* editorialized: "In issue after issue *Harper's* writers put their own lives on the line in passages of personal revealment and commitment [and] provided pieces of penetrating journalism." George Frazier wrote in *The Boston Globe,* "In four years Willie Morris converted a moribund, stuffy, utterly humorless *Harper's* into one of the very best magazines ever published in America." Norman Mailer was quoted in *The New York Times,* "[Willie's loss] is the most depressing event in American letters in many a year because *Harper's,* under Willie Mor-ris, had become the most adventurous of all magazines. Morris is a great editor. I never saw him take a backward step on a piece." Bill Moyers, who had quickly declined a Cowles invitation to replace Willie, said of him, "He knew how to feed writers' egos, to make them want to write their best." Gary Hart, manager of Senator George McGovern's presidential campaign—and soon to be a U.S. senator himself—wrote directly to William S. Blair: "I find it incredi-ble that you allow a man of Willie Morris's talent and integrity to get away. I guess money is just as important in corrupting literature as it is in [corrupting] politics and all of American life."

Many other publications and writers, and a few editors, lauded Willie while not a few excoriated *Harper's* management. There is no doubt that Willie won the public relations battle big time—but eventually all the supportive quotes and accolades faded away without changing anything.

I ALTERNATED BETWEEN BEING PISSED at Willie for what I thought was a bumbling handling of all those Minneapolis meetings he'd kept us in the dark about, and, yet, remembering with great affection the opportunities he had provided me and others, the excellent magazine he delivered, the camaraderie among those he had gathered around him, and the great fun he sometimes provided with his gift for changing his voice.

The first time he victimized me was when my second book was about to be published and he called alleging to be a *Time* writer who had been assigned to write a long feature story about me. Well, my God, you talk about a career breakthrough: With the influence and readership of the newsweeklies in 1968, it was like going from being an unranked prelim boxer to being considered a challenger who thereafter would fight only main events. It was simply too good to be true—which I would have known had I not been so blinded by ego, excitement, and hope. So under the questioning of the "*Time* writer" I began posturing and postulating, claiming the influences of many of The Old Dead Greats on my writing style, inventing rules of writing, and perhaps judging the literary rankings of some writers I had read scantily if at all; it would not surprise me to learn that I even tried to affect a British accent. And of course, at the height of my folly, Willie Morris said in his own voice, "Why, Larry, I didn't know you knew so much about writing!"—whereupon two or three friends Willie had let in on the joke—listening on extensions—began to guffaw and mock me.

A year later, as I was preparing to leave for Harvard for my Nieman year, a young lady asked me to hold the phone for Dwight Sargent, curator of the Nieman program. "Mr. Sargent" conventionally asked how I was and I cheerfully responded that I was even then packing my bags to head for Cambridge and much looking forward to a great adventure.

"Well, yes," the "Nieman curator" said, and perhaps coughed discreetly. "I find it is my duty to, ah, ask what I fear is a rather personal question."

"Uh, all right. Go ahead."

"Mr. King, have you ever been convicted of a felony offense?"

"I beg your pardon?"

"A crime. Have you ever been convicted of a crime?"

"Well, ah, no. Good God! What's going on here?"

"It's certainly distressing, Mr. King, but a member of the Harvard Corporation has received information that you're a convicted felon. If so, I'm afraid we'll be forced to reconsider your Nieman Fellowship. Not that we'd preclude you without official inquiry and judicious study—"

"*What?* Preclude me? This is the damndest thing I've ever heard!"

"You irrefutably deny it, then?"

"Goddamn right! Irrefutably!"

"There's no need for profanity, Mr. King. I *am* duty bound to inquire! Have you, perhaps, been convicted of a misdemeanor offense? One short of a felony, though involving incarceration?"

"No! *Hell* no!"

"So then you unequivocally state, Mr. King, that you *never* have been in jail? . . . Hello? . . . Mr. King? . . . Hello? . . ."

"Ah, well now, Mr. Sargent. See, ah, it didn't really amount to much, just silly little kid stuff really, just ha-ha, you know, laughable little things youngsters will do."

"Oh dear, I find this *so* distressing! I must ask you to elucidate."

"Well it was for, you know, fighting and drinking and little stuff like that, back when I was just a kid in Texas. It was, you know, quite common in the culture of that time and place. Ha-ha-ha. Kind of a rowdy frontier culture you know, but at least we didn't kill any Indians, ha-ha-ha."

Under the agonized queries of "Mr. Sargent" I confessed to having "accidentally killed" a mean old dog when I was a teenaged postman "but no charges were filed," to having run over a gas pump in Texas and *that* had led to a dispute with the service station owner, and the cops came, yeah, and I had been "temporarily handcuffed" but released after I agreed to pay damages. I was just beginning to confess a peace march arrest when Willie, chuckling, said, "Hello, Larry, you old outlaw!"

"Willie Morris, you sorry son-of-a-bitch!"

Those were not the only times Willie zinged me by phone. You ask, "Didn't you ever suspect him?" Yes. Once. A young woman told me to hold for New York Governor Nelson Rockefeller and I thought *Willie Morris knows that two members of Rockefeller's staff have talked to me about becoming a speechwriter for him in his upcoming presidential campaign. That's Ol' Willie about to come on the phone!* So after "Governor Rockefeller" had made a short pitch and asked me to catch a shuttle to New York the next day for a 3 P.M. meeting in his office, I said, "Sure I will. And as soon as I sprout wings I'll fly to the West Coast. And you can go butt a stump."

You see it coming don't you? I was speaking to the real Governor Rockefeller. I don't think I merely imagined that his zeal for me almost immediately waned.

One day in the summer of 1969 I was at my typewriter in Washington when I received a telegram reading "YOU HAVE JUST BEEN TRADED TO NEW YORK REVIEW OF BOOKS FOR EDGAR FRIEDENBERG, JASON EPSTEIN AND TWO MAJOR LEAGUE EDITORS TO BE NAMED LATER. YOU HAVE DONE US VALUABLE SERVICE BUT WE NEEDED MORE LEFT-HANDED HITTERS. MORRIS."

IN LATER YEARS, after he had gone home to Mississippi, Willie persuaded his friend Ed Yoder—as they drove through the kudzu-plagued countryside—that the man who had imported to the U.S. what Yoder called "the now uncontrolled anti-erosion groundcover plant" was still alive in Oxford, Mississippi. As Yoder recounted it in "A Personal Memoir" in *The American Oxonian,* a Rhodes Scholar publication, shortly after Willie's death,

When I asked if I might be able to interview him, Willie said that the man was so mortified by the vine's fecund rampancy that he had become a hermit and withdrawn from all human society. When I naively reported the story in my newspaper column, a southern editor I knew was on the phone within minutes.

"What is this shit about kudzu?" Claude Sitton demanded.

"Shit? What do you mean, Claude?"

"If the man who imported kudzu is still living, he's one hundred and fifty-eight years old!"

Claude knew; he had once written about the menace of the plant for *The New York Times*.

David Halberstam told at Willie's funeral of a telephone call he got shortly after his best-selling *The Best and The Brightest* had been dethroned from the top of *The New York Times*'s list by a diet book; ostensibly the call was from the diet book's author. Affecting a "donnish voice," Willie as the "diet doctor" apologized to Halberstam for leap-frogging past him on the best-seller list, then proposed that they collaborate on a book to be called *The Best and the Fattest*.

During the *Harper's* years, Willie at a party told the *Sports Illustrated* writer Edwin (Bud) Shrake, that his black lab retriever, Ichabod Crane, had fallen out of a window in Willie's and Celia's apartment and plunged six stories to the sidewalk—but landed on his feet and was virtually unhurt. Shrake, amazed, quizzed Willie, who added the fillip that, oh, maybe Ichabod had sore paws but that was all. Shrake, knowing that his magazine was closing its current issue, rushed to the phone and dictated a couple of paragraphs about the "miracle dog" for use in the front of the book. A bit later Shrake mentioned to Celia Morris the miracle of Ichabod's fall, "and she gave me a look that said I was an idiot and said, 'Did you fall for that? It never happened. It's pure Willie bullshit.'" Shrake almost pulled up lame rushing to call *SI* and retract his "scoop." For a long time he was kidded and razzed by his colleagues at *Sports Illustrated*, some of whom barked on sighting Shrake.

Years later, when ex–Ku Klux Klansman David Duke, a member of the Louisiana legislature was running (unsuccessfully) for Congress,

Willie called his campaign headquarters election night and asked that Eva Braun be paged. He shortly heard the P.A. system at Duke's headquarters broadcasting, *Telephone call for Eva Braun . . . Eva Braun, telephone call . . .* When Willie eventually was told "Eva Braun" didn't answer, he assured the person on the other end of the line she was supposed to be there. "What does she look like?" the campaign worker asked. "Well," Willie said, "she looks very Germanic."

Sometimes in the night now, when sleep won't come, rather than counting sheep I rerun those old Willie Morris brain movies in my head, and eventually drift off, smiling.

AFTER THE *Harper's* debacle, Willie soon decided that he "had given too much of myself to someone else's property and to their caprices about it." He knew he wanted to be his own man, and write, but couldn't decide what: fiction, nonfiction, kiddie books, or all of that? He had published a second book in 1971—*Yazoo: Integration in a Deep-Southern Town*—a book that again contained a great deal of autobiographical material, one that received good reviews—including a *Time* rave about the twenty-two-page excerpt that *Harper's* used as a cover story: "thoughtful, deeply personal and brutally honest." But, somehow, after his fiasco with Cowles and Blair, Willie seemed paralyzed, incapable of new beginnings. The *Harper's* setback was the first time the fair-haired boy had failed at anything in his career, and rather than fighting back with a vengeance—to re-prove his worth—Willie sank deeper inside himself, closing out everyone, including those to whom he had been closest.

David Halberstam wrote Willie a letter saying, "You cannot arbitrarily cut yourself off from us . . . it is not good for you, it is not good for us . . . it makes us look like people who ride only winners. Your title had nothing to do with the affection we held for you in the good old days; your lack of a title should not be held against us now." Willie didn't respond.

A bit later—on July 6, 1971—I wrote Willie to report on my travels promoting a new book, beginning it, "This may never reach you. Your whereabouts is a pluperfect mystery." Then, attempting jocularity in hopes of reaching Willie emotionally, I wrote, "Everywhere I went, bragging on my book, people wanted only to talk about *Harper's*. And *you*. I got damn tired of answering the question 'What is Willie Morris going to do?' I varied my answers so as not to bore myself: 'He has just been named assistant football coach at Tatum, New Mexico. . . . He is in Osteopath's School in Joplin, Missouri. . . . He has gone blind and is in the County Home for the Blind and Deaf at Post, Texas. . . . He is living in sin on a Greek isle with Ethel Kennedy, except on weekends, and then he pastors the First Baptist Church of Homa, Mississippi. . . . He went to pee and the hogs ate him.'" I heard nothing more than had Halberstam. It was months before Willie contacted any of us and began to renew friendships; eventually, he would dedicate books or stories to several of us—but that was after decades, not just years.

Even Willie's mother could not reach him. On March 10, she wrote imploring him to call—collect if need be—and expressing disappointment that he had not done so since the *Harper's* upheaval began. "I called Harper's and asked your secretary if you were coming in soon. She said the telegrams were coming in from everywhere to you"—but, apparently, the secretary offered no further information. Mrs. Morris continued, "You simply must have some way I can get in touch with you. You can't expect me to lose sight of you entirely. I have been calling your apartment for three days. If you are going to do your writing at home, you have got to have a way for people to get in touch with you. I can't stand your being another Thomas Wolfe, writing day and night and neglecting yourself physically." When repeated attempts to reach her son failed, Mrs. Morris eventually resorted to calling him in the name of his grandmother, Mamie. Willie was furious when he took the call and found he had been tricked, seemingly not at all understanding of his mother's concerns though she had in her letters told him of her strong support of him and that she was canceling *Harper's* subscriptions she had earlier sent to a few Mississippi libraries.

Willie did stir himself to draft a note in longhand, which he arranged to be typed and sent to the secretaries, proof readers, and other support troops in the *Harper's* office. Dated March 8, it ran:

Since I am about to move out of my office, I want to thank each of you for your loyalty and hard work on our magazine. I will not soon forget the fun and achievement of these years; working with all of you has been one of my deepest pleasures.

Abe Lincoln told the story of the boy who stubbed his big toe on an old tree trunk. The boy said it hurt too much to laugh, but he was too big to cry. My warmest gratitude to all of you.

Willie

And yet motivation to start *anything* in the way of work was lacking until, when Willie complained to Bill Moyers of having no certain goal, Moyers said, "Willie, you're only thirty-seven and you have a good typewriter." And that, somehow, got him started. ("I wasn't *frightened* of making a new start," he later said. "Just terribly bereft.")

He fled the Big Cave like a bear was chasing him, going 100 miles east of Manhattan to the South Fork of Long Island, an area he first had discovered while riding through it on a bus for a joint weekend meeting of the *Harper's* and *Atlantic Monthly* sales forces. The flat terrain and potato fields reminded him of Delta cotton patches back home in Mississippi; the land had the same brooding quality, he thought, of his native place; perhaps it would be a good place to mend and to work. But it *was* lonely and he knew absolutely no people there, though Muriel Oxenberg Murphy—then traveling abroad—owned a sizeable duplex near Georgica Pond, near Wainscott. That's where Willie moved in, more or less camping out, because he didn't know how long he would remain on Long Island. He missed Muriel, had hoped she would postpone her European trip after the *Harper's* disaster, but she had declined to do so. Indeed, though Willie then had no way of knowing it, his relationship with Muriel would never regain its old intimacy—being off-again-on-again for about a year before winding down to a close. It is easy for the suspicious to conclude that Muriel Murphy found Willie somehow less the desirable swain, less the public trophy to be displayed, once shorn of his cachet as the popular and much-heralded editor-in-chief of *Harper's*. But that may be a bad guess: Even after they were no longer lovers, Willie and Muriel continued for years to be friends; indeed, she sent a wedding gift when Willie married JoAnne Prichard.

The summer crowd of artists and writers would not flock to the Hamptons for some three or so months, so Willie was among strangers. He took solitary walks at night by the water near Bridgehampton, the least posh of the several Hamptons, or drank in small bars where—very uncharacteristically—he avoided conversations. He did not yet want to know anyone or make any friends. Soon, he thought, he likely would be gone—though to where, he didn't know. He would have been astonished had someone told him he would spend ten years in Long Island exile, experiencing both the best of times and the worst of times.

WILLIE OCCUPIED ONE SIDE of Muriel Murphy's duplex on Wainscott Pond, though a casual observer might have thought he was packing up to leave rather than settling in. Most of his books, papers, clothing, and a few personal effects, still packed, were dumped hither and yon in an uncoordinated jumble. Untidy stacks of letters, appearing unsorted and mostly unopened, littered the floor.

Though Willie Morris *intended* to immediately write, soon establishing on a sturdy table the tools of his trade—an old manual typewriter, stacks of typing paper, yellow legal-sized tablets, sharpened pencils, a dictionary, *Roget's Thesaurus,* a couple of books of quotations—he was restless and had trouble staying in his chair. No matter if typing or writing in longhand, he would put down a few words or sentences, then crumple the paper and abandon work with sighs or curses.

He wanted to write a book for youngsters—even had the title in mind—*Good Old Boy*—and knew he would draw on some of his own boyhood experiences. But he knew, too, the story needed a bit of jazzing up, fictional adventures he had never known, characters more exotic than the real people from his childhood—or than he had ever imagined. But, somehow, the exotic characters hid themselves in his mind and the words simply wouldn't come. His concerned friend Ed Yoder has recalled that Willie seemed interested only in "chitchat" and said, "On the stereo, Morris played the same two records over and over again: an album of Mahalia Jackson spirituals, and someone reading Robert E. Lee's farewell address to the Confederate army." That, to me, is a sad image.

Willie Morris obviously was still going through withdrawal symptoms resulting from his sudden dislocations following the *Harper's* fiasco. Even his mailing address—"General Delivery, Wainscott, Long Island, N.Y."—shouted of impermanence and dislocation; one had to call for one's mail at the post office, seeing an impersonal clerk at a window frequented by those with no fixed addresses on any established mail routes—the next-to-homeless. Willie's fresh anonymity and his lowered status had to strike him anew every time he visited the post office.

At least he *got* mail, quite a lot of it. Offers continued for some weeks to pour in, forwarded by a friendly *Harper's* secretary who was one of the few people Willie had told how to reach him. Most of the offers or invitations Willie Morris dealt with by not dealing with them at all, though some few he responded to, once the events were safely past, with varied excuses: He had been away, a writing deadline prevented his participation, he had a schedule conflict, the invitation had not reached him in time; so sorry.

The Twentieth Century Fund wanted Willie "to conduct a study of the book publishing industry." Yale invited him to appear at a series of seminars on modern journalism under its Poynter Fellowship Program. Colorado College asked him to give the Demarest Lloyd Memorial Lecture in the Humanities; shortly thereafter it proposed that Willie join its faculty as a visiting professor, who would lecture and host seminars. The University of Alabama and Bucknell University, in Pennsylvania, asked him to be their commencement speakers. Duke gently reminded Willie that it needed a response to its invitation to become its writer-in-residence. The American Association of State Colleges and Universities wanted him to conduct "an in-depth study of campus newspapers, their rights and responsibilities." Will you lecture at Columbia University on *North Toward Home?* Or speak at Mercer University in Georgia? Or participate in our upcoming college workshop on writing here at Oberlin College in

Ohio? Will you speak at the YMCA on campus at the University of North Carolina, Chapel Hill? Canfield Press, San Francisco, solicited a book about writing, "not a textbook or a grammar book, but a *personal* book on writing, its joys, problems and pitfalls for students who have been ossified by twelve years of diagramming." Robert Manning of *Atlantic Monthly* asked about the possibility of Willie's writing "East Toward Oxford" for him. Ray Cave of *Sports Illustrated* offered the opportunity "to write an occasional piece for us about sport and leisure and southern attitudes." Someone at Random House wrote to inquire whether Willie was still interested in writing a book that had been discussed with him earlier, but did not specify its subject. All of these well-meaning folks were, frankly, just pissing in the wind.

Some letters brought disappointment. Caroline Hobhouse of Macmillan turned down the right to publish *Yazoo* in England, saying that the English market, always small, "now seems to be shrinking as far as excellent books of non-parochial interests are concerned." This occurred after another British house, citing similar problems, had withdrawn an earlier offer to pay him 2,500 pounds—roughly $6,000 and change.

Willie was left with very little but hen-scratch money. A royalty check from the four-year-old *North Toward Home*, issued on June 21, 1971, in the amount of $1,463.10, was for the sale of 345 copies of the book in the previous six months. That money, and $1,000 Willie's mother had kindly sent him, represented all the money he had on hand or in the pipeline—and Celia's lawyers, alarmed by Willie's not having a job, already were getting testy about his alimony and child-support payments. And still the words wouldn't come.

WILLIE IGNORED CELIA'S LAWYERS, but he did write his ex-wife a stern letter saying he could not write so long as she "harassed" him for money and that if she expected him to "support you for the rest of your life" then she should back off from any pressures that might make his writing more difficult. Celia was angry, feeling that Willie had the option of taking a job, if that was required in order for him to meet his obligations to her and to David Rae. She did, eventually, voluntarily suspend about one-third of the monthly alimony Willie owed, provided that once his financial condition improved he would pay the amount she had suspended. He agreed, Celia says, but never paid it; she has lost track of the amount he was in arrears but reckons it might be around $40,000. (David Rae Morris comments, "He was not very good at paying child support. He did, however, foot the bill for my four years at Hampshire College, which cost about $50,000. When my grandmother Morris died in 1977, my mother told me to tell my father that she would forgive the debt provided he paid for my college. He did, although in retrospect I felt guilty about asking him this on the plane heading to Mississippi to bury his mother.")

But the biggest crisis with Celia came after Willie "kidnapped" the family's black Labrador retriever, Ichabod H. Crane.

"It was horrible," Celia Morris says. "Willie at his narcissistic worst. Ichabod really was David's dog and after Willie kept him over the Christmas holidays [in 1971] when we went to Minnesota, he refused to give him back. I wrote him, called friends and asked them to help, David begged. One of my notes, I remember, said, 'Most people can't believe that a man would steal his own son's dog.' David's friends talked about drawing up a petition."

"'He belongs in the country,' was one of my father's excuses for not returning Ichabod," David Rae Morris says.

The standoff continued through the winter. I remember driving with my father, alone, that winter and telling him we would take him to court if he didn't give Ichabod back. He said nothing, but when we returned to Muriel's house he vanished. Muriel emerged and told me my father was quite upset by what I had said. Being only twelve, it was difficult to stand my ground, especially against her (I did not like her very much) and I was forced to say that I never would really do it. Spring came and then summer, with the Ichabod issue still unresolved. July 22, Ichabod's seventh birthday,

Willie Morris and Celia Buchan as University of Texas undergraduates in 1956, two years before they married. (PHOTO COURTESY CELIA MORRIS COLLECTION)

Rhodes Scholar Willie and Celia in Cambridge, England, in 1959 on the day he received his degree in History from Oxford. (PHOTO COURTESY CELIA MORRIS COLLECTION)

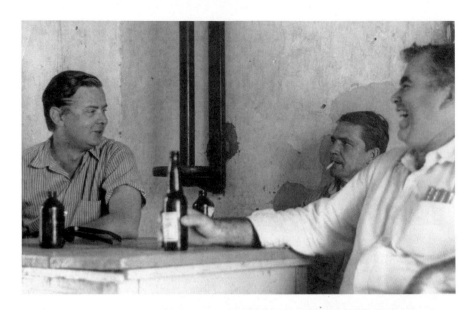

ABOVE: Willie Morris, during his days as Editor-in-Chief of *Harper's* magazine, relaxing in a Mexican border town bar with two Texas lawyers, Warren Barnett (with cigarette) and Malcolm McGregor.
(Photo by Neil Caldwell, courtesy of Southwestern Writers Collection)

BELOW: Larry Wells, left, and Dean Faulkner Wells—owners of Yoknapatawpha Press—bracket Willie Morris on the day in 1979 that he visited Ole Miss to determine if he wanted to come there from Long Island to teach. Far right is writer Adam Shaw, who accompanied Willie to Mississippi. (PHOTO COURTESY OF WALT MIXON)

ABOVE: Mississippi dignitaries in "The Grove," near the Ole Miss football stadium, just before the Rebels played University of Georgia on Willie's exploratory trip. *Seated, from left:* Willie Morris, Judge Grady Jolly, Mrs. (Bettye) Jolly. *Standing, left to right:* Artist William Dunlap. Ed Morgan, U.S. Senator Thad Cochran, Adam Shaw, Larry Wells, Dean Faulkner Wells, Carl Downing and William Lewis, Jr. (PHOTO COURTESY OF WALT MIXON)

BELOW: Willie Morris and Larry L. King at Ole Miss in 1982, while King was answering questions from students and faculty after a speech. Willie presented King with a bogus "literary prize," which was, in truth, an old bowling trophy. (PHOTO BY OXFORD *EAGLE,* COURTESY OF SOUTHWESTERN WRITERS COLLECTION)

Willie Morris at Oxford, Mississippi, Little League game.
(PHOTO COURTESY OF WALT MIXON)

Dean Faulkner Wells and Larry Wells with Willie Morris at a book
signing in Vicksburg in 1980. (PHOTO BY JANET BEASLEY, COURTESY
OF THE *VICKSBURG EVENING POST*)

Winter, 1980 photo of Willie Morris and "Pete"—just after he moved to Oxford—in the yard of #16 Faculty Row. (PHOTO BY SUSIE JAMES)

Willie and his wife, Joanne, outside Elaine's, the Manhattan watering hole of writers, before a party celebrating publication of *New York Days* in 1993. (PHOTO BY DAVID RAE MORRIS)

Willie and Eudora Welty, probably the most famous writer Mississippi has produced other than William Faulkner, at a restaurant in Jackson.
(PHOTO BY DAVID RAE MORRIS)

Willie Morris, Ole Miss History Prof. David Sansing, and author William Styron picnic at the grave of one "James Crow" in Charleston, Mississippi.
(PHOTO COURTESY OF JANE RULE BURDINE)

ABOVE: Willie waving to crowd assembled at the Hoka, a cinema-cum-coffeehouse-and-BYOB watering hole in Oxford, for the world premiere of the film *Good Old Boy,* made from his book. Driving: Jon Mallard, whose dog Denver was so frightened by the crowd's roar he tried to jump from the car, to the amusement of Ole Miss tennis coach Billy Chadwick.

LEFT: Wearing a rare tuxedo, Willie is interviewed by an Ole Miss coed at the premiere. He called Ole Miss coeds "Goldfish" because "they put on makeup and good clothes even to jog, and most are searching for a M-R-S degree."

(PHOTOS COURTESY OF JANE RULE BURDINE)

Jack Bales—a writer, editor, and reference and humanities librarian at Mary Washington University in Fredericksburg, Va., just before introducing Willie to students and faculty at the university in 1998. (PHOTO COURTESY OF WILLIAM B. CRAWLEY, JR.)

Willie Morris placing red roses on his parents' graves in the Yazoo City cemetery he played in as a boy. (PHOTO COURTESY OF JANE RULE BURDINE)

fell on a Saturday. The night before, my father let the dog out to roam. When Ichabod had not returned by morning, we went searching for him in my father's Volvo.

We were driving down the Sag Harbor Turnpike when we saw something on the side of the road. Once my father realized it was Ichabod, he became inconsolable. Two passers-by stopped and helped us load Ichabod's body into the back seat. My father continued to weep uncontrollably. "I don't want you to see me like this," he wailed. I told him it was okay.

I don't remember sobbing on the phone [as Celia says he did] when I called my mother to tell her the news. With my father so distraught, I had to play the straight man. When a friend of mine came by, I told him not to say anything that might upset my father. At that point, my father was sitting on the couch in a state of shock. I don't remember him talking or moving, just sitting alone weeping quietly to himself.

Somehow it was arranged for Ichabod to be buried at Muriel's house in the woods near Georgica Pond. A yard man dug a grave and Ichabod was placed there covered by my father's sheepskin coat. Periodically, Dad would get down on his knees and lean into the grave to pat Ichabod's body. His sobbing continued. Julie Murphy, Muriel's daughter, read from what I believe was the Book of Common Prayer. I think she thought it was silly, because she appeared to be close to laughing several times. My father took it *very* seriously. I didn't know what to think.

That evening we had a cookout on the beach. My father had recovered his composure but still managed to forlornly exclaim, "My dog's dead." But I never forgot that my father had stolen MY dog and let him die. It was a great burden to carry. In 1993, when my father sent me the manuscript of *New York Days*, he made the comment that Ichabod was his dog. I referred to the page number and simply wrote, "Ichabod was *my* dog." He responded as if amused, but conceded, "Of course Ichabod was your dog." It allowed me to let go of my old pain and resentment—and was another sign that he was, by the mid-90s, becoming a better person.

BUT WILLIE'S MOTHER WAS ON HIS CASE far more persistently than was Celia Morris. It was almost as if Willie's having lost his "respectable" job qualified him for additional flayings. She demanded to know "who that woman was that answered the phone at your house and what is she to you?" She cautioned Willie against adding to the "filthy trash" being published—including Larry McMurtry's *All My Friends Are Going to Be Strangers*: "I believe it is the vilest book I ever read." (McMurtry's book was far from vile in my opinion.) She hoped that Willie's books would not embarrass her with her friends or with the *good* people of Yazoo. She had read in *Time* that "you and Mailer are heavy drinkers" and "it hurt"; another magazine referred to Willie as a "playboy" and that drew Mama's admonition that he had departed from the way he had been raised. She cautioned that drink had made Thomas Wolfe fat and that Willie himself would look less fat if only he would wear suits and ties rather than turtleneck sweaters on television.

Mothers want their sons to do well, yes; the benevolent can perhaps give Marion Morris credit for good intentions—though I doubt that entitles a mother to accuse her son of not caring about her, even her son's *son* of not caring about her, or writing, "I am beginning to wonder if my only son is losing his mind." Time and again Willie is told that—because of him—Mama Morris cannot sleep, walks the floor, has anxiety attacks, feels desolation, is thinking of selling her home in Yazoo because Willie so rarely comes to see her and, after selling it, she hopes to find a loving family that will take her in as one of their own. She eventually wrote him of his first novel: "There are plenty of books that don't deal with sex that sell. For God's sake, don't try to pattern your books after Norman Mailer! People in town say this book [*The Last of the Southern Girls*] is *not* Willie Morris." On Willie's fortieth birthday he received from his mother a check for $50 (still uncashed, as are numerous small checks Mrs. Morris sent him at one time or another, all now in the Willie Morris Collection at Ole Miss) and an original poem, scrawled on a "Happy Birthday!" card, that simply boggles the mind:

I prayed once to have a son/ A strong one to lean on/ When my days are done./ I have a son, unreachable, not there/ And my strength must be found in others, somehow, somewhere./ Birthday wishes to you, Willie/ Days of success for you./ But where has this boy gone?/ This son I thought I once knew. Love always, Mama.

Little wonder that Willie once took a pen and, in mad scrawls, blotted out his mother's face in a photograph published in a Mississippi newspaper alongside a story touting one of Willie's books. When I told David Rae Morris about it, years later, and asked what he thought about it, he said, "That it sounds like it was done about three A.M."

"My grandmother had many problems," David Morris says,

not the least of which was that she had no sense of personal boundaries. Her paranoia and oppressive attitude was always evident. In 1971, I was left alone with her in Muriel Murphy's house in Wainscott. I don't honestly know if she knew I was there. I was in a bedroom across the hall, and listened for what seemed like hours as she wailed to herself (and to the Lord "to take me home"). I could tell she had been drinking. I was absolutely terrified and didn't make a sound, fearing she might accost me.

On another of her visits, my father let me spend the night at a friend's house. The next day when I returned, my grandmother was gone. Apparently my father had left her alone in his house in Sagaponack, which was not close to anything. My grandmother had gotten scared and tracked him down at Bobby Van's or wherever. I don't know what words were exchanged, but apparently my father got angry and told her to go home.

On one of our visits to Yazoo City when I was thirteen, she insisted on cutting my shoulder-length hair. She was happy that I looked somewhat more "respectable" in her eyes. However, the next time I had my hair cut the barber asked who had cut my hair last, because they had done such a horrible job.

I know she complained that my father rarely came to see her. In reality, we saw my grandmother a good bit—both on visits to Mississippi and when she came to Long Island. I remember trips to visit her in 1972, 1973, 1974 and 1975, and she came to visit on Long Island in 1971, 1972 and 1975.

SHORTLY BEFORE the *Harper's* shakeup, Willie Morris had met at a Manhattan cocktail party a comely young woman, Barbara Howar, most often described as a "Washington socialite." Though Ms. Howar had worked in local television, co-hosting a midday talk show with Maury Povich, and had written articles for *The Washington Post, Ladies Home Journal,* and *Redbook,* she largely was known for being well-known. A North Carolinian with a finely chiseled face, a sweep of blond hair, a trim figure, great legs, and a tart tongue, Howar attracted attention wherever she went: "a real-life Golden Girl," *The Los Angeles Times* described her.

Always, by her own admission, this native of Raleigh—born Barbara Dearing—had "a thirst for the limelight" and a rebellious nature not normally indigenous to young Southern women raised by nannies and indulged by doting parents. Barbara Dearing soon became the bane of priests and nuns at each of the several Catholic schools she attended, starting unauthorized campus newspapers in which she attacked everything she didn't like about the school or its faculty or teachings. More than one school refused to have her back after her repeated clashes with those in authority. She graduated from St. Mary's College in Raleigh in 1955, but without distinction, and "actually had more fun at Miss Bootsie's School of Tap and Toe."

After working briefly as the assistant to the liberal editor of *The Raleigh Times*—himself a rebel who drew the ire of some readers for endorsing the Supreme Court's decision to integrate the nation's public schools, although North Carolinians generally were much less critical than residents of the deep South—she moved to Washington, D.C., "with the foolish notion that I was ready to conquer it." Not much came of a job as the lone woman on the staff of the

House Interstate and Foreign Commerce Committee, where she manned a mimeograph machine, hand-delivered messages to congressional offices, occasionally took dictation by memorizing what she was told—with the aid of her own original bastard shorthand—and, yes, in the custom of the times, sometimes fetched coffee and snacks for her male "superiors" on the staff.

But there's more than one way to skin a cat: Young Miss Dearing climbed the social ladder as if she had brought it with her from Raleigh, attending party after party, meeting and charming more and more Washington insiders who had clout, and eventually getting invitations to fly in private airplanes to the Kentucky Derby, to Broadway shows, to the Mardi Gras in New Orleans; she rarely turned down a promising invite. It became time, soon, "to do the only thing I had not tried: marriage."

As she wrote years later in her best-selling autobiography, *Laughing All the Way*, "All I had to do was choose a man from among the available crowd who was going places, and move on to something new and more fulfilling." In 1958 she chose Edmund Howar, in the construction business, big time, and in his bride's blunt words, "The richest Arab in America."

Barbara Howar first came to general public attention as an associate of the LBJ family in 1964 as a "Lady for Lyndon" on the Lady Bird Special—called by Republicans and damnyankees "The Cornpone Special"—a campaign train working the South during President Johnson's re-election campaign against Republican Barry Goldwater. Somehow, she had been designated as Mrs. Johnson's hairdresser on the Cornpone Special, though having no particular affinity for the job. It kept her in close proximity to Mrs. Johnson, however, and they got along well.

After LBJ's landslide victory, Barbara Howar served on numerous committees planning the Inauguration and, in time, she became the fashion advisor, shopping escort, and sometimes chaperone for the Johnson daughters, Lynda Bird and Luci Baines. LBJ, who had a keen eye for shapely ladies, was fond of dancing with Ms. Howar and once said of her, "I like that girl but she talks too much." Howar's quips, not always kind, caused careful politicians to shy away from her, though she remained in good odor so long as she had her LBJ–Lady Bird connection.

She lost that connection when private detectives hired by Edmund Howar discovered her in a Florida hotel room with the president of a major airline—himself a former White House aide—well, shucks, in flagrante delicto. With pictures, yet. The White House reacted almost as strongly as did "the richest Arab in America," the Johnsons quickly canceling a posh engagement party the Howars had planned for Luci Baines Johnson and her intended, Patrick Nugent.

Luci Johnson had earlier asked six-year-old Bedar Howar to be her flower girl at her wedding. No cancellation notice was given about *that* so Barbara Howar struggled with what course of action might traumatize her daughter the least: having her role canceled, or going through with it in difficult circumstances. Typically, Ms. Howar decided on a damn-the-torpedoes strategy. Bedar served, indeed, as the flower girl, though—excepting the bride, a long-time Johnson maid, Helen Williams, and the also tart-tongued Alice Roosevelt Longworth—just about everyone at the wedding and the White House reception that followed treated her mother as if she smelled like three-day-old fish. Not too long afterwards, Barbara and Edmund Howar were divorced following a failed reconciliation.

Barbara Howar recalls that she and Willie Morris "got along famously" at that Manhattan cocktail party, chatting about politics and their mutual Southern heritage. "A few sparks flew," Howar said in later years. Nothing immediately came of that promising beginning, Willie's *Harper's* ship soon sinking and casting him rudely upon the beach.

In the summer of 1971, however, Barbara Howar learned that Willie Morris was living in one side of Muriel Murphy's large duplex in Wainscott. Conveniently, Howar and her children—Bader, then eleven, and son Edmund Jr., seven—were renting a summer house not far away. Even more conveniently, Polly Kraft, married to the syndicated columnist Joseph Kraft, and a friend of Howar's as well as her neighbor back in Georgetown, was renting the side of Muriel Murphy's house that was only a wall away from Willie Morris. More conveniently still, Muriel Murphy was again abroad. It is not surprising that Barbara Howar called on Polly Kraft soon after all these converging conveniences were revealed. And it did not take long for the Howar-Morris mating dance to begin.

PART FIVE

HARDSCRABBLE TIMES, TROUBLES WRITING, AND FICKLE HEARTS

"I tried to buy a new car yesterday. I put down a small down payment and traded in my yellow Volvo and signed the financing where I'd pay the remaining $2,000 over three years, at a paltry $68.00 per month. The bank wouldn't finance it because I have no credit. I owe the federal government X thousands. I've run out of money on my book advance, and I'm generally about as pissed off as a man can be and still be alive. . . . I believe I've hit rock bottom and can't go anywhere but up."

—WILLIE MORRIS

in a 1972 letter to Muriel Oxenberg Murphy

CHAPTER 12

UNLIKE THE COWBOY TWO-STEP, it was not a simple or an easy dance. And it was complicated by Willie's duplicity in pretending to Barbara Howar that Muriel Oxenberg Murphy was no longer a factor in his life, and for concealing from Ms. Murphy that he had something going with Ms. Howar.

Willie made up fictions as to where he was and what he might be doing when he was dallying with one to the exclusion of the other. I recall that at some point in late 1971 or early 1972, Willie said he was going from Howar's home in Georgetown to Arkansas for research on the novel he was writing, *The Last of the Southern Girls*, some of which was, indeed, set in that southern state. He was vague about how he might be reached in Arkansas, however, and when it increasingly became obvious something was amiss, Willie claimed that well, see, he really had needed to clear his head of all but working on the novel—so while he had *said* he was going to Arkansas, he really had holed up in a small rented room in Washington for a couple of weeks and had done his research in the Georgetown Library so as not to be tempted by socializing and romance. I doubted that story then, and I doubt it now.

For one thing, just a few days before his "trip" to Arkansas, Willie had borrowed a minor sum of money from me—$50 or $60, I believe—so how would he have paid for a rented room for a couple of weeks? And why would he have *needed* to, Barbara Howar's Georgetown home being commodious enough to have accommodated any need for privacy, and she—then working on her book that would become *Laughing All the Way*—knowing enough of a writer's requirements that surely she would have granted Willie such privacy as he needed. Also, the Georgetown Library was but a stone's throw from Howar's home and Willie, by then well-known in the neighborhood, likely would have encountered someone who knew him if, indeed, he had been where he said he was. And, lastly, Willie could no more have stayed out of Georgetown's bars, come night, than he could have resisted a free bottle of bourbon. And Georgetown then had too much of a small-town atmosphere and small-town habits for him not to have been discovered. I have no proof of where Willie was or what he was doing during the "Arkansas" charade, but my suspicion is that he was in New York with Muriel Murphy.

Years later, in an article published in the *Bridgehampton Sun* on July 1, 1980, Willie began with what sounded like a confession that might answer many questions I had long harbored about his juggling of Howar and Murphy:

> Once, several years ago here on Eastern Long Island . . . I was in love with two women at the same time. It was terrible. No sooner was I with one than I started missing the other. I dissected their characters piece by piece, taking them apart bit by bit for my perfervid scrutiny, casting a faulty coil here and a cantankerous bolt there for the sake of a finer amalgam, reassembling their disparate elements out of the mortal puzzle. I began comparing their children and dogs. My friends suspected me of self-indulgence, failing to comprehend my prickly guilt.

Alas, the confession ends there, as abruptly as his affairs with the two women had, and it becomes clear that Willie was using them only as a hook to write an article comparing "my Mississippi and my Long Island." But it is more than he ever said to me personally about his triangular relationship and offers evidence—if not the particulars—of his several mysterious disappearances and no-shows during his wandering heart period.

Before Willie and Barbara Howar hooked up, I had met her but once when she, Maury Povich, and Robert Novak had interviewed me on television about an article I had written on the double standards of Congress in exempting itself from many laws it imposed on the rest of us ("Congress Is Hypocritical") in *The Saturday Evening Post*. I made such a smashing impression on her that Ms. Howar recalls it not at all. Rosemarie and I began to see a great deal of Barbara and Willie, however, once they became lovers and Willie frequently came to Washington. But there were periodic gaps in Willie's attentions: After he failed to show up for a birthday party Sally Quinn gave for Howar in September of 1971—not only didn't attend, he neither called nor sent a message or a gift—Rosemarie said we must give Barbara more time when Willie neglected her. Howar now says she does not recall Willie's failure to appear at her thirty-seventh birthday party, but I clearly recall her as then being embarrassed if not devastated.

At any rate, we began to see more of Howar and less of Willie. There came a time when Barbara virtually quit mentioning him and changed the subject when I mentioned him; she obviously wanted no questions. Occasionally, Sally Quinn—later the queen writer of *The Washington Post* Style section and then Barbara Howar's best friend—would join us or we would meet at some public place in Georgetown for drinks. Sally now says that Howar openly flirted with me and that I responded, though I swear to having no memory of such conduct. It is true, however, that not long before she died, Rosemarie said to her long-time best friend, Ella Ward Udall, "Barbara Howar's waiting around for Larry. And I guess he could do a lot worse."

The last five months of her life, Rosemarie was home less than two weeks, as her condition rapidly deteriorated. I spent almost every day in the cancer ward at the National Institutes of Health in Bethesda, Maryland—and, increasingly, almost every evening at Barbara Howar's house in Georgetown. Barbara fed me, commiserated with me, listened to my laments, included me in her dinner parties, and was, indeed, a comfort in a time when comfort was most needed. And, inevitably, nature took its course. We began an affair.

IT ALSO WAS INEVITABLE that Muriel Oxenberg Murphy would discover Willie's affair with Barbara Howar. It must be presumed she was not overjoyed by that discovery.

It is hard to chart the exact chronological order of the ups and downs in the Morris-Murphy relationship, though it is clear from an undated letter that Ms. Murphy wrote to Willie from her Manhattan townhouse, apparently in the spring of 1972—when Willie and Howar were not together, and he was living in one side of Ms. Murphy's Wainscott duplex—that Willie had, in the fairly recent past, proposed marriage to Muriel Murphy, which she more or less finessed, by noting that—in contrast to the marriage proposal—during the same period Willie had accused her of not caring about him, had hung up the telephone after making unspecified accusations, and had thrown objects in a fit of rage, though apparently not at Ms. Murphy.

Willie apparently had recently borrowed an unspecified sum of money from Ms. Murphy, then soon left on short notice for Manhattan (from Wainscott) with his book manuscript in hand, plans to buy a new Volvo, write Ms. Murphy a check for his debts to her, and then go to Washington—the inference being that Ms. Howar was the reason for his trip. Willie's taking his book manuscript with him, and his "plan" to write her a check for old debts, apparently was interpreted by Ms. Murphy as being tie-cutting actions.

Hers is a long, rambling letter and while it is full of various declarations of love for Willie, it also dwells at length on Ms. Murphy's being some fifteen years older than Willie, and how that likely will grow to be a bigger problem as time goes by. She also mentions in passing that should she marry Willie, they might have—at least by her standards—financial problems.

More immediately, she writes of her awareness of Willie's many signals of discontent, concluding that come summer—when Ms. Murphy will leave her Manhattan townhouse for her usual summer sojourn in Wainscott—they should maintain separate quarters. She had, she said, talked with her friend Shana Alexander (a prominent magazine editor of the day), and they planned to share Long Island quarters for June, July, and August.

If Willie immediately responded to that letter, there is no available record of it. It is possible, of course, that he and Ms. Murphy discussed its contents by phone or even face-to-face. But from an angry letter Willie wrote to her several months later, it would appear that he had permitted the issues at hand to go unchallenged or unanswered for quite a long time. There may have been reasons for this, as we soon shall see.

WHEN ROSEMARIE DIED ON JUNE 8, 1972, Willie called from Long Island within hours to say he was coming to Washington for her funeral. I attempted to discourage that, because Barbara Howar had said that once Willie discovered our romance, he "likely won't go quietly." That puzzled me: By Howar's account she had broken off her relationship with Willie—not the other way around—because, once she and her children had returned to Georgetown after their summer on Long Island, he had immediately resumed with Muriel Murphy. Then why, I asked, would he be upset by *our* affair? Ms. Howar said that Willie couldn't stand rejection and that—because of my long friendship with Willie—he would be particularly chagrined that I had replaced him in her affections.

We met Willie at National Airport. After perfunctory condolences to me, topped by one quick embrace, Willie attempted to kiss Barbara on the lips; she turned her head enough to make it a cheek peck. Willie also took her hand as we walked toward her car, but she soon freed it; when we reached Barbara's car, by prearrangement I got in the front passenger seat as she slid under the steering wheel; Willie got in the back seat but said nothing. He said more of nothing all the way back to the city—perhaps a fifteen-minute ride—only grunting or speaking in monosyllables when I attempted small talk, especially after Ms. Howar said she had reserved a room for him at the Georgetown Inn, and then used a couple of mild terms of endearment when addressing me. I could see Willie beginning to puff up like a toad. He checked into the Georgetown Inn, giving his bag to a bellhop, but not going to his room, as Barbara Howar had said we would wait for him in the car. As we parked near Barbara's house, Willie suddenly blurted, "I don't like what I think I'm seeing here." I ignored the comment, and Barbara chattered through it. Willie fell to quick, hard drinking and gave me looks to match.

Others of my friends, and Barbara's friends, were gathered at her house. Willie could not effectively isolate us and verbally have it out. It might have been better had we faced the matter head-on, but we didn't and the time for that soon passed. Willie's anger obviously deepened; he drank almost in silence, answering only perfunctorily when others attempted conversation. I recall an evening of great tension.

Late in the evening—*very* late—Willie began berating Ms. Howar in my presence and that of a few remaining guests. I felt compelled to intervene. I don't recall what I said, but I do recall that each of us spoke forcefully, even harshly, and Willie invited me outside, saying he would kick my butt. We fought in the street across from the house owned by Jackie Kennedy Onassis's mother, Mrs. Auchincloss; Jackie O., indeed, was in residence, accompanied by her Secret Service agents, when Willie and I—in the words of visiting Texas trial lawyer Warren Burnett—"brought the combined cultures of Odessa, Texas and Yazoo, Mississippi to the very heart of Georgetown."

Ultimately, I got in a punch that knocked Willie down. He retreated to the Georgetown Inn a couple of blocks away, leaving behind a string of oaths. There he began a series of angry calls to Barbara Howar's house, variously claiming to have suffered a fractured jaw and broken teeth—none of which proved true—in between berating Ms. Howar and telling her what a sorry back-stabbing SOB I was. She tried to appease him, without success, and several times hung up the telephone as his anger escalated. Willie called back each time, until Barbara Howar took her phone off the hook.

It is not an event I am proud of. I still regret it in this moment.

I TOOK A COWARD'S WAY OUT. A week from the day Rosemarie had been eulogized by Congressman Mo Udall, I bade Ms. Howar farewell to go to Texas to visit old friends. I simply needed to get away, I said; see you later, alligator. She was sweet about it, and understanding. Looking back, I think I was having a tardy reaction of guilt, maybe even unfairly blaming Barbara Howar for our affair's occurring at the most awkward and inappropriate of times.

I stayed for a bit in Austin with Bud Shrake, and with my cousin and soul-brother Lanvil Gilbert, going on to Odessa to visit Warren Burnett, visiting Taddy McAllister and her family on Mustang Island, and then—getting away from just about everybody I knew—roaming Texas and parts of Louisiana and Oklahoma, without purpose, drinking and crying and fighting and carrying on as if deranged. And I believe I was.

Barbara Howar called me once, in Austin; she was having some sort of problem with her book-in-progress; I do not recall the details and fear that I was not very attentive, pretty shabby treatment considering that Ms. Howar had given me sustenance and comfort when I was sore in need of both. When I had a little better grip on myself, I went to Nantucket to spend some time on that lovely island with David Halberstam. He was, as always, a port in a storm—but he also told me it was time to stop my aimless wandering, super-heavy drinking, and, yes, feeling sorry for myself. Life must go on, he said: so must you.

At some point I had talked to Barbara Howar again, just as she and her kiddies were leaving for their summer vacation on Long Island. The agreement was that I would call when I was ready to see her. So on a given day I called from Nantucket to tell Ms. Howar I had in mind coming to Long Island in a few days. She er-ed-and-awed for a moment and then said, "Well, I fear this is not truly a good time." Oh? Well, see, she was sort of nursing Willie through a bad time: He had broken his ankle in a softball game in the annual Artists v. Writers contest in Bridgehampton, so she had gone to see him, to take him some food, and . . . well . . . well, he really was dispirited and needed somebody to look after him . . . and . . .

I said, "It sounds as if there is no time that might be 'a truly good time' to see you." She forthrightly said, "That's right!" I used the old saw about how you win some, lose some, and some are rained out. And on that mundane note our brief fling ended.

WILLIE AND BARBARA HAD NO TROUBLE rekindling the embers in that summer of 1972. Ms. Howar recalls a couple of "memorable parties" including one that Willie gave for "an enormous tree, supposedly the oldest tree in the Hamptons, in the back yard of my house on Ocean Road. He called it a 'birthday party' for the tree and all who were invited had to come dressed as some sort of tree. So kids and parents and dogs came, some with gum drops pasted on their clothes, some with dollar bills glued to themselves. Willie wore a stethoscope and a white jacket, saying he was a 'Tree Doctor.' It was a real 'happening,' and but one of Willie's many delicious ideas."

At a celebrity-studded sit-down dinner party Willie stuffed the guests' after-dinner fortune cookies—which he personally placed by their plates—with messages he had himself typed. Betty Friedan's asked, "Why don't you go back to Peoria?" and she was dazzled because she was, indeed, from Peoria. Lena Horne's fortune cookie said she must sing for her supper, Truman Capote's was along the lines of "Writing is not your road to riches" and so on. I, frankly, would have lasted about two minutes at a tree party or a fortune cookie party before seeking larger amusements, but there was in Willie a kind of child's wondering glee that not only allowed him to enjoy such entertainment but somehow carry many others along with him. Not for nothing did Willie often say he was "the world's oldest sixth-grader."

Bud Shrake visited Willie several times; Ms. Howar recalls that he slept on her couch and that her children, encouraged by Willie, called Shrake "Uncle Drunk," as did David Rae Morris. Shrake also recalls waking in the night when he was in bed at Willie's rented house, hearing a bugle blowing "Taps" and looking out to see Willie Morris astride the roof like a cowboy, he and his bugle outlined against a big moon. "I thought I was dreaming. But, no, that really was Willie out there." Broken ankle and all, one presumes . . . (Actually, Shrake isn't sure it was the same summer of the broken ankle. The 1970s, he now says, remain in his mind as "one vague blur.")

There were many trips to Bobby Van's, a piano bar-restaurant with the owner often at the keyboard. Willie, indeed, put Van's on the map. It had been a place for locals and day tourists, more or less, until Willie Morris choose it as "his" hangout, bringing along his writer friends Truman Capote and John Knowles—Hampton summer residents. Soon writer Wilfrid Sheed became a regular. Later, once James Jones moved to the area he, too, sometimes joined the group. Bobby Van's was the first place Willie took writers who came for brief visits: Bill Styron, Shrake, Larry Wells, Winston Groom, and eventually—once Willie and I had made up and Ms. Howar had become the best of friends with the playwright Herb Sargent—he took me there.

The summer passed all too soon for Barbara Howar, but September came as September will, and Bedar and Edmund had to return to the private schools they attended in Washington. And it was not long until Willie's mood became much less sunny than it had been during the lazy, hazy days of summer.

I HAVE THE WORD of two trustworthy people who don't want to be identified that when Barbara Howar was not around (or Muriel Murphy or whomever was heartthrob-of-the-moment) Willie's solitary drinking took over and he easily crossed that line where Dr. Jekyll became Mr. Hyde. Sometimes he could become morose, melancholy, or even mean-spirited when nobody was with him except the bottle, and perhaps old ghosts of discontent.

"But nothing could get Willie as riled up as his long wine-soaked lunches with like-minded pals who often tended to encourage his alcohol-induced 'poor me paranoia,'" one woman said. "[They] buttressed both their own and Willie's sense of being used and victimized by literary know-nothings, while perceiving themselves as in no way responsible for their shortcomings or culpable in any failed endeavor." Willie sometimes would come from such outings as angry and vindictive as a boy, wrought up by an adult world that he considered venal and banal and, somehow, out to get him. "There was no reasoning with him then," my source said. "The more he drank the more he wondered if he drank because he was crazy or was crazy because he drank. It was a theme he returned to repeatedly, and it could be frightening to see such a generous, helpful, accommodating man blown so far off his normal course."

This conduct was so far from anything I ever had witnessed personally, that I have trouble grasping it. Oh, yes, I heard Willie complain about not being appreciated by the Cowles clan in Minneapolis, and I saw him angry and violent when we had our fistfight, but blaming others for his own shortcomings, or questioning his own sanity—no, that was as far from my experience as distant foreign shores.

WILLIE WAS IN THE FALL AND WINTER OF 1972 struggling to write his novel *The Last of the Southern Girls,* and we know from his later writings that things were not going well as he worked "mostly alone and in a drab and snowy wintertime in an old house near the Atlantic on eastern Long Island." He was, he later wrote, "severely discombobulated," so much so that "a few of my trustworthy comrades thought me momentarily deranged." He was broke, and booze was looming larger in the picture.

All those factors probably were at work, then, when on October 3, 1972, Willie wrote two drafts of a letter to Muriel Oxenberg Murphy—though, apparently, they had not seen each other, unless in passing, since her letter of the previous spring. It is not known which of the drafts became the letter Willie mailed, the totally harsh one obviously written in the white heat of anger, or the second draft in which Willie tried to be more civil but could not, in spots, contain himself. (Willie's widow, JoAnne Prichard Morris, doubts if he mailed either. Willie, she says, often drafted letters he never mailed—a way of getting something off his chest—though he saved the drafts among his papers. Still, such documents are helpful in knowing his mind-sct.)

That second draft letter, like Ms. Murphy's letter of an earlier time, rambled and zigged and zagged into many mood changes. But let us first consider the original:

> I went over to your house today to get the old files from my days on *The Daily Texan* and found some strangers moving in, with new refrigerators and God knows what else jammed against the boxes of my papers, and then all of my possessions and my son's scattered around in two garages, attics, alcoves, and corners. All this sent such a stabbing pain through me that I felt compelled to write [you]. I'm afraid the sight of it made me very bitter.
>
> You decided somewhere along the way this spring that I would not live in the small side of your house and that you would rent a large expensive place with Shana Alexander. This baffled and hurt me. You may rationalize that your decision was somehow for my own good, but to the contrary I believe it was done out of the most zealous self-regard. . . .
>
> You know nothing of the loneliness of hard work because you've never had to do it. You know nothing of what it's like to be uprooted and displaced because you've never been without the money to own fine apartments and your own incomparable house. When I moved my few things out of there in June, from the house where I had lived for three years, seeing David's things and mine crammed into dark corners, I felt like lashing out at the whole world. Today was as bad—maybe even worse.

Willie goes on to somehow blame Ms. Murphy for the death of his son's black Labrador retriever; his logic, apparently, was that Ichabod would have been safe from traffic accidents had he and Willie still lived on Georgica (or Wainscott) Pond; he also complains of "the meanness and disregard of your friends and relatives" who allegedly had "despised and belittled" him and he decries "your frequent jaunts to Europe in the bloom of our love and your trek to Africa one week or less after I had resigned myself from the sources of all my old ambitions"—meaning *Harper's* magazine. Quite a boatload of blame, that! Oh, and Willie included this postscript: "I have this house in Sagaponack through the winter. After that I may leave this place for good. By your example, I'll never marry again. . . . I hope the summer was worth it to you. Would it had been worth it for Ichabod H. Crane."

The second draft is not wholly accusatory—though it's not free of blame-placing—and seems, on the whole, calculated to make Ms. Murphy feel sorry for him. After perfunctory opening remarks, Willie wrote thus:

Let me tell you a little about what it feels like for a person like myself, with a strong sense of place and belonging, to be so rootless and displaced now. The closest thing to a home and a family I've had in my whole adult life, with the possible exception of a few months during my marriage when I had my own house, has been with you. I've had to move from one house or apartment to another twelve times in the last ten years. I suppose the fact that I've continued to produce good work in such a constant state of dislocation must mean I have fortitude. And my love and affection and respect for you have been real.

All this, of course, has been very deceptive. I'll confess that there have been times, fool that I am, that I've actually felt your house there by the pond was *mine*. I fell in love with it, with the whole splendid setting, and despite the frequent loneliness I believe I was as much at peace there with you as I can ever be. . . .

I've been struggling away stone broke . . . to do a book that was worthy of a man of talent who has never tried fiction, after a painful break in my career and the most intense early success that turned sour. My discipline, though I seem to have little of it on the surface, has never let me down. You've never known what it's like to struggle this way with your talent. You've never known what it's like to have no money, and you never will. . . . I doubt if you really, genuinely, comprehend what's it like for a man like me to feel so homeless, even though you've known the author of a book not fortuitously named *North Toward Home* over three years.

Your decision to rent out the other side of your house and move in with Shana Alexander in that expensive house in Sagaponack baffled and hurt me. Perhaps a long time from now you'll try and tell me why you did it. The day I moved Ichabod and my manuscript and my rather tawdry possessions into this unsatisfying little house in Bridgehampton was one of the most depressing of my life.

I've tried to tell you why my grief over Ichabod's death has been so profound. Aside from the fact that I loved him so much and that he was my best friend in the whole world, he had grown to represent a certain stability and certitude to me. He was so very important to me. And I sensed when I moved into this house on these busy streets, in the midst of that lonely toil of trying to finish a novel, that this was Ichabod's death sentence.

I had of course come to expect, spending so much time in your new house in Sagaponack, that it was partly mine, too, that I could feel free and relaxed to come there with my son and my dog and not feel those awful tensions that a sensitive interloper must feel. Again I was wrong. And then that happy night with my [visiting] Southern friends when we had the lobster, to overhear Shana Alexander and that headshrink whispering to each other making jest of those people was entirely too much.

This mood will mellow, but right now I accuse you of letting me down. Your attitude toward me has ranged from the most loyal to the most inexcusably cavalier, depending on your own uncertainties and calculations. I've been anything but faultless, of course, and I'm sure this emotion will pass, leaving in me the soft lingering sadness that we loved each other. But I believe you can grant me this momentary hurt and bitterness.

I tried to buy a new car yesterday. I put down a small down payment and traded in my yellow Volvo and signed the financing where I'd pay the remaining $2,000 over three years, at a paltry $68.00 per month. The bank wouldn't finance it because I have no credit. I owe the federal government X thousands, I've run out of money on my book advance, and I'm generally about as pissed off as a man can be and still be alive. Maybe bad luck just comes in streaks. But I believe I've hit rock bottom and can't go anywhere but up.

I'll pay you back every cent I owe you if it takes ten years. But maybe you ought to go ahead and marry that rich fellow so you won't have to worry about the likes of such Southern boys again. Or if it's not him, I'll bet a thousand that whoever it is will be very rich.

I'll be over the day after Labor Day to get my things. Please be there and show me where my mildewed belongings are. When I'm long gone from this place and back home you may think of me off and on again when you drive through the fields I've grown to love. And if you and Julie will put a flower on old Ichabod's grave every month or so I'll be in your debt, as if I'm not forever already. I'm not talking about money debt in this instance, but the debt of the spirits.

Love, Willie

Those letters (or drafts) are curious in more ways than one. Barbara Howar, after a happy and restoring summer with Willie, hardly had been gone from Long Island for a month—yet one would not know from Willie's writings to Muriel that he had even *seen* her that summer. Ms. Murphy surely knew the score. It therefore seems unlikely that anything Willie said to her would have a great impact. Was Willie so out-of-touch with reality that he surmised Ms. Murphy did *not* know the score or, even that if she did know, he might somehow persuade her to . . . what? Take up with him again? Apologize for old sins? Or was Willie merely venting his spleen, settling old scores, indulging improbable fantasies, choosing a dramatic exit?

Nothing in the available records indicates that Muriel Murphy responded by letter. If she had, it probably would be among Willie's papers at the University of Mississippi; he apparently rarely threw away so much as a scrap of paper, no matter whether its contents made him look good, bad, or indifferent. (Two known exceptions: David Rae Morris notes that two letters he sent his father about excessive drinking—written several years apart—"apparently somehow made it to the fireplace.")

As to whether Ms. Murphy was in place to point out Willie's "mildewed belongings" on the day after Labor Day, as he requested, I have no way of knowing. From all I can discern, only sporadic contact occurred between Willie Morris and Muriel Oxenberg Murphy after the fall of 1972, though David Rae Morris says they visited on good terms as late as 1974, and that Muriel attended the publication party of *New York Days* at Elaine's in 1993. And JoAnne Prichard Morris says that she and a friend, visiting New York in 1977 or 1978, had tea with Muriel and Willie at Muriel's house. Nothing of record indicates that romantic entanglements were part of those occasions, however.

CHAPTER 13

WILLIE DID NOT SPEND MUCH TIME GRIEVING after the split with Muriel Murphy in the fall of 1972. He resumed his courtship of Barbara Howar, visiting her in Washington fairly frequently. She recalls they spent time with the writer Larry McMurtry, who owned a Georgetown bookstore within the proverbial stone's throw from Howar's house. They saw Sally Quinn and her boyfriend of the time, a New York newspaperman, Warren Hoge, and they hung out at Martin's Tavern, an unpretentious neighborhood watering hole with a history of better days*; Howar recalls "a parade of people" who joined them at Martin's, largely people Willie knew. (Ms. Howar never much valued hanging out in bars.) I was not among the invited, still being persona non grata where Willie was concerned. Most of the time, however, through the remainder of 1972, Willie was on Long Island writing *The Last of the Southern Girls* and Ms. Howar was in Georgetown finishing rewrites of *Laughing All the Way*.

There were a few relatively carefree weeks once their books were done. They went to Haiti, staying at the same hotel where Sally Quinn's parents, General and Mrs. William Quinn, were registered along with their good friends Barry and Peggy Goldwater. Willie, Barbara, and Senator Goldwater went into the Haiti "bush" in a helicopter the United States had, for reasons defying logic, given to the

---

*It was there, on June 24, 1953, in Booth #3, that young Senator John Fitzgerald Kennedy purportedly proposed marriage to Jacqueline Bouvier.

notorious Haitian despot François ("Papa Doc") Duvalier before his death in 1971. He was succeeded by his son, Jean-Claude ("Baby Doc"), whose regime was only slightly less repressive than his father's; three armed, uniformed, and scowling guards—whom Willie thought had the look of "Papa Doc's" *tontons macoutes* (secret police)—were on board the helicopter, ostensibly to protect Senator Goldwater.

It was a light-hearted outing despite the demeanor of the grim-faced guards: Willie dubbed them "The Mouton Cadet," saying he'd rather think of them as a mellow red wine than as the sinister sentinels they truly were. Senator Goldwater wore Bermuda shorts exposing his incredibly bony and knotty legs, so when at one rural stop the chattering natives gathered close around him as he took pictures, despite their wariness of the armed guards, and Goldwater said it was probably because they were seeing their first camera, Willie Morris said, "No, Senator. It's because they're fascinated by your legs."

Not many such carefree sojourns remained for Willie and Barbara, though neither knew it at the time.

Each of them had known disappointments and setbacks as they wrote their books. Willie fretted because he originally had little faith in himself as a novelist—never having completed a novel—and, of course, he had money worries, lectures from his mother, and disputes with Celia or her lawyers, none of which assisted his concentration or his confidence.

Ms. Howar, writing her first book, suffered a near trauma when Putnam—her original publisher—rejected the book after she had turned in the first half of it and demanded its advance money back. (It was that act, I have recalled after prompting, that caused Ms. Howar to track me down in Austin when she needed advice and/or comforting, and I was too preoccupied, drunk, and crazy to decently respond.)

Sterling Lord, Barbara Howar's agent, loaned her money to live on while she continued to write and while he looked for another publisher. He found one, in Stein and Day, actually getting a better contract than Howar had with Putnam. I know enough of the writing process in general—its uncertainties, fears, bogs, hopes, dreams, and drainings—to know that both Willie and Barbara had to have felt like they'd been through a war by the time they finished their respective books.

Although in later years Willie would write that he had been "seriously discombobulated" and that some thought him "deranged," he wrote several friends during the writing of his novel—and shortly after finishing it—in an optimistic tone. "A year ago today," he wrote his friend Ed Yoder,

> was the *Harper's* business and I just finished the first draft (today) of *The Last of the Southern Girls*. . . . It's been a rather strange and rough time for me, but God I think it's good, most assuredly the best thing I've ever written. It's as if it had been inside me for a very long time. It's set in Washington, D.C. and Long Island, with flashes to certain places in the South. The protagonist is a woman. I'm afraid I've fallen in love with her and hence will be looking for her all my life, though this does not delude the author that she has certain bitchy qualities—but goddammit she can be redeemed, and she will survive and endure as the last full measure of what she's been, and what she is. Shit I love her. . . . Writing is so lonely, so pray for me Ed that this one is good.

He had been a bit more muted when writing to Bill Styron some three weeks earlier (in February of 1972), as if trying for a light tone:

> I'm hard at work and well into my book. . . . I've promised myself I'm going to master this form if it kills me, and if this one doesn't hit the mark I'll keep on plugging away until they put me in the black earth of ol' Miss'ippi. I'm learning just what an agony the act of the imagination can bring down upon you—it's so much more different than non-fiction as to be almost another form altogether. Between you and me and about eight others I also have a wholesome desire to make some money for a change so I can buy a new car and a (country) place and spawn one

more white child, in or out of wedlock, before I Hang My Saddle
On The Wall. . . . Why don't you and Rose hop another plane
and come over here some weekend? Or if not, maybe Muriel and
I could do the same that way. It's really quite lovely here at this
time of year, although when I am alone, which is about three
days a week, the wind and the fog make me slightly looney, so
that when my big black dog starts howling, I howl too.

Willie also sent a draft of the book to old friend Ronnie Dugger. I
have not been able to turn up what Willie wrote to Dugger, but Dugger's response, while saying some few good things about the manuscript, reads as if he is taking care not to be as critical as he perhaps
would like to be. He more or less apologizes for such mild criticisms
as he makes, and warns Willie that due to his past successes, some
critics may have their stingers out for him. It is a friend saying to another friend, *Don't get your hopes up too high.*
    That painful advice would prove also to be very sensible.

BARBARA HOWAR'S *Laughing All the Way* took off like a jet plane.
By comparison, *The Last of the Southern Girls* waddled down the run-
way like a one-engine biplane made of canvas and bailing wire,
barely clearing the airport fence.
    Barbara's best-selling memoir, by and large, received much better
reviews than did Willie's first novel, though a number of critics
seemed to enjoy pummeling both authors. Typical of the double-
caning reviewers was Christopher Porterfield, who wrote in *Time*,
under the heading SUCH GOOD FRIENDS,

It must have seemed like a good idea at the time, which was probably a year or two ago in some Georgetown parlor or Southhamp-
ton sun deck. Washington Socialite Barbara Howar would write a
memoir of her already copiously documented career as a ringmas-
ter of Washington's social capers, her marriage to—and divorce
from—the heir to a construction fortune, her affairs and flirta-
tions with the mighty, her fall from grace as a lady in waiting to the

Johnson White House. At the same time, her constant companion, ex-*Harper's* Editor Willie Morris, would write a novel transparently based on the same material. Alas, it might have been better if Morris had ghosted the memoir and Howar attempted a novel. . . . The reader is left with the dispiriting sense that Barbara still believes her own publicity, and Willie is now writing it.

He also fetched these licks:

Like any clever woman [Howar] is less revealing than she pretends to be . . . most of what she seems to have gleaned from the Washington social circuit are banal generalities. . . . *Laughing* is only incidentally an anatomy of power in the nation's capital. Howar's story is much older: how a girl with looks, sass and plenty of hustle cultivates powerful people and becomes the next best thing to powerful—famous.

If *Laughing* is what one might have expected from Howar, *The Last of the Southern Girls* is a disappointment from Morris. Admirers of his editing career and his other books . . . may not know what to make of it, unless they shrug it off as the indulgence of every man's right to do something silly to impress his girl friend. A few passages—earthy scenes from his heroine's childhood, vignettes of her stumping through a rural state with her Congressman lover—hint at the book that he might have written.

But *Girls* most resembles a political novel in the way its narrative keeps jerking to a halt like a campaign train, while Morris hops off to deliver a high flown speech. ("An aura of romance and beauty surrounded her, there was a rare electricity to her movements, she seemed touched with gold. . . ."

Myra McPhearson in *The Washington Post,* was just about right on in writing:

The books are reviewed together, hers often more favorably than his. They are asked to speak on talk shows, and questioned about each other, all of which they find annoying and a strain on their relationship. The suggestion that they are the Bonnie and Clyde of the publishing field, either actually collaborating, or ripping off any excess publicity they can get from their personal situation, sends them and their publishers into fits of expletives.

Mrs. Howar . . . says they were on one of their many "outs" while writing. "We didn't even talk to each other during the nine months I was writing my book." A Knopf spokesman said "From our point of view, it's perfectly horrible. It's all turning into a piece of gossip. That's not what my publishing house is like. I worked on Willie's book not knowing there was any real person. When someone said it's based on Barbara Howar, I said, "Who is Barbara Howar?"

Willie Morris . . . says he's written a "serious work of fiction." He stops his car during an interview and says, "Now you get this down. This is a terrible situation we're living through. It's very, very bad timing. I have worked seriously in the vineyards of American writing all my life. It just so happens that a woman, whom I love deeply, has come out with a book about herself that coincides with my first novel."

The publicity, however, does not seem to be hurting. Mrs. Howar was criss-crossing the country, speaking and signing autographs as her book made number 10 on the *New York Times* list this week. Both have sold their books to paperback firms for six-figure sums, and Morris is negotiating a movie contract.* They have agreed, after much backing and forthing, to one joint public appearance at Thursday's *Washington Post* book and author luncheon.

That luncheon was on May 17, 1973; the following day's *Post* published a large picture made at the event, in which Willie Morris—in profile—stands behind Barbara Howar while sucking on a cigarette with a glass in his hand, staring into the distance; he looks as if he might prefer to be in hell with a broken back. Howar faces the cam-

---

*Willie actually received no paperback sale until LSU Press bought the rights for a modest sum twenty-one years later; no movie deal ever occurred.

era, apparently talking directly into it, waving an arm, looking on-message and hot to trot. They were two very different people when it came to promoting their respective books. Howar was adept at zingers calculated to claim newsprint space; Willie seemed more concerned about his image than in selling books.

Ms. Howar, for example, said that when she read Willie's book, "I swallowed a lot. I'm sure it never crossed Willie's mind that he was ripping me off . . . but, well, I like to skim my own cream for myself. One learns not to talk in one's sleep around a writer." On the fact that Willie's protagonist, Carol Hollywell, had an affair with a con-gressman, Howar said, "I'm such a snob *I* never dropped below the Senate."

Asked about such zingers, Willie offered a gentlemanly response: "Just a few handful really know Barbara Howar. She's so different a private human being from what her so-called public posture is. I see brilliance and growth." Willie also argued that "Carol Hollywell" was based on himself: "I don't care if people think its about Perle Mesta, Martha Mitchell OR Barbara Howar," Willie told *The Austin American-Statesman*, whose reporter added that "Morris spoke with an em-phatic force that could be mistaken for caring."

The she-is-me ploy was a contention that many could not take se-riously. Willie answered goading questions about his bad reviews by saying he never read his reviews—another questionable assertion—and added a third dubious statement in saying, "I never drink when I write, and I never write when I drink." He was playing so much de-fense you might have thought him a middle linebacker trying to turn away a foe who faced second and one inside the red zone. There is no doubt that Willie was very much hurt by the response to his book, and perhaps by some of Barbara Howar's barbs.

Ms. Howar seemed oblivious to that at the time. She recently in-sisted that things were fine between them when Willie came down from New York for the *Washington Post* book-author luncheon; in-deed, she said, Willie stayed at her Georgetown house. Willie said in his opening remarks to an overflow crowd of 1,200 that he had called his mother in Mississippi from the "Hay-Adams Hotel" the night before and it's a fact that much of Willie's speech was scrawled on Hay-Adams stationery in his own hand. Howar's memory in this instance would appear to be at fault.

"Willie never begrudged my success with *Laughing All the Way,*" she has said. "And when he sat in my Lumber Lane dining room [on Long Island] and read my galleys, his eyes welled with tears of pride and he said, 'You are going to be an important writer, Barbara, and never let anything or anybody tell you otherwise.' That, from a man who knew his own concurrent novel wasn't good, is a testament to the quality of person Willie was then, and continued to be."

I don't doubt for a moment that Willie Morris said what Barbara Howar quoted. But it's obvious that somewhere along the line Willie, in his anger and frustration at the poor reception his book was getting, had a change of heart. Because on letterhead stationery (Willie Morris, Box 299, Wainscott, New York 11975) he typed under date of May 7, 1973—a full ten days *before* the *Washington Post* book-author luncheon—and here and there corrected by hand, a rather astonishing memo headed To Whom It May Concern:

As a writer and as an editor, I made one of the large mistakes of my life in becoming associated with Mrs. Howar's work. I persuaded her to write her book, I gave her her title *Laughing All the Way,* and I edited her rough manuscript line-by-line, as I once did for raw writers when I was editor of *Harper's,* often re-writing whole paragraphs for her, providing words for her, and getting so far in the restructuring of her book that I was, for instance, responsible for her whole ending, and for the remaking of whole passages.

I admit this with a profound regret, for although I see my own novel *The Last of the Southern Girls* as an independent effort, I also understand in retrospect that I was also feeding on another being too closely, and for this I apologize to those who have supported my writing from *North Toward Home* to *Yazoo.* It is not easy to admit this, but I must do so because of Mrs. Howar's allegations about my own work. I only hope that those who care about my writing will understand the depth of my admission.

Yours Sincerely, WM

Well, what to make of that? It seems to be a radical reaction to Barbara's attention-grabbing "zingers" about his having ripped her off and "one learns not to talk in one's sleep around a writer." It might be that Willie's paranoia seized him when he was gazing on the wine; perhaps in that state he truly feared that Ms. Howar *might* sue him and was preparing the memo as the first step in his defense. Indeed, Willie had written his editor, W. H. Swanson, back in February that he had feared Barbara Howar might sue him—but that if she intended to "she probably would have done so before now." Then why, some 100 days later, was that possibility still on his mind?

"I may be hazy on some things, but not on this," Ms. Howar responded when I told her of Willie's surprising memo and his representation to his Knopf editor that she might sue him.

There were never EVER any [such] discussions between Willie and myself. I doubt that Willie suggested my title to me, since it came from one of my favorite writers, e. e. cummings, a perfect line for a "memoir" title that said "looking forward into the past and backward to the future, I walk along the highest hills and laugh about it all the way," or something to that effect.

The book was both titled and written without any input from Willie, since we were estranged during the writing process. Other than the fact that I would never stoop low enough to sue Willie or anyone whose friendship was such a valuable part of my life, he and I both remained loyal to one another and kept in some kind of touch, usually via messages to and from other people, until the day he died.

So where all this "suing" business came from, I don't know. And what, for God's sakes, would I have gotten from a law suit? Willie was dead broke and his own book, supposedly about me, didn't earn a dime.

I quarrel only with the contention that *The Last of the Southern Girls* "didn't earn a dime." For all the knocks it took, that book brought Willie $54,000—a pittance compared to what *Laughing All the Way* earned for Howar, yes—but money not to be sneezed at by most writers. Indeed, until Willie received a six-figure sum for *New York Days* (1993) and a comparable advance for *My Dog Skip* very late in his life, *Southern Girls* made more money for Willie than any other of his works. The breakdown: $10,000 advance on signing; $25,000 as a Book-of-the-Month Club selection; $14,000 for serialization rights from *Ladies Home Journal;* and $5,000 for British rights from Andrè Deutsch. (It is true all that was prepublication money; so, in effect, Howar was *close* to right because royalties on sales after publication returned "not a dime.")

The pre-publication excerpts sold to magazines, the book club sale, and the sale of rights in England, no doubt gave Willie very high expectations at a time when he had little in his pockets except lint and cigarettes—and when he also had persuaded himself he had written a very good novel. Thus the critical bashings, and modest sales, of his novel likely came as a greater shock than they might otherwise have.

Willie's accusations and claims in his memo relative to Ms. Howar suing him remain a mystery and are at odds with his usual practices in that he never, just *never,* boasted about the editing or rewriting help he gave to many many writers. The timeline favors Ms. Howar in this dispute, as does her contention that her salty and sassy brand of humor, which permeates *Laughing All the Way,* never was indigenous to Willie. There is no evidence that Willie ever sent a copy of that puzzling memo to anyone, or made any use of it, though he did save it among his papers. JoAnne Prichard Morris thinks Willie probably wrote it "for posterity—people who would read it in later years." But the why of *that* is a mystery, too, since the memo seemingly had little to do with the realities.

I THINK WILLIE, in his own mind, had "divorced" Barbara Howar before—by *her* edict—they officially called it quits. I believe this because I know the depths of Willie's despair as his book failed; he even told some few friends he had considered suicide. He cared more about his work, and how it was judged or perceived, than he cared about anything else. Consequently, he just had to be more upset by Howar's public quips about his book than he let her know. And despite his "never begrudging" the success of *Laughing All the Way,* he could not have been exceedingly glad that her book stayed on *The New York Times* best-seller list for a glorious seventeen weeks in a time when his own book was being widely criticized, even mocked, and plunging like a stone.

All this is not to say that Barbara and Willie never laughed or loved again after the book wars, but Willie's increased heavy drinking, accompanied by jealous rages, or his making angry scenes about small matters, and not writing at all for weeks stretching into months, are signals that their relationship suffered tensions not previously present.

It was during this period that the writer Irwin Shaw, concerned that Willie was not working and was drinking so heavily, volunteered to submit himself along with Willie to an alcoholic rehabilitation program, though Shaw did not need such treatment himself. Willie, as usual, refused even to discuss his drinking and Shaw came to realize that if Willie wouldn't help himself, nobody else could do it for him.

Howar made up her mind to leave Willie one night in the back room of P. J. Clarke's, a Manhattan watering hole with great burgers at high prices, rude waiters, and a celebrity-dotted clientele. "Jim Jones, Bill Styron, and Willie went off to make 'men talk'—they frequently did that—and suddenly Rose Styron and Gloria Jones began telling me I had 'a duty' to look after Willie, to help him reach his full potential and brilliance, to—in short—play the Muse. My hat is off and my heart goes out to such noble ladies, but I've no regrets or apologies for not being one of them. Willie was dear to me in many ways, but I wasn't cut out to be a nurse-maid."

"We didn't part rancorously," she says. "I simply had to get on with my life."

What Ms. Howar tries to soft-pedal is that Willie would not go quietly when she called a halt to their affair. (David Rae Morris recalls "some pretty big fights" between them near the end of their involvement.) Willie called Howar at all hours after the split, sometimes sweet-talking her but usually angry, accusing, and upset at being rejected. This was a pattern: Willie had not paid all that much attention to Celia until she insisted on a divorce, whereupon he began an eccentric wooing: part cajoling, part angry accusations and—by Celia's account—harmful uses of their son, David, in a battle that was not the boy's and that he should not have been in. (For that matter, almost *any* rejection—bad reviews, criticism of his drinking or conduct caused by it, being challenged as to the facts of one of his tales—pushed Willie's temper button.)

Shortly after Ms. Howar took up with Herb Sargent, the television writer-producer and sometimes playwright, Willie in the middle of the night crashed his car through the greenhouse connected to his former love's bedroom on Long Island; immense breakage and damages occurred; neighbors, awakened by the considerable commotion, called the cops.

The two policemen who answered the call knew and liked Willie—one had once reluctantly arrested him for driving under the influence, fearing Willie might seriously hurt himself or someone else while grogged up behind the wheel—and so they were easily persuaded that Willie had been involved in an accident rather than mischief when he plowed into the greenhouse. They therefore took him home rather than to jail. A comic opera scene was added later: When Willie ultimately came to claim his car, he inspected to make sure he had not lost the potato he kept stuffed in his gas tank, the potato replacing the gas cap he had long before lost.

Willie over the years often called Ms. Howar, generally in the wee hours, to lament what might have been. Sometimes he was civil, even friendly as in the old days, sometimes not so friendly. When I visited him once in Mississippi, in 1984, he insisted that we call Barbara together at an ungodly hour. I tried to talk him out of it, but he made the call anyway. Aroused from sleep, Ms. Howar was not noticeably highly honored nor excessively amused. I felt awkward in the extreme, said little, and went to bed when Willie took the phone; as I tried to woo sleep, I heard him raise his voice in apparent anger before slamming down the phone. He had seemed in a good mood, so I was puzzled as to the cause of his ire. When I asked Willie about it the next morning, he said I had not heard what I thought I had and he puffed up when I said, "I have no doubt as to what I heard, Willie." Barbara Howar, understandably, no longer recalls the details of that call but says that random and often eccentric wee-hour calls came from Willie "almost until he married that marvelous woman in Mississippi."

There is a gap in the relationship that surprised Ms. Howar as to length when I told her that, from the available paper trail, it appeared Willie had not been in touch with her for four years when—in October of 1978—he sent her an inscribed copy of his book *James Jones: A Friendship*. Howar responded warmly on October 31: "I'm very grateful to you and I am glad we are friends again. Somehow we always were." They periodically exchanged warm, gossipy letters after that, though neither mentioned Willie's pre-dawn telephone calls.

Howar does not regret her long affair with Willie. "Our romance was great when up, horrid when down, but always memorable." A pause. "But oh, were there ever a lot of laughs in the interim!"

As for Willie, after his romance with Ms. Howar ended he had a few brief flings, and two relationships that son David Rae thinks were more than passing fancies. One was in the mid-1970s with a young reporter from *Newsday*, Janie Schneider, whom the teenaged David Rae considered "like a big sister, who bought me records and took me to the movies," and one in the mid-1980s with a woman named Julie Cass, a *Philadelphia Inquirer* reporter based in New Orleans. On the whole, however, there is literally nothing in Willie's papers about those two relationships; Willie's old friends largely consider that after Barbara Howar he did not have a truly serious or lasting relationship with another woman until he fell in love with JoAnne Prichard.

CHAPTER 14

WILLIE OFTEN TALKED of the Hamptons as a good place to write, but in truth he did not produce at the rate one might have expected of a freelancer who didn't ride the tiger of a nine-to-five job.

In the time he lived on Long Island—only four months short of nine years—he produced *Good Old Boy: A Delta Boyhood* (1971), *The Last of the Southern Girls* (1973), *A Southern Album* (1975), and *James Jones: A Friendship* (1978). *A Southern Album,* subtitled *Recollections of People and Places and Times Gone By,* really was a coffee-table book and required Willie to write only a 6,000-word introduction to complement the book's photographs.

He also completed Jim Jones's *Whistle*—the last of the trilogy of war novels Jones wrote (the others being the classic *From Here to Eternity* and the near-classic *The Thin Red Line)*—from notes Jones had compiled and from a tape recording he made on his deathbed. Wisely, Willie did not try to imitate Jim Jones's writing style but gave a straightforward summation of the final three chapters his good friend did not live to finish.

Such work could not have taken long. In an oral interview in 1971, asked to describe a typical writing week, Willie said,

> Well, I work—I'm an afternoon writer. I work from shortly after noon until, it depends on how I feel, I can't, or I don't, put in more than four hours a day of actually trying to work, I mean sitting at a table and writing. Sometimes I think it's a mistake, at most I can go

five hours. I fiddle around. I go into the village for coffee, sleep late, late in the morning, go into the village for coffee and I come back. I'll go to the beach down the road and then, I ah, work in the afternoons. I usually have a date or meet friends in a restaurant here early in the evening, home by midnight. Something like that.

I was amused reading that, because Willie—an articulate man who normally never paused or er-ed-or-ah-ed—obviously was backing and filling in trying to leave the impression that he was a man of regular habits. Most of the time he was not. He *did* sleep late and he *did* go out almost every night, but unless there was absolutely nobody to revel with I very much doubt that he rushed home at midnight to prevent his potato-gas-capped chariot from turning into a pumpkin. And if he had partied late and partied well, I double-guarantee you that Willie Morris wasn't up and headed to the village for noon coffee.*

More than once—and in at least four cities—in times ranging from 8 A.M. to noon I banged on Willie's hotel door with blunt objects, let the telephone ring in his room for minutes on end, and shouted threatening imprecations, all to no avail. Willie got up, then, when he damn well wanted to—whether at 2 P.M. or 6 P.M. and never mind what may have been planned for that day, or with whom. When *The Best Little Whorehouse in Texas* was playing at Memphis State University (produced and directed by a friend formerly from West Texas, Dr. Keith Kennedy) I persuaded Willie to drive to Memphis from Oxford to see a performance: "Willie, dammit, you are one of the few adult Americans not to have seen *Whorehouse*. I insist you come over here. We can visit in the daytime or whatever, and go to the theater that night."

For four consecutive days I banged and whooped and phoned, trying to get Willie out of his bed at the Peabody Hotel. Of success I

---

*JoAnne Prichard Morris agrees with my "double guarantee," but David Rae Morris disputes it. He says his father did not stay out drunk "every night" and often got up at noon, went to town, got *The New York Times, Newsday,* and one of two New York tabloids, and drank coffee while reading them cover to cover before writing for "three or four hours."

had none. I never saw Willie anywhere but in the bar of the Peabody, when I came in from the theater each evening; always, he had an enthralled group of strangers hanging on to his every word, and always he pledged that *tomorrow* night, for sure, he would go with me to see *Whorehouse*. On the fifth day, when I returned to the Peabody from a long lunch with Keith Kennedy, I found a note that had been pushed under my door. In Willie's bold scrawl it read: "'Fesser' King"—Willie's nickname for me after I spent two years at Princeton as Visiting Ferris Professor of Journalism—"Sorry, but I got a call from David and I must go to Oxford to help him move."*

My first thought was, *What did he use to get you to answer your phone? Dynamite?* My second thought, accompanied by a chuckle, was of Willie's having emphatically told me the day he arrived in Memphis not to tell *anyone* where he was because he was trying to *avoid* helping "a friend" move!

Even giving credence to David Rae's testimony that his father practiced more regular writing habits than I thought, I know from my own experiences and observations that he—as with many writers, myself included—sometimes had writer's block: maybe from exhaustion, maybe from depression, maybe for reasons not even understood by the writer in question, maybe for a simple want of words. Blocked writers who avoid working soon worry whether they still *can* write, and the longer they lie fallow the greater becomes their desperation. Editors or agents or spouses or lovers screaming about deadlines or money needs cannot start the blocked writer's internal machine. Nothing identifiable can. It is then the blocked writer most desperately drinks, fights, break things, sobs, curses, or otherwise manifests craziness each according to habit and taste. When the writer *does* come suddenly alive anew and begins producing, he or she likely is afraid to quit writing for fear of not being able to get in gear again—so they often work until physically and mentally exhausted. I have no doubt that Willie Morris went through every one of those stages—and more than once.

---

*It occurs that perhaps, for complex reasons, Willie preferred not to see an international hit play I had co-authored—especially in my presence.

Maybe in his later years—after JoAnne Prichard provided an orderly home, meals, clean clothes, a warm presence, and artistic encouragement—Willie became *routinely* a writer of regular habits. But before then, no.

Good Old Boy had been conceived as a kiddie book—and for the most part it was—but it also roped in Southern men who found in it familiar echoes of their own childhoods. Some twenty-five years after its publication, when Jack Bales accompanied Willie and JoAnne into a Mississippi restaurant, "A big rough-looking dude recognized Willie and approached him very respectfully to say that *Good Old Boy* was the first book he'd read all the way through since high school, and he thanked Willie for writing it." Bales asked JoAnne if that happened often and she said, "All the time. And often in almost those same words."

Originally, the book had modest sales: Willie's agent wrote him on April 13, 1972—roughly a year after publication—that it had just passed the 5,000 sales barrier. But *Good Old Boy* sold fairly steadily over the years as more and more teachers, largely in the South and especially in Mississippi, taught it in their schools. Yoknapatawpha Press in Oxford reprinted it in 1980; Yazoo Delta Press published a teacher's guide with suggested questions for students and outlines for class discussions.

In a foreword to the 1980 edition published by Larry and Dean Faulkner Wells at their Yoknapatawpha Press, Willie had this to say:

When I wrote this book in 1971, I did not expect the response which came to it. I received hundreds upon hundreds of letters from children all over America. . . . I was impressed by the diversity of emotions expressed in these letters. The emotion of wonder and excitement over the small-town America of a generation ago seemed to predominate. Many of my young correspondents told me that the places in which they were growing up were not much different from the Yazoo of my tale. Others suggested to me their disappointment in not having had these small-town adventures. To the latter I would reply: Never mind, adventure lies deep in the heart of any young person who wishes it, just waiting there to be summoned, depending on how much you want it.

The two questions most asked of me, time and again, were: where is Spit McGee now, and is everything in the book true? Spit McGee now lives, as always, far out from Yazoo in the swamplands, in a tent surrounded by twenty-six stray dogs, eighteen stray cats, six beautiful tame deer, and a pet rattlesnake. He comes to town once a month for his supplies. I ran into him on a recent trip home, buying some flour and bacon on Main Street. "That was really sumpthin', what we did at the Clark Mansion that night, wasn't it?" Spit said. He confessed to me that he still wanders around that doomed mansion sometimes. Mostly Spit McGee lives close to nature under the stars and the faraway planets and takes orders from no man. He has not changed.

As for the second question—was everything in the book true?— Spit himself had found a copy and read it, and he said to me: "You told it like it was." This question in itself elicits the old and abiding things. Yes, everything in *Good Old Boy* is true, although as Mark Twain once said, sometimes you have to lie to tell the truth.

That foreword also contained Willie's letter to his son, David Rae, which contrasts David's growing up in New York City with Willie's having grown up in Yazoo City. Yazoo was, Willie writes, "different from New York but I hope you will never forget that my town and its people are part of what you are now. So this book, in a way, is a letter to you."

David Rae Morris and his little friends made suggestions for the book, Willie always said, but he never specified how many of them he used. He did claim, in an interview published in *The Jackson Clarion Ledger,* that David wrote at least one paragraph in the book, though David was only about twelve years old when *Good Old Boy* was published. "The kids were out of school when I was in the middle of that book," Willie said. "I'd work on it all day and come down in the evening. They'd sit around the fire in front of me and ask me to read what I had written. When I'd finish they'd say, 'What's going to happen next?' I'd say, 'I don't know. Make some suggestions.'" At various times Willie said the kids came up with ideas about the "haunted" Clark Mansion and actually invented the seven giant—ten feet tall—tattooed Choctaw Indians, but to me, at least, all that bears Willie Morris's indelible personal stamp.

The reviews of *Good Old Boy* were almost all positive, including notices in *Publishers Weekly* ("an affectionate, nostalgic story, full of humorous incidents—some fact, some fiction—and an appealing atmosphere"); *Time* ("drenched in crawdads, squirrel dumplings, Delta woodlands and Peck's-bad-boy jokes. But Morris eases out of realism into fantasy and back with no strain, and it's nice to think that somebody more contemporary than Huck Finn remembers it all that way"); *Christian Science Monitor* ("A fine example of just how exciting an adventure tale can be when it's well-written and filled with action. . . . [There] is a haunted house that will make your hair stand on end.")

In March of 1972, *Good Old Boy* won the Steck-Vaughn Award for the best book of the year for children, and Willie got a modest $200 in prize money. The gratification had to be worth more than that, writers often seeing awards as an affirmation of their work, talent, place on their profession's ladder, and how they've chosen to spend their lives; awards are small, stabilizing anchors in a job that often seems to drift, rudderless, like a ship without a port of call.

The only thing that went wrong—and it was no small thing—is that whoever supervised the drawing up of the contract for movie rights of *Good Old Boy* inexcusably neglected to see that it included residual monies for each time the show played on television. So Willie got $8,000 up front—but not a cent more for the many times the movie played on the Disney Channel over the years, or from a PBS video called *The River Pirates,* in a time when he often was scrabbling for nickels and dimes.

He did receive immense satisfaction, after moving back to Mississippi, from appearing in classrooms to speak to kiddies who loved his book and were eager to ask questions of the author.

Jack Bales thinks there may be "thousands," not mere hundreds, of *Good Old Boy* letters among Willie's papers, letters that have not yet been catalogued. "I saw them in Willie's house, bundled and then stored in garbage bags," Bales says. Such letters, says Prichard Morris, "were Willie's greatest satisfaction."

It could be that a "mere" kiddie book was one of the more influential works Willie Morris left behind. And there's absolutely nothing wrong with that, mighty oaks growing—after all—from little acorns.

AFTER THE CRASH OF *The Last of the Southern Girls* in 1973, Willie's published work for the next four years consisted only of his 6,000-word introduction to *A Southern Album* and a few magazine and newspaper articles.

He also was paid for some speaking dates, though it does not appear that Willie was at all aggressive in pursuing any jobs, despite being as poor as Job's turkey. Twin examples: in April 1973, *Family Circle* magazine offered Willie $3,000 and expenses to go to Texas and interview Lady Bird Johnson; that same month, *Ladies Home Journal* wanted Willie's recollections of the day John F. Kennedy was shot—a "thumb-sucker piece," as we say in the trade, one he could have written without leaving the house. Nothing on record indicates Willie so much as responded to either opportunity. And though he made some few speeches for money, he perhaps declined—or ignored—more than he accepted.

During this period Willie said in interviews that he also was working on two novels: "The Chimes at Midnight," which we know never advanced much beyond 100 pages, and the troublesome *Taps,* that we know he worked and reworked and kneaded and massaged and fattened up and slimmed down, repeatedly, over twenty-five or thirty years and that was not published until 2001, two years after Willie's death. So the era from 1973 to 1977 was not a good time, in terms of productivity, though it was then that he cemented his friendship with James Jones.

He also played first base on, and became the manager of, a softball team, the Golden Nematodes—named after a potato bug—made up of writers and a few Bridgehampton workingmen, a pursuit in which he took great delight. Managing the softball team gave him prime time with his son, David Rae, who played center-field and as a budding photo-journalist wrote reports of the Golden Nematodes games for the Bridgehampton weekly newspaper. David Rae and his father worked together "scouting" new talent for the team, discussed game strategies, and grew closer in the process. More than once Willie told his son how his earliest memories in-cluded his own father's teaching him to hit a ball when he was little more than a toddler.

Indeed, the softball job gave Willie connections with locals out-side of the usual bar-stool associations, and he began to feel like a member of the community, and to act like one. He participated in community events, unlike most writers in the Hamptons, who had gone there to avoid people more than to interact with them. But Marina Van, wife of Bobby and director of the Bridgehampton Chamber of Commerce, said, "Willie became a goodwill ambassador for Eastern Long Island." He was liked both by writers and locals and, in the words of resident writer Wilfrid Sheed, had a talent for bringing people together. "He could make you feel he was as inter-ested in *your* writing project as he was in his. He made being a writer sound like something really important." But he could make oth-ers—non-writers—feel as if he cared about *their* jobs and lives too, asking them questions no one else thought to ask or cared to ask. Most felt flattered by his attention. Willie quizzed these people be-cause, I believe, he was seriously interested in their lives both as a human being and as a curious writer always examining whatever turf he then occupied.

A long op-ed piece Willie Morris wrote for *The New York Times* about Bridgehampton, its small-town rhythms and changes of sea-sons, its flat-land potato fields reminding him of the Mississippi Delta, and Bobby Van's restaurant-and-bar being a social center, originally was a big hit with the locals; it brought in tourists, espe-cially to Bobby Van's place: Larry Wells was astonished, when he called Van's attempting to locate Willie and the bartender who an-swered said, "Willie Morris is not here!" before Wells could ask for him. "He was by then using Van's as his message center, as he would later use our Yoknapatawpha Press office in Oxford."

Eventually, however, some felt that Willie's article had, in the end, attracted too many "outsiders" and caused unwelcome changes in the community. Ironically, Willie Morris was one who, in time, bayed in full cry against the changes he had inadvertently helped bring about.

WILLIE WAS PAID $5,000 FOR HIS WORK on *A Southern Album*. Though John Logue of Oxmoor House (Birmingham) enthusiastically told Willie after receiving his introduction that it was a lightning bolt and would break every other heart in the South, the *Album* received decidedly mixed reviews.

On the plus side was Sammy Stagg's comments in *Library Journal:* "the introduction by Willie Morris is lyrical and nostalgic, evoking love of the legendary South." *Publisher's Weekly* applauded "the blend of regional pride, grace, candor, and a sense of human community that emanates like an aura from photos and text. . . . Willie Morris's memory-laden introductory memoir illuminates the entire book most beautifully." These, unfortunately, were minority reports and largely read by a trade and not commercial audience.

Edward Hoagland, reviewing what he dismissed as four "picture books" in the Sunday *New York Times Book Review,* sounds as if he would have liked to have thrown all of them on the floor, stomped on 'em, and maybe even pissed on 'em. He derided "an appalling piece of balderdash called *A Southern Album*" and grumped that "Willie Morris's unfortunate prose contribution is derivative drivel. . . . The whole zombie narrative . . . is so mercifully brief that it might be more accurate to describe him as lending his name to this book rather than contributing to it." (Willie—who never read reviews, right?—goes on at some length in his later book, *James Jones: A Friendship,* about what a talentless wimp Hoagland was and how and why he was wrong.)

BY THE SPRING OF 1974 my estrangement from Willie Morris had lasted almost two years. We'd had absolutely no contact, didn't even bump into each other despite having many friends in common as well as the same Manhattan restaurants and bars.

When my book *The Old Man and Lesser Mortals* was published by Viking that spring, I thought that sending a warmly signed copy to Willie might open the shut door. It did. He called me soon after receiving the book, and we chatted at length, neither mentioning the old trouble between us.

Willie invited me to come visit him in Bridgehampton in about ten days, on a given weekend; I accepted, and told him I'd let him know when I would arrive. Congressman Mo Udall, pleased that we were making up, volunteered to fly me in his private plane from Princeton to Long Island; once he had located a small airfield, he told me its name and location so I could tell Willie. I called Willie and got him—not always a sure thing, as you have seen. He was delighted that Mo Udall was coming along and said he would meet us at the small airfield on Long Island and drive us into town. "We'll have a good ol' time," he said.

Unfortunately, an unforeseen glitch in Udall's life caused him to apologetically recant, almost at the last moment. I began calling Willie, to give him the news, and tell him I'd be arriving on a Long Island Rail Road train. He was nowhere to be found. A guy who answered the phone at Bobby Van's said he hadn't seen Willie in a day or two but he'd have him call me. I got no call. Ultimately, I called James Jones—though I then had not met him—but got no answer there, either. *Uh-Oh! Were they off somewhere together?*

By Friday night, I was getting desperate; I was to leave Saturday morning. "Oh yeah," said the Bobby Van's guy. "We heard Willie's gone to the city." No, he didn't know where in the city or when he might be coming back. That seemed vague enough to prompt a cancellation of my trip.

I half-wondered if Willie had intended to pull a no-show—either because he still secretly harbored a distaste for me, or as one of his pranks—leaving me and Mo Udall scratching our heads on the tarmac of an isolated airfield while awaiting rescue in vain. No, I decided, Willie would not want to be rude to Udall, and he probably wouldn't pull a prank on me so soon after our first step toward making up. I felt certain Willie would call to apologize and explain, very soon, but you might say I'm still waiting for that call. In time I presumed that Willie simply forgot that Mo and I were coming on the given date, and—if and when he remembered—he was too embarrassed to call. Or that some sudden, if mysterious, opportunity had offered itself in Manhattan, and Willie couldn't resist because he considered it an adventure superior to a visit from me. Given his known eccentricities, that seemed within the realm of the possible.

A few months later, visiting South Hampton as a guest of the actor Peter Boyle and his live-in lady friend, I called Willie. He came to fetch me with apparent enthusiasm, introducing me first to Bobby Van's saloon and then to James Jones, whom he persuaded to join us. A few months later I was the guest of a record producer, whose name I have forgotten, who invited me to his posh Hampton digs because—it turned out—he was under the mistaken impression that I somehow had great influence on the Texas singer-songwriter Willie Nelson, in whom he was professionally interested; I think he must have confused me with Bud Shrake. When the truth came out the music man quite rapidly lost interest in me, so I went to Bobby Van's in search of Willie Morris.

I heard him before I saw him: ". . . and then he said, 'Lookie yonder at that ol' dawg drivin' that ol' car!'" A whoop of laughter from a nearby booth guided me to Willie. We again had a fine time; he promised to come speak to my Princeton students in the upcoming fall, but I never was able, then or later, to pin him down to a specific date. But at least we were friendly again, and for that I was grateful.

FROM JANUARY 10 TO MARCH 5, 1976, Willie was a writer-in-residence at the *Washington Daily Star* newspaper, writing three columns a week on subjects of his own choosing, for which he was paid $4,000 plus $1,500 expenses. The visiting writer program had been established by Editor James Bellows, former editor of *The New York Herald Tribune,* which many thought the "most readable" of

Gotham's sheets in a time when it had several daily newspapers. Some of the writers Bellows attracted to the Washington newspaper (now long defunct) had written for Bellows's *Herald Tribune*, among them Jimmy Breslin, Jane O'Reilly, and yours truly.

I did not see Willie during his *Washington Star* stint as I was living in New York and also was a Thursday-to-Saturday Communications Fellow at Duke, during the school year. His columns were not particularly outstanding, but, for that matter, neither were mine when I took the same *Washington Star* job in late 1976 and early 1977. Such an experience will cause a writer to gain new respect for columnists who turn out several columns per week for years and years: Russell Baker, Robert Novak, Tom Wicker, Jack Germond, Molly Ivins, Mike Royko, and Jimmy Breslin. Royko is dead, and with Breslin's retirement in late 2004, only Novak and Ivins soldier on as columnists.

Besides not being outstanding columnists, Willie and I shared another distinction at the *Star:* Jerry O'Leary, long a writer there and a recovering alcoholic, hectored any and all whom he thought had a drinking problem and might benefit from membership in Alcoholics Anonymous; he did not have to be a master detective to discover that Willie and I might be appropriate fodder. And, of course, we avoided him and his offer of the gift of sobriety as if he might be a fanged vampire thirsty for our blood. (Willie had a harder time avoiding Jerry than did I, since he had rented a small house in Alexandria, Virginia, that O'Leary owned.) We might have done well to listen to O'Leary: Willie was arrested for DUI during his *Star* stint. What he most feared was that the rival *Washington Post* would discover the police record of his arrest and publicize it, but that didn't happen. David Rae discovered it, quite by accident, when he opened a letter to Willie from the District of Columbia Department of Motor Vehicles, thinking it might contain a parking pass. What he found was a letter notifying Willie that his driver's license had been suspended because of his failure to attend what I call "drunk driver's school." David Rae then advised his father against driving without a permit, but "he pretty much would have nothing to do with that. I don't know when he had his license reinstated."

Willie encouraged a young writer at the *Washington Star*, one Winston Groom, a Vietnam veteran who was attempting a novel about the war, that eventually was published as *Better Times Than These*. "It might not have happened without Willie's encouragement," Groom says. "I had written a little of the novel, but Willie's talks to me about literature and the importance of it gave me the spark to get going." Groom, indeed, was so encouraged that he quit his newspaper job cold turkey—"which still scares me when I think about the chance I took"—and moved to Long Island, near Bridgehampton, into a house rented by another young writer, Adam Shaw, son of the celebrated Irwin Shaw. It was almost "right around the corner" from a small house Willie Morris was renting. "When the summer celebrities went back to the city in September the writer's population was reduced to just a few of us, so I was with Willie at Bobby Van's and at our house or his frequently." Jim Jones also taught Groom some few "tricks of the trade," several times sitting down with him after reading portions of his manuscript. "I learned something every time," Groom says. Not a bad couple of mentors, Morris and Jones.

Groom went on to write a number of successful novels after *Better Times Than These*, among them *As Summers Die, Gone the Sun,* and *Such a Pretty Pretty Girl*. He also wrote nonfiction books: *Shrouds of Glory: The Last Great Campaign of the Civil War; A Storm in Flanders: The Ypres Salient, 1914–1918; 1942: The Year That Tried Men's Souls;* and a labor of love—since he was a graduate of University of Alabama—*The Crimson Tide: an Illustrated History of Football at the University of Alabama*.

Groom also wrote a book he didn't know what to think of from one minute to the next. Was it really good or was it truly bad? His agent had not wanted him to write it, his publisher was not keen on the idea. But Groom pressed on with his novel of an idiot savant who became an All-American football player at Alabama, a Vietnam War hero, a world-class ping-pong player who helped open relations with Red China, a very successful businessman, a man who over three decades somehow bumped into the mighty—LBJ, Nixon, others—and in childlike wonder observed insanity all around him. Groom *knew* that the novel, narrated by his protagonist, was highly unusual. But that, he thought, was a plus. Or was it too far-fetched, too out-of-the-mainstream? He sent his manuscript to Willie Morris. "Willie's eyes were the first to see it, other than mine. He read it and told me, 'Don't change a word! Not one!'"

And, of course, *Forrest Gump* became a huge best seller, and an even larger movie that, according to *Publisher's Weekly* grossed $329 million in the U.S.A. alone, making it fourth on the all-time list of books turned into the biggest smash-hit films. (Groom says the film grossed an astounding one *billion* dollars worldwide.)

I am sure Willie was happy for his friend Winston Groom, though *Forrest Gump* was one in a series of money-making works delivered by writers Willie had helped and encouraged, while he still had trouble picking up a nickel off the ground—a bittersweet irony that Willie never mentioned publicly though he sometimes confided his dissatisfaction to select intimates when in his cups. In later years and during lighter moments, according to David Rae Morris, Willie joked that he was going to demand 1 percent of the money earned by the many writers he had helped launch. "If you added up the take from just Winston Groom, Donna Tartt, John Grisham, and Jill Conner Browne," David Rae said, "my dad could have retired in style!"

After I had co-authored the libretto of the smash hit musical comedy *The Best Little Whorehouse in Texas* and bought a nice home in one of Washington, D.C.'s better neighbors, Willie visited me and my wife, Barbara Blaine, and enjoyed asking me, "What would your old Daddy say about this big house and grounds, and your kiddies riding horses while dressed like English squires riding to hounds?" "I believe he was sincerely happy for you," Barbara said after a private talk with Willie one evening as they sat under big trees in our backyard, sipping wine. "Willie said, 'I know Fesser King had nothing growing up and struggled for years. It's really good to see him in better circumstances.'"

PART SIX

LOSING A GOOD FRIEND AND A MOTHER— AND HEARING, AT LAST, THE SIREN CALL OF HOME

"This has been a homecoming for me. I find myself happier than I've been in years—that curious serenity in one's middle years which derives from coming back to the sensual textures of one's childhood—the landscape, the wood-smoke on wintry Mississippi days which Bill Faulkner wrote about, the unflagging courtesy among people, the way people talk, all of it. I think I may stay this time. . . ."

—WILLIE MORRIS

in a letter to novelist and poet Robert Penn Warren
on January 28, 1980

CHAPTER 15

THE ONE CONSISTENT BRIGHT LIGHT in Willie's life in the mid-1970s was his close friendship with James Jones, or "Jim" to his real pals. Morris idolized Jones as a writer and looked on him as a personal hero: one who had fought in the world's biggest war and not only survived but lived to write about war about as well as war ever has been written about; his work captured both the horror and tedium of military life, both the heroic and the craven among combatants, both the quick and the dead—or, put another way, both the lucky and the unlucky. Jones judged and defined more often than not: The title of *The Thin Red Line,* possibly the most authentic book written about combat, came from a Kipling poem assisted by an old adage, "There's only a thin red line between the sane and the mad."

Willie, like many who never had served in the military, stood almost in awe of men like Jones who had been in the thick of it. "I like the way Jim deports himself," Willie once told me. "He's confident in all that he does, but not cocky." Jones did, indeed, strike me as old-shoe regular; what you saw was what he was and what you got. If worms of doubt or fear worked his soul, as they do in most of us, he hid it well. "He was small but built large," the novelist-screenwriter Budd Schulberg said, "with a barrel chest and a lantern jaw and a craggy face I would put on an ex-drill sergeant or a tank town middleweight. His vocabulary was a string of four-letter words and, in the field of literary gossip he was an ignoramus ... he didn't talk about the human condition ... [but] about people he had grown up with in Robinson [Illinois]."

Talking about their early lives and their respective small towns began a bonding between Willie Morris and James Jones early on. Jones grew up in "copperhead country," Yankee territory largely sympathetic to the Confederacy; that probably struck a chord with Willie. And Jones soon revealed that as the son of a father who had killed himself and a mother he hated, he'd had—in Willie's words–"a tortured and lonely childhood." Having mothers they each found difficult may have been another factor in their quick bonding. Whatever, the two writers traded intimate confessions almost from the first, evidence of quickly sharing a mutual trust. (David Rae recalls that when his Grandmother Morris came to visit Willie in 1975 on Long Island, "We were driving her to dinner with Jim and Gloria Jones and she kept having Willie repeat the titles of Jones's books. As soon as she saw him, my grandmother said, 'Oh, I am so happy to meet you! I have read *all* of your books: *From Here to Eternity, The Thin Red Line*. . . .' Willie had to leave the room to keep from laughing out loud.")

Jones and his wife—the former Gloria Mosolino, a native of John Hara's hometown of Pottsville, Pennsylvania, and a beautiful, busty blond bombshell, a fearless extrovert, a former actress who had been a stand-in for Marilyn Monroe, and who could, and often did, match her husband in preaching four-letter gospels—had lived for fifteen years in Paris; their apartment on the Ile St. Louis was so close to the city's famed river that Jim Jones wrote Bill Styron, "I can stand in the window and piss in the Seine, but I don't do it." Every American writer of note who visited Paris almost always gathered at the Joneses to play poker—where the stakes somehow kept creeping higher from the friendly sums bet early—to tell stories, laugh, eat, and most of all to drink.

"He lived extravagantly and his time in Paris was a fifteen-year fête," Irwin Shaw remembered of Jones. "His liquor bills alone were shocking, but he was constantly worried about money. He was haunted by the fear of poverty and lived on a lordly scale."

Jones sometimes "doctored" film scripts for goodly sums, but wouldn't allow his name to be attached. Darryl Zanuck, preparing to produce *The Longest Day*, sent Jones a wire asking him to repair "a small piece" of dialogue a British screenwriter had botched. Jones wired back, "How much?" "Fifteen thousand," Zanuck responded. Jim Jones fired back, "Okay, shoot." Zanuck wired a single line of dialogue: "I can't eat this bloody old box of *tunny* fish." Jones wired back, "I can't stand this damned old tuna fish"—and got his fifteen thousand. Jim Jones often told that story, not to brag, but to illustrate how Hollywood frequently stepped across that "thin red line" between sanity and madness.

Though he worked hard, and usually well—as his track record shows—Jones drank like a true alcoholic in his Paris years and, as drinking men will, had a few fights and once got some ribs cracked. By the time I met him his wild-man days were over, and I had difficulty matching him with the rowdy he once had been. By then Jones drank relatively sparingly, due to a heart problem, though old friends who drank—including Willie, of course—were welcome to imbibe in his home in the midst of a Long Island potato field, and dubbed "Chateau Spud" by Willie. But when Willie persuaded Jones to join us at Bobby Van's three or four times when I was visiting, I had the notion he came strictly to accommodate Willie. He never stayed long, saying he had to "go work." By then, I later would learn, Jones feared he might not live to finish the final novel of his war trilogy as well as other books he wanted to write.

Jones was first put on notice that he had a serious problem in 1970, when, visiting Bill and Rose Styron in Connecticut, he repeatedly mentioned not feeling well. They took him to doctors in Boston, who soon discovered he had congestive heart failure. *Don't drink,* they ordered him. *Above all, don't drink.* Like most veteran boozers, Jones originally compromised: He would drink only white wine, though he often complained that it wasn't Scotch. There came a time—in late 1975—when he was forced even to give up wine. Thereafter he drank only grapefruit juice on the rocks but groused about it having "no kick."

Several things prompted Jim Jones to return to his native land for good and all in 1974. First, his tax lawyers said the advantages of foreign residency had diminished, and the dollar's value had, too; in short, it simply became too expensive to live in Paris. And Jones's most recent novels, *The Merry Month of May* and *A Touch of Danger,* as well as his nonfiction book *Viet Journal,* all had disappointing sales. Second, Jim and Gloria thought that their young children, son Jamie and daughter Kaylie—about to become teenagers—needed "Americanizing." And, thirdly, since his congestive heart condition had been discovered in 1970, Jim Jones increasingly thought he needed to get back to America, get back in *touch* with America, and work there in his final years.

In 1973 he began looking for a place to teach in America, one to provide a base salary that would underpin his writing income. He hoped to go west—the University of Texas, perhaps, or the heralded University of Iowa Workshop program. Texas, however, expressed little interest. Iowa could provide only about $20,000. Three-year-old Florida International University, ambitious to grow and seeking attention, offered Jones $27,500 for the nine-month term and the title of visiting professor and writer-in-residence. He accepted. FIU then was, in the words of novelist Michael Mewshaw—who had explored the possibilities of teaching jobs for Jones—"a school for commuters, workies, blacks and Hispanics."

Say for James Jones that he gave FIU, and his students, honest weight. He seemed at home in academe, thrived on it, worked hard; he brought Willie Morris and Irwin Shaw to FIU as guest lecturers. He got along well with his faculty colleagues, never playing the big-shot writer, which may have surprised them and certainly gratified them. Jones also picked up another $1,000 and expenses as a participant in the University of Florida's annual Writers' Conference in Gainesville.

Still, living in a rented house and watching his pennies was a long way from being the acclaimed, extravagant host in Paris. And teaching took away precious hours from *Whistle,* the novel-in-progress that Jim Jones then valued above all else.

Another writing job got in the way of *Whistle,* too, but it proved to be well worth doing. Working with the former art editor of *Yank,* the

World War II military newspaper that often vexed the generals but was the irrepressible voice of GI Joe, Jim Jones provided the text for a nonfiction book, simply titled *World War II*. It was the kind of project that easily could have turned into an undistinguished coffee-table book, but it did not because of the picture selection and Jones's prose. The book received good reviews—his best since *The Thin Red Line*—and was highly promoted; it made money. At a dinner honoring Jim in the Georgetown section of the nation's capital, the commanding general of the United States Army rose to give a unique toast: "To Pfc Jones, who understood us all."

Shortly, Jim and Gloria sold their Paris apartment for almost half a million dollars, which permitted them to buy "Chateau Spud" in that Long Island potato field. Buoyed by the success of *World War II*, the sale of his Paris place, and surrounded by his cherished artifacts in an attic office he established, Jones happily settled down to work on *Whistle* and he and Willie Morris began to grow closer by the day.

IF JONES WAS AWARE that he likely had but a short time left on earth—and certainly he was—he also was aware that while finishing *Whistle* was of paramount importance, so was spending time with his children, with his wife, with a friend like Willie, and in doing some few things he liked or wanted to do.

Willie Morris has recalled in *James Jones: A Friendship* how Jones deported himself with his children. On Saturdays, when TV stations ran and reran old Western films, Jim Jones and his son, Jamie, both dressed in cowboy clothes and wore cap pistols they occasionally shot at the TV screen when the Bad Guys rode into view; virtually nothing was permitted to get in the way of that ritual. Jones also talked to his daughter, Kaylie, as if she might be an adult and answered her questions about writing; little wonder she turned out to be an accomplished novelist. Jones, in fact, rarely tried to shield his young ones from hard truths about the real world. No matter what they asked about war, how he had won his medals and why he didn't wear them, about death or whatever, he usually gave them truth with the bark off.

Willie and Jim Jones took their sons to baseball and football games, and when Willie was doing his *Washington Star* stint, the four of them—in February of 1976—visited Civil War battlefields at Antietam, Chancellorsville, The Wilderness, Spotsylvania, and Harper's Ferry. It was at Antietam, where was fought—as Willie wrote in his *Washington Star* column—"the bloodiest single day's fighting in the Civil War, some say the bloodiest in the history of mankind until then"—that Jones climbed a small tower and after looking over the field where more than 23,000 fell on September 17, 1862 (compared with 6,600 who fell in France on D-Day, June 6, 1944), shook his head and said, "I don't think that men could go any farther than these men did in this battle and still be members of the planet."

It was a raw, misty day when they visited Antietam, and after they had returned to their motel, and while Willie was phoning in his story to the *Star,* Jones disappeared. He did not return until after dark, "soaking wet." Yes, he admitted, he had gone back to the battlefield. "Why did you go back in this weather?" Willie asked. "I don't know," Jones said. "I guess you really have to be alone in a place like that."

BEGINNING IN 1975, Jones had several attacks of breathlessness and other complications, at least two of which caused him to be hospitalized. A severe attack as Christmas approached caused him to make an appointment with his doctor in Huntington, a sizeable commuter city about halfway to Manhattan from Bridgehampton. Apparently anticipating bad news, Jones didn't want Gloria to go with him. Instead, he asked Willie to accompany him.

"When we got there, he went through a series of tests which lasted nearly two hours," Willie later would write in his *Friendship* book.

> Then he came out into the waiting room. The doctor had told him that his lungs were filling again and that his heart was seriously enlarged. The doctor had reserved a bed in the hospital and told him to check in right away.

We got in the car and drove down a steep hill toward the hospital. The streets at noontime were festive with Christmas decorations, and flurries of snow swept by in the wind.

"He told me I can't drink no more, goddamn it. Not if I want to live." He said it faintly, with resignation.

We were driving by a huge restaurant and bar called Glynn's Inn. "Let's go in that place!," he suddenly exclaimed. "The hospital can wait. Fuck the hospital. I want to have two or three drinks."

"Are you sure?"

"Yeah. My last ones."

The bar was dark and deserted at this hour. There was Christmas music on the Muzak, and the dining room next door bustled with the chatter of commuters' wives at their lunches. . . . We sat down at the bar and ordered a bottle of white wine. He took a sip and said, "What I'd give for a big-assed tumbler of Scotch."

They sat in the bar talking "about how a man's life changes, about the inevitability of sorrow, about death." Jones remarked how he had never been able to pace himself, like Styron, who—Jones once noted—always had about one drink to his three. "It was hard enough when I realized I couldn't fight no more," he said. "Fight some son-of-a-bitch who was acting mean or trying to make out with my wife." The Christmas tunes wafted out from the music machine. The bartender poured another wine.

"Hell, Kaylie was asking me about death the other day. I told her life is a great adventure and death is one of those adventures. I advised her to try and look at it that way. That's hard for a kid, though. . . ." Death was, with good reason, much on Jim Jones's mind. He spoke at length of being on burial detail in the army, what a tough duty it was, and how the detail's members always laughed a lot to keep from cracking. He stared into his glass until Willie said it was about time to go to the hospital. Jones gulped the last of his wine, said, "That's that!" and they went out into the blowing snow.

JONES WAS PERMITTED TO GO HOME from the hospital on Christmas Eve and attacked his *Whistle* manuscript almost immediately, though he did take time off for the tour of Civil War battlefields with Willie Morris, Jamie, and David Rae in February.

Willie would write of that outing: "On our drive back to Washington . . . we decided the four of us would make another trip someday soon: first, to Robinson, Illinois which [Jones] had not been back to since '57, and then through Kentucky and Tennessee. We would stop in Memphis to look for whatever landmarks remained of his days there, in the hospital in '43 and later in the trailer camp when he was working on *From Here to Eternity*—then on down to Yazoo City. It was a trip we never made."

In January of 1977 came a scary night when "we had to get [Jim] to the hospital in Southampton in the blizzard, Gloria and I following the ambulance down the Montauk Highway, going slow as could be to avoid skidding off the road into snowdrifts. They almost lost his pulse in the ambulance."

James Jones seemed to be deeply into denial. "'There ain't nothing wrong with my old heart,' he said in the bed in the Cardiac Care Unit, 'I got a good heart.' For two or three days we thought he was dying. He asked me to get a notebook. . . . I sat by the bed and between whiffs of the oxygen mask he talked about the few remaining chapters of his novel.

"He survived that attack but he was extremely weak. When he got out of the hospital in February, the doctors warned him not to work at first. But, gradually, he started back into the hard routine." Jones also began taking Gloria to Bobby Van's for lunch, a regular routine in better times, lingering over a cigar after his meal, drinking his punchless grapefruit juice on the rocks, and chatting up the locals. This seemed almost miraculous to those who had seen him fighting for breath and gulping oxygen only days before.

Soon Jones's brother, Jeff, died in Roanoke—also of congestive heart failure—at age sixty-seven. The writer had not seen him in years but concluded he was not in physical shape to attend his brother's funeral. He lost himself in his work, reading new passages aloud to Gloria and Willie. One night, having read a scene about an old soldier who wore life's scars and—like himself—was nearing the end, Jones wiped away a tear and then laughed at himself.

Willie wrote, "I was so saddened by his physical condition. As the days passed, he became more wan and pale. In his farmhouse, there were times I went into the bathroom to fight back tears."

EVEN AS WILLIE MORRIS NURTURED JAMES JONES through the hardest of times, he also had to listen to a drumming of discontent from his mother. Marion Morris, true to a lifelong pattern, continued to advise, instruct, harass, snipe at, or guilt-trip her son about . . . well, almost everything. Some typical random shots:

February 10, 1972: Says by letter that she has reached the time in life when she needs love and security; her friends have kids and grandkids to comfort them, but she only has "a son I see once a year, and a grandson who cares very little for me." (JoAnne Prichard Morris recalls Willie visiting his mother in Yazoo City in May of 1973 and "making at least two or three more trips to see her before she died. And Willie's mother visited his Long Island home at least twice. Once he took her to Dick Cavett's summer house in Montauk, so she could meet her favorite talk-show host." And David Rae Morris, in response to his grandmother's accusation that he cared little for her, said, "I think she was being a little hysterical. As I have noted, we did see a good deal of her, and I spoke on the phone with her periodically. I remember especially calling from New York once and putting on a mock Southern accent. I told her I was from Memphis and was doing an 'Organist Almanac,' highlighting the church women of Mississippi and I had a few questions. I kept her going for ten or fifteen minutes. She was telling me her life story. And then I asked, 'Mrs. Morris, do you have a grandson?' 'Oh, yes!' 'Does he like to play tricks on you?' I then revealed myself, and she laughed a hearty laugh.")

January 8, 1973: Says that Barbara Howar, when asked why she and Willie had split up, responded it was because of Willie's drinking and "your drinking" (this is Mrs. Morris writing to Willie) "is one of the things that has helped to get me in the shape I am in" and put her in the hospital. "Dr. Chapman says I am in a terribly nervous state and is giving me B12 shots at $5.00 a shot" and also has put her on tranquilizers.

July 7, 1973: "I seem to make you *mad* with everything that I say about your writing. I do not intend to do that—it's only that I'm interested and concerned." She adds that plenty of good books sell without being about sex and again warns Willie against emulating Norman Mailer.

January 20, 1974: "I need you, Willie, so badly and I am *begging* for *help.* I have no appetite and my sleep at night is troubled . . . when I don't hear from you, I feel as if I am losing my mind."

March ?, 1974: Writes that Celia Morris wants her to leave money directly to David Rae in her will because, as Celia understands it, Willie has not filed income tax returns for some five years and that "could amount to a horrendous debt." Marion Morris is "terribly disturbed" by this report and instructs Willie to call her collect because "I need to hear the truth about this."

September 28, 1974: Thanks Willie for a *Reader's Digest* he sent her, containing his article about his beloved grandmother, Mamie, but adds, "I am trying to understand you, Willie, for I can't seem to penetrate your 'outer wall.' Don't close me out, Willie."

December ?, 1975: "I am beginning to wonder if I have a son anymore. He is too busy writing a book to pen a few words to his mother."

January 3, 1976: Writes that when she telephoned Willie at 1 P.M. David Rae answered and said his father was still in bed. Referring to his upcoming three-month stint at the *Washington Star* she admonishes: "You are going to have to get to bed at a reasonable hour so you can get to your job. . . . Remember you will have a boss." Reminds her forty-two-year-old son to lock his Long Island house when he leaves for Washington.

January 27, 1976: Chastises Willie for not lately having written to his high school English teacher, Omie Parker: "She is your *best* friend in Yazoo City and loves hearing from her former students." (Somewhat earlier, she had threatened not to send Willie "any more money" unless he wrote to someone identified only as "Mrs. Ramsey"; probably this was Lizbeth Ramsey, who had a gift shop and who had hosted book signings for Willie on some of his visits to Yazoo City.)

February 14, 1976: Writes that Celia Morris "could have done a better job of teaching David Rae that a grandmother's love is important." Says that she doesn't know David. On Christmas Day of 1976, a long-time friend of Marion Morris writes to Willie—cautioning that "if you ever tell your mother I wrote to you, I will hate you *forever*" (What's with Yazoo City women and their stingray letters?)— and tells him his mother is in bad shape. "I understand when you were here you said you are aware of the problem but didn't know what to do about it. Well, believe me, there *is* a problem but what it is none of us knows (or) what to do about it—and have no authority if we do know."

The litany: (1) Mrs. Morris has become a menace to herself and others when driving a car; (2) she is "falling down on her music" as church pianist by "suddenly changing key, missing a page, etc"; (3) she "walked into Fellowship Hall at the church on Sunday recently minus her shoes—wanted to know if she had left them and her purse in the church [but] they were outside in her car"; (4) sometimes, "according to some" she has "the smell of alcohol on her breath" and this upsets friends who fear she might be taking tranquilizers in tandem with liquor, a dangerous combination. Marion says, however, she is not taking tranquilizers (but she told Willie to the contrary); (5) Marion "borrowed a glass of sherry from me on occasions, to help her sleep, she says. I was glad to tell her last Sunday that I had already given her all I had"; (6) she "cannot remember anything for any length of time. . . . She picks up a package from downtown [then] two hours later goes back for the same package"; (7) "in one short conversation she will tell you the same thing at least three times. And she doesn't *listen* to anyone"; (8) "She is restless, restless, restless and I think it is beginning to get the best of her. You know how nervous she has always been."

The woman concluded:

Most definitely, *something* is radically wrong with Marion. Her face is quite bloated, her eyes droop, she staggers on occasion and her tongue is sometimes quite thick. I am not in the least suggesting Marion is a drunkard. She is, you may remember, a border-line diabetic. She may have a quite serious physical disability.

I would suggest that you make an immediate trip home (sometimes money counts for little) and take your mother to a good clinic for a thorough examination. Something *must* be done. . . .

Nothing of record indicates that Willie went to Yazoo City then, and there is nothing to indicate he answered that letter—or, as JoAnne Prichard Morris says, "that he even read it." It was, apparently, among letters not opened until after Willie died. Prichard Morris recalls that Willie visited his mother in November of 1976 and brought her to a small dinner party JoAnne gave. "And Willie was extremely upset about her condition."

On April 7, 1977, Mrs. Morris wrote her only child apparently what was her final communiquè: "I don't understand you anymore, Willie. There is no need to tell you when I go to the hospital for an operation, because you wouldn't care."

One week and one day after her last note to Willie—on April 15—Marion Weaks Morris died of a cerebral hemorrhage.

"I WAS SITTING IN RICK'S, a bar on Main Street in Bridgehampton, talking with Rick and a couple of potato farmers about baseball," Willie Morris wrote in *Atlantic Monthly* of March 1978. "From outside the big window I saw him park his car behind mine and cross the street in our direction, a pale figure in blue jeans and a sweater, and a green-and-yellow baseball cap and the leather satchel with the strap flung over his shoulder in which he carried his cigars and a few of his knives."

James Jones walked up to Willie and said, "Your Mom just died. I'm sorry."

"She had gone into the hospital that week in Mississippi," Willie wrote. "Nothing serious, the doctors said, but I had made reservations on the plane for the next day. She had died suddenly that morning." Mississippi friends, unable to reach Willie, knew enough to call Jim Jones's house.

"I been looking all over for you," Jones told Willie in Rick's place. "The cops had it on their radio. Come on home with me. You shouldn't be alone."

Willie had two hours to kill before going to LaGuardia Airport. He called David Rae, in school in New York, and arranged for his son to accompany him to Mississippi, and made other calls relative to his mother's death. He watched Jim Jones, writing in a notebook, thinking that he looked "gaunt and tired."

When it came time for Willie to leave, Jones "came downstairs in the chairlift he had rigged up after his last attack to take him to and from the attic. He stood for a moment in the airy sunshine. The first touch of spring, always late to eastern Long Island, was all around us. We shook hands, in that shy, casual way old comrades do. 'You know I'd go with you if I could,' he said. 'I have to finish *Whistle.*'"

Willie was in Yazoo for almost a month. When not attending to business, he often wandered in the Yazoo graveyard, as he had so many times, and this go-round he had

the most acute awareness that my son and I were the last of our line.

I had to close down the house where I grew up and put it up for sale. No brothers or sisters to share that trial of finding things in the back corners of closets—a program for my mother's piano recital in 1916, a faded photograph of my father in a baseball uniform in 1920, another of my great-grandmother holding a parasol in 1885, yellowed clippings, trinkets from high school. The movers came to take away the furniture. The last item to leave was the baby grand, which would go to the church.

Willie telephoned Jim Jones his last day in Yazoo, to tell him he would be seeing him soon. Jones, sounding "gruff and breathless," said he wasn't feeling too good.

"The moment came that I stood alone in that empty house. Did I know then how it would grow to haunt my dreams and nightmares? In the gloom of it that day I strained to hear the [piano] music again, my father's footsteps on the porch, the echoes of boys playing basketball in the back yard, the barks and whines of Tony, Sam, Jimbo, Sonny, Duke, and Old Skip. I locked the front door and did not look behind me."

Willie Morris revealed much less emotion in writing of his mother's death than he actually experienced, according to his son. "When we went to the funeral home in Yazoo City," David Rae Morris told me, "my father became very emotional and had to stop talking for a few minutes to regain his composure. The undertaker asked if my father wanted to see his mother and he said, 'No.' During the visitation at the funeral home the casket was open, a Southern tradition. . . . I stayed in the back of the room. Later, I told my father that I couldn't look at [his grandmother]. And he confessed: 'Neither could I.'" Later, in the church during his mother's funeral—with David Rae beside him in the family pew—Willie suddenly grabbed his son's knee and began crying long, deep sobs.

FROM A MOTEL IN TENNESSEE late the night after he left Yazoo, Willie called Jim Jones again. Gloria answered, saying she had hospitalized her husband that afternoon, and he was very sick: "I think it's time for you to get on back." Willie got on a freeway near Nashville and kept the speedometer on or near seventy miles per hour, the legal limit,

> stopping only for coffee or for gas or to sleep or to empty my bladder, I felt the South recede as an element of nature recedes. Ever since my boyhood, driving through the South had never failed to suffuse me with a bittersweet sadness, the sadness of love and belonging, and now something there had ended for me, something irretrievably lost in the land I knew in my heart, some connecting vein with one's own mortality. In the trunk of the car, sealed in a cardboard box, was the family silver, which I had not entrusted to the movers—the same family silver which my great-grandmother

had hidden from the Northern troops when they took the town in 1863.

On these interminable stretches of freeway, in a drive I managed to make in only slightly more than two days, I thought of my friend who lay dying in a hospital out at the easternmost littoral of America. His fate, and the solitary farewell in Mississippi, became enmeshed for me on this drive, one of those junctures which, once passed, becomes symbolic, almost, and makes a man ask: What now?

WILLIE SPENT HIS FINAL NIGHT of that trip somewhere in Pennsylvania, calling the Southampton hospital to learn that his friend was sinking fast. He arrived there the following afternoon. Gloria Jones, Jamie and Kaylie, and a few friends were in a waiting room. Gloria told Willie to look in on her husband but warned he might not be able to stay awake.

"Jim was lying in the bed with wires in him for the monitors (checking his pulse and heartbeat) and the glucose. He took my hand." They exchanged pleasantries before Jones asked, "Did you inherit anything?" Willie said yeah, the family silver was in the trunk of his car—a Plymouth with Yazoo County license plates. Jones grinned. In a moment he reached for his oxygen mask and said, "I'm scared, Willie." Willie assured him they would stay with him, that he wouldn't be alone. "Aw shit, it ain't that! I'm scared I ain't finished *Whistle.*" Willie said no, Jim, you have, really. "Just them three short chapters," Jones said. "I gave Gloria two more tapes while you were gone." His eyelids seemed to grow heavy; when Jones dropped off to sleep, Willie left.

Willie, Gloria, and a few friends sat in the waiting room all afternoon, some drinking in paper cups from a bottle of bourbon Willie had stowed under the couch.

We huddled together, as old friends will. Now, in the early evening, a doctor suddenly appeared. He took Gloria and the children aside. He told them it was just a matter of time, perhaps an hour. They went in again to see him. In about an hour Gloria emerged. "Quick!" she said. "He wants a drink!" I poured a paper cup full of bourbon. She hurried inside with it.

All that evening we waited; Gloria, Adam Shaw and I took turns sleeping on the floor. The doctor later said that he had practiced heart medicine for twenty years, and had never seen a patient come back like that from the edge of death; he had never seen a patient want to live so much.

At about 2 A.M. Jones sent for Willie, who must have entered with great trepidation, given the circumstance. "I think I'm going to pack it in," Jones said. "I want to talk to you. But I got to get unhooked. I can't talk with all this shit." He ripped out the various wires, picked up the tape recorder, and told Willie to listen carefully because he hadn't made clear two points he'd tried to cover earlier and that bothered him. "He talked for a long time, weakly but lucidly. When he had finished, he sat back, exhausted . . . 'God, I'm sleepy.'"

Amazingly, Jones hung on through the weekend and had a brief, teasing visit with old friend Irwin Shaw, who had just flown in from Europe; Gloria stayed by her husband's side almost constantly. Sunday afternoon she came out and said that Jones wanted a copy of Yeats's poem "The Lake Isle of Innisfree," which he wanted read at his service. Willie and his son David Rae drove to Bridgehampton and got the poem. When they returned, the death watch crew had gone home to take naps and the nurse said that Willie and David Rae could stay only a minute.

Jones read the poem to himself and said, "It's a strange poem . . . it makes me want to weep," and brushed away tears.

"Slowly," Willie wrote, "in the old familiar gruff voice, he read it aloud:

I will arise and go now, and go to Innisfree
And a small cabin build there, of clay and wattles made:
Nine bean-rows will I have there, a hive for the honey-bee
And live alone in the bee-loud glade.

And I shall have some peace there, for peace comes dropping slow,
Dropping from the veils of the morning to where the cricket sings;
There midnight's all a-glimmer and noon a purple glow,
and evening full of linnet's wings.

I will arise and go now, for always night and day
I hear lake water lapping with low sounds by the shore;
While I stand on the roadway, or on the pavements grey
I hear it in the deep heart's core.

The moment Jones finished reading, the nurse told his visitors they must go. Willie paused at the door, turned back and said, "I'll see you tomorrow, ol' Jim." Jones responded, "I'll see ya, ol' buddy."

But it was not to be. Shortly, James Jones lapsed into a final coma. Gloria and the children stayed with him through the afternoon. Early in the evening of May 9, 1977, the old soldier suddenly struggled up as if trying to get out of bed, then fell back dead.

As Irwin Shaw said at a small private funeral, the adventure—for Jim Jones—was over.

CHAPTER 16

THINGS WERE JUST NOT THE SAME with his pal Jim Jones gone. Willie for weeks visited his grave almost daily and, he later said, "Talked to him at times." He still saw a great deal of Gloria, especially when writing *James Jones: A Friendship,* using her as a source and to check his memories of past events.

Probably the closest friend Willie ever had was Jim Jones, though Bill Styron, Ed Yoder, and Larry and Dean Faulkner Wells rated high. The rest of us were, by comparison, also-rans—no matter that we'd had our innings. Neither was there a woman of note in Willie's life at the time of Jones's death. In short, there was a lack of intimacy: no ear to whisper confidences in, no one to share memories of the good times, no crutch to lean on in time of need.

Willie still had writer friends in the Bridgehampton area, year-round residents at the time to include Winston Groom, Wilfrid Sheed, and Truman Capote—the latter of whom was in social exile since the rich ladies with whom he had shared many lunches and much gossip had turned on him like pit bulls when they were too easily identified in a story published in *Esquire* and said to be an excerpt from what proved to be a famously unfinished Capote novel, *Answered Prayers.* And Willie still hung out at Bobby Van's with Van, bartender Cal Calabrese, who played on the Golden Nematodes softball team Willie coached, and other favored locals—but none could come close to replacing Jim Jones.

James Jones: A Friendship was published by Doubleday in October of 1978, evidence that it was quickly written. Willie said he pushed it to completion "before I could forget things that needed remembering," but it was also, I think, his way of holding onto Jones a little longer by again immersing himself in that which was suddenly gone.

The book was not a "big book" in terms of sales (16,000 copies) and even those critics who liked it best saw it as an illumination of a warm friendship rather than a deep probing of Jones's work; some few faulted Willie for too strongly defending Jones against his critics. Willie probably made such comments inevitable, by his own Author's Note in the front of the book: "This is not a work of scholarship or literary criticism. Rather it is an illumination of a friend, and perhaps of myself and others of us, and I hope it tells something about writing, especially American writing."

Kirkus Reviews damned with faint praise: "For the most part, Morris is clear-eyed about Jones' victories and failures. . . . The only flaw in this labor of love is that the quotes from Jones' works are so much more vigorously hard-edged than the book we're reading."

Christopher Lehmann-Haupt in *The New York Times* questioned Willie's "critical objectivity" for extolling his friend's books within "the framework of his personal devotion to the man" and for "closing his eyes to Jones's shortcomings as a writer." But he then admits that Jones "comes off as an appealing person" whose "small-town values and 'bedrock integrity'" Willie shares. The book, therefore, "is as much autobiography as it is a portrait of another, and as self-exploration it stands as a fitting embellishment to *North Toward Home.*"

I liked the book simply because it reveals how much Willie Morris loved a friend he both admired and enjoyed, and it humanized Jim Jones, warts and all, in ways Jones's own work may not have. Jones's death, I believe, had more to do with Willie's decision to return home to Mississippi than any other event.

REMEMBER WHAT WILLIE MORRIS TOLD JIM JONES when Jones asked if he had inherited anything? Yeah, the family silver "is in the trunk of my car, a Plymouth with Yazoo County license plates." Not exactly the whole truth, it turns out. According to a CPA's tax document dated April 15, 1978, Willie inherited a total gross estate of $180,620 broken down thusly: Stocks and Bonds: $133,828; Mortgages, Notes and Cash: $25,396; Real Estate: $14,896; Miscellaneous property (household furnishings): $6,500.

That was far from a fortune, even in 1977–78 dollars. But the amount astonished ex-wife Celia Morris and David Rae, along with a few friends who learned of the inheritance; how had a working widow, teaching piano, accumulated that much in a Delta backwater? Whatever, by Willie's flat-broke standards it was a small fortune.

So what became of the money? It might appear to the unknowing that Willie ran through it in about two years, after ignoring the pleas of a money-wise and honest lawyer in Yazoo City—Herman DeCell, an old family friend—who virtually begged Willie to let him handle the money and invest it. But Willie's widow says that the $133,000+ in stocks and bonds largely was in old railroad stock that "crashed" not long after Willie inherited it—and it was not Willie who told her that, but Herman and Harriet DeCell. Willie, according to JoAnne Prichard Morris, actually got only about $40,000 in real money. In his late years, Willie said of his inheritance that "much of the money" had put David Rae through college and kept him in cars.

It is true that David Rae's college tuition was about $12,000 per annum, with another $2,000 to $3,000 for extras, and it's true that Willie once bought him a new pickup truck. So, those expenses would have gobbled up around $70,000, which would be pretty consistent with what Willie once told me: that he largely paid for David's college by "writing for *Reader's Digest, Playboy, Parade,* and other magazines paying top dollars" and from "book advances."

IT SEEMS PROBABLE that Willie Morris began thinking of returning home to Mississippi not long after he finished his James Jones book. He accomplished little other work, a few magazine or newspaper pieces, though he may have done some of his incessant rewriting of his novel long in progress, *Taps.* His lack of productivity would have made him restless and, perhaps, seeking. He had no money; being broke may have inspired him to look for greener pastures. When he did leave Bridgehampton, indeed, he owed his land-lord eight months back rent, an unspecified sum to Bobby Van, and $14,487.38 to a local bank. It was about that time that he urged me to approach two mutual friends—Texas trial lawyers Warren Burnett and Malcolm McGregor, the latter a pal since Willie's *Texas Observer* days—"To let me have, between them, say twenty or twenty five thousand dollars."

"Well, uh, what would I say about your prospects for payback?"

Willie said he hoped they'd consider it a . . . well . . .

"A *gift?*"

Well, yes.

"Jesus, Willie! Do you realize what you're asking? That's a hell of a lot of money to give away!"

Well, Willie said, they were rich men; they had the money. He insisted that I call them and solicit in his behalf; I was to tell them that twenty or twenty-five grand would solve all his problems, get him out of debt and ease his mind so that he could get back to doing quality work. He believed, as friends, they might appreciate his dilemma.

Reluctantly, I called Warren Burnett and made the pitch. I was startled when he said, "No problem." Then he added, "I'll match any amount McGregor gives." I burst out laughing; not for nothing was McGregor a Scotsman; he could squeeze a nickel until the buffalo double-humped. That put it in perspective, and I gave up the chase. Willie must have accurately assumed that I struck out—or perhaps had not even solicited the lawyers—because he never mentioned the subject again.

Willie long had said that he could never return to Mississippi so long as his "crazy mother"—his words—remained alive; that condition, obviously, had changed. Still, though in his work he praised the South in general and Mississippi in particular, he didn't return that often of his own volition, nor stay long when he did. In one of his wee-hour calls, Willie told me he liked the idea of moving back but wondered if he might have become a little too "citified" to enjoy his old haunts. He also discussed that factor with Truman Capote, who had made his famous remark that exiled southerners always returned home "even if in a pine box." So we know that Willie mulled the possibility of returning home, not long after James Jones died, even if he was not yet committed.

In 1980, Willie told the Memphis *Commercial Appeal* that while speaking to the Delta Arts Council in Greenville in 1978 (for $2,000 and expenses) he had told Larry Wells he would like to become writer-in-residence at Ole Miss. No, Wells says, that was the first time he and Dean Faulkner Wells had met Willie—but that subject didn't come up then. They had seen Willie standing alone, smoking a cigarette and looking vaguely ill-at-ease and when they approached, "The first thing Willie said was, 'Would you mind standing here between me and these little old ladies?'" Larry and Dean connected quickly with Willie, and they left him feeling they had made a great new friend. "Willie loved the idea that we were running a small press in Mississippi, making us kissing cousins of Don Quixote," Larry Wells recalls. "He asked us a lot of questions.

"We had no idea that one day we'd publish Willie. It was enough just to meet him and get to know him. Dean had admired him from the moment she first read *North Toward Home* while living in Panama—her first husband was in the Air Force—and she couldn't have imagined that five years later we would reprint *North Toward Home* and keep it in print for almost twenty years."

A few months after that initial meeting, Larry Wells went to New York on a sales trip for his Yoknapatawpha Press, which soon was to publish a photo-biography, *William Faulkner: The Coffield Collection*, which he had edited. By prearrangement, he borrowed a Manhattan friend's car and drove out to Bridgehampton to visit Willie. Willie then lived in a small house on a side street behind Bobby Van's, so they didn't have to go far to dinner.

"It was one of those pivotal moments for me, an inexperienced editor and sometimes writer, getting to have dinner with *Willie Morris* at his favorite watering hole. Bobby Van himself sat at the piano and played 'As Time Goes By,' Willie's favorite song next to 'Darkness on the Delta.' The famous picture by Jill Krementz—of Willie, James Jones, John Knowles, and Truman Capote—was hanging over the bar and it came to symbolize the literary golden age of Bridgehampton. It was pretty heady stuff, but I was not much of a drinker so much of our conversation is lost in the haze." Wells got out of bed with a terrible hangover before 8 A.M. but didn't disturb a snoring Willie Morris, who might have awakened had a fife and bugle corps piped music into both ears.

Wells next saw Willie in mid-1979 when, with Dean, he attended a "Sense of Place" Symposium at the University of Southern Mississippi in Hattiesburg, where Morris was the guest speaker. Willie rhapsodized to them and to Hunter Cole of University Press of Mississippi over the brightness and apparent nearness of the stars—"in a soft voice and in childlike wonder"; Cole recalls Willie saying, "The whiteout of Gotham's lights has erased all but the moon from the night sky."

"We sat up drinking and talking in Willie's hotel room," Larry Wells recounts. "He woke William Styron at his house on Martha's Vineyard to introduce him to us. And that's the night, when we were finally alone with Willie, that he asked if we would look into the possibility that Ole Miss might hire him as a writer-in-residence or to teach."

The idea thrilled Larry and Dean Wells; they thought Willie would benefit the university and that coming home would benefit Willie. Wells went straightaway to Chancellor Porter Fortune and found him receptive. Fortune sent him to talk to Vice-Chancellor Robert Khayat about how to bring it off. There was no money in the English Department budget to pay a writer-in-residence, so the money had to be raised outside the university. That took a bit of doing—and, in addition, the university powers insisted that Willie actually teach, not just float around as a ghostly campus presence.

Larry Wells, eager, had in February presented his "money raising kit"—a form letter and a suggested mailing list of potential donors—to Ole Miss authorities. "They"—he wrote to Willie— "smiled indulgently and remarked that they would revise my letter so it would speak money talk." They must not have been whizzes at writing "money talk" letters themselves, since in November they were still writing them: $9,825 had been collected and another $1,325 had been pledged, but $3,850 still needed to be raised. This money, the pitch ran, would be used to pay Willie Morris, to cover the expenses of famous authors who visited his classes (John Knowles, William Styron, and Irwin Shaw were named) and would help pay for receptions for Willie and his various "notable guests."

Larry and Dean Wells wanted Willie to come to Oxford for a football weekend in late October, ostensibly to meet Ole Miss officials whose goodwill would be needed. But they also thought that if Willie could meet some of Oxford's more interesting people, at the type of parties created by home-game fevers, the circumstances could erase any fears Willie might have about Oxford being too small, or too dull, or too remote. They had learned that Willie loved football and figured him to respond to the color, excitement, and community unity brought about by the Rebels' home games. "It's literally the only game in town," Larry Wells said. "*Everybody* gets involved. Tailgate parties in The Grove, packed stands, camaraderie. When the Rebels win the joint is jumping, and when they lose the streets are empty and as sad as a morgue."

But where would the money come from to bring Willie to town? Sid Graves, an old friend of Willie's who ran the public library in the city of Clarksdale, was enlisted. He said he would put his entire annual lectureship budget on the line—only a modest $500, yes, but who can fault a man who gives all he's got?—provided Willie would agree to speak at his library. And, of course, Willie did. In fact, Larry and Dean picked Willie up in Clarksdale after his speech there and drove him to Oxford.

"Willie was impressed with Oxford and its people, *truly* impressed. Oxford, per capita, is probably the most sophisticated city in Mississippi and Willie saw that," Larry Wells says. Dean Faulkner Wells recalls, "We got back from Clarksdale late, but we stopped at Rowan Oak and walked the grounds, swapping stories about Pappy [Faulkner]." "There was Pappy's grave, too," her husband injected. "And you know how Willie loved cemeteries." Wells saw "an immediate" new enthusiasm in Willie with respect to moving to Oxford. "It didn't hurt that just about everybody in town flocked to him. At the parties you'd hear over and over, 'There's Willie Morris!' and they'd go over and pay their respects." At one such party, hosted by Larry and Dean on the eve of the Ole Miss–Georgia football game, "staunch admirers included Chancellor Fortune, U.S. Senator Thad Cochran, and Mayor John Leslie," according to Dean. "After the party, a group ended up in Taylor, six miles south of Oxford, eating catfish and, as is traditional, signing the walls. Artist Bill Dunlap sketched a mural—a crop duster flying over Delta flatlands—and Willie wrote an inscription evoking Gavin Stevens and Temple Drake, from *Sanctuary*." As Willie might have said, it was an "ineluctably" perfect evening. Even the weather cooperated: "It was unseasonably cool for the first week in October, cool enough for drinks by the fire, yet summer enough for a bouquet of zinnias picked from our garden."

Willie Morris had brought along young Adam Shaw who said to him, when Willie was mulling what to do, "These are good people, Willie. This is a good place. You'd be crazy not to come here." Dean Wells says that Adam Shaw was "a major positive influence" in Willie's decision.

Willie and the Ole Miss officials put on their best faces for each other. He agreed to teach two courses—Creative Writing and The American Novel—to meet, respectively, on Tuesdays and Thursdays. Enrollment would be limited to sixteen in the writing course and thirty in the American novel course—though when Willie imported his famed writer friends, much larger audiences would be accommodated. Potential donors were told they would get special invitations to these gatherings, and also to receptions for the honored guests. Those promises pushed the fund-raising drive over the top.

Willie did not know it, but some faculty members in the English Department originally objected to his being brought in. Their official reason was that Willie had no Ph.D. As if maybe his master's from Oxford in History wasn't worth the paper it was written on, and as if being a Rhodes Scholar wasn't maybe just a little bit better than having graduated from Mississippi Military Academy. Knowing a smidgen about human nature, I'd guess that some were jealous of Willie Morris, some may have been intimidated by his popularity, and others, well . . . almost every organization has a few natural born chickenshits.

Evans Harrington, acting English Department chairman at the time—himself a historian who admired Willie's work—somehow put down the budding revolt before it spread and before many even knew of it. He remained a staunch supporter of Willie Morris throughout.

Very late in the game, Larry and Dean Wells learned the university people somehow had overlooked providing housing for their new hire. "I rushed out there and talked to them," Larry Wells said,

and Willie was assigned a little frame house at Number 16 Faculty Row. Nothing fancy, but perfectly adequate. Then I learned that *somebody* had to pay the rent on that house! You'd think, it belonging to the university, they could just assign it as a perk. But, no, that's not how they operated. So a wealthy outside donor came up with $4,800 to pay Willie's rent, and it was officially carried on the books as part of his salary.

Then Dean asked if Willie would be bringing furniture, bedding, cutlery, china, silverware, kitchen utensils and such. I hadn't even thought about that, but I immediately sensed, no *knew,* that he wouldn't. I was right: All he brought was his car, his son David Rae, his dog Pete, his clothes, a carton of Viceroy cigarettes and a bottle of bourbon—nothing approximating what you'd need to furnish a house.* Thank God, Dean and her friends had scavenged their own houses to furnish Willie's, and stocked his refrigerator with basics so that he had coffee, milk, bread, and stuff. We rented a bed from a furniture store and got pillows and blankets for it. We knew Willie loved a fire, so we laid the makings of one in the fireplace.

Willie and David Rae drove up to the Wells's house about mid-afternoon on January 5, 1980, Willie repeatedly honking his car horn as an indication of a festive mood. After dinner with Larry and Dean and a few locals who had helped prepare for his homecoming,

* A bit later, Willie and David Rae drove back to Long Island and brought Willie's papers and books to Mississippi.

Willie and David Rae joined a small caravan of cars to Number 16 Faculty Row.

Willie Morris was delighted with his instant home, and immediately touched a match to the fireplace kindling, lit a cigarette, poured a drink, and with the faithful dog, Pete, lying at his feet he began telling stories in the little frame house that would be his nest for the next ten years.

CHAPTER 17

"WILLIE'S CLASSES OVERFLOWED IMMEDIATELY," Larry Wells remembers.

> People would sit in the aisles, and his dog, Pete, would lie down in front of the stage and sleep through the proceedings. Nobody else slept: those first classes generated more excitement on campus than anything except, maybe, an Ole Miss Rebels' football game.
>
> Faculty members as well as students paraded in to check out the action, including some in the English Department who'd opposed Willie's hiring. They would sort of sneak into back row seats, but they were *there*. A young fellow in the Law School sat in several times and asked Willie to look at a manuscript of a novel he was attempting. Years later, he would set up a program to bring visiting writers to the Ole Miss campus because of how valuable and enjoyable he'd found Willie's classes. His name was John Grisham.

Willie Morris gave John Grisham a few pointers and supplied the first dust-jacket blurb he received for that first novel, published as *A Time to Kill*. He also made telephone calls to New York on Grisham's behalf, checking out editors, agents, publishing houses, and, in general, trying to help him get off to a good start in a profession where the young neophyte writer knew nobody.

A local fireman, Larry Brown, asked Willie to look at his early work—a novella and some short stories later made into an odd but interesting movie called *Big Bad Love;* Brown got off to a promising start, but, unfortunately, died of a heart attack during the Thanksgiving holiday in 2004, at the young age of fifty-three.

One day a young Ole Miss miss—Donna Tartt—having a drink in the Holiday Inn bar felt a hand on her shoulder and turned to see its owner who said, "My name is Willie Morris and I think you are a genius"; he based that opinion on several unpublished stories the young woman had written, which had been slipped to Willie by a faculty member.

Willie persuaded yet another writer on the faculty, Barry Hannah, like Willie a native of Mississippi, to permit Miss Tartt, a small-town Mississippi girl, to enroll in his graduate student writing workshop, although she was only a freshman. The two writers convinced Tartt to transfer to a liberal arts college in New England—Bennington, in Vermont—so as to broaden her cultural, social, and geographic base. Tartt has proved to be a deliberate, exacting writer, having produced only two novels in about twenty years, but what fine novels they have been. Her first, *The Secret History,* fetched a $450,000 advance, won critical acclaim, and was translated into twenty-four languages; *The Little Friend,* did almost as well, both as to sales and acclaim.

"Willie became my best friend," Donna Tartt later said. "The year I was at Ole Miss we drove all over the countryside, talking about writing and history and Mississippi. When I was going out on my first book tour with *The Secret History,* I was nervous and didn't know what to expect. Willie Morris came to New Orleans and calmed me down."

"Willie helped everybody who asked," Larry Wells says, "and just about *everybody* asked Willie to read their stuff. Of course, he had his fun: each time some little old blue-haired lady brought him a hopelessly flawed work he would say it was 'a natural' for Yoknapatawpha Press and sic 'em on me!"

There is ample evidence that Willie Morris originally was delighted to be back. On Christmas Day, 1979—shortly before leaving

Bridgehampton for Mississippi——he penned Truman Capote, "Please come down and talk to my class and hang around Oxford for a couple of days. 'Knowlesie' is coming, and Bill Styron, and Irwin Shaw, and Walker Percy, and Eudora [Welty]. Ole Miss is poor and can only pay expenses, but I need you and so does Miss'ippi."

A bit over a month later—January 28, 1980—Willie wrote, in longhand, a "Dear Red" letter to his friend Robert Penn Warren: "This has been a homecoming for me. I find myself happier than I've been in years—that curious serenity in one's middle years which derives from coming back to the *sensual textures* of one's childhood—the landscape, the wood-smoke on wintry Mississippi days which Bill Faulkner wrote about, the unflagging courtesy among people, the way people talk, all of it. I think I may stay this time. . . ."

Inside Sports published in May of 1980 Willie's first public reaction to his new life; it was later in the Yoknapatawpha Press book *Terrains of the Heart:*

I finally came home. It was not too late. Much of being back has to do with the land, its sensual textures—one's memory reawakened by the rising mists on January afternoons, the oscillation of bitter winter days and the swift false springs, the jonquils piercing through the ice, the slow-flowing rivers and the hush of the pine hills. In a moment of despair once in New York City, involving lost love and the Manhattan *angst,* in the Sunday morning of an autumn mist with the church bells chiming, an honored friend said: "But you have Mississippi. It never left you. . . ."

I enjoy moving amidst the people and places Faulkner wrote about. It gives me a curious serenity, these things he owns. At 25, being a writer and a Mississippi boy, I believe his aura might have intimidated me. When asked what a Southern writer could do after the example of Bill Faulkner, Flannery O'Conner said: "You get off the tracks when the Dixie Special comes through." At 45, I no longer want to leap off the tracks, for I have learned that I own a piece of the railroad, too.

I like the way they sell chicken and pit-barbecue and fried catfish in the little stores next to the service stations. I like the way the co-eds make themselves up for their classes. . . . I like the un-flagging courtesy of the young, the way they say "Sir" and "Ma'am." I like the way the white and black people banter with each other, the old graying black men whiling away their time sit-ting on the brick wall in front of the jailhouse, some of them wear-ing Rebel baseball caps. I like the intertwining of old family names. I like the way people remember their dead. . . .

I find strange mementos, unusual objects of obeisance or piety, or perhaps *duty*, left by enigmatic visitors on Mr. Bill's grave. Many twigs of holly were deposited there after Christmas. Once we found a full pint of bourbon. An old, soggy edition of Yeats' po-ems was there one day. On Valentine's there were several small chocolate Kisses for Mr. Bill, and on Mammy Caroline Barr's up the way in the black section. She was Dilsey.

Almost every time a visiting writer or reporter came to see Willie, over the years, he took them on a post-midnight tour of the Oxford cemetery, always ending at William Faulkner's grave. There, by the flickering flare of a cigarette lighter, they read Faulkner's tombstone and—invariably—they would water the old master's resting place with token splashes of whatever was in their cups or glasses or bot-tles: bourbon, Scotch, wine, beer, you name it.

Willie's homecoming seemed to spark a new spirit of fun. "He must have sold my wife a hundred and fifty pounds of sweet pota-toes," historian David Sansing once said. "He'd call up and tell her he was a poor boy trying to work his way through school, or some old farmer raising money to pay his taxes. And she'd fall for it every time, no matter the price he'd quote her."

An invitation to sit on the bench with the varsity basketball team at a home game—a routine public-relations courtesy extended to one faculty member at each game—happened to coincide with Glo-ria Jones's visit to Ole Miss to speak to Willie's students. Gloria is not the world's greatest sports fan, so she didn't question Willie when he told her that in addition to teaching writing and being the writer-in-residence at Ole Miss, he also was the varsity basketball coach. Willie saw to it, of course, that Gloria was at "his" game. She watched

Willie, carrying a clipboard, having "strategy huddles" with players during the game—subs unlikely to play, and in on the joke—and as he "supervised" the warm-up shoot-around before the game and at halftime. He told Gloria in a quick aside, as halftime began, that he had to go in the locker room and give "my team" a pep talk. Back in New York, Gloria ran into novelist Winston Groom, who asked how Willie was faring at Ole Miss. "Frankly," she said, "I'm a little worried. They're keeping Willie too damned busy. He's not only teaching literature, and shepherding his writer friends he brings in to speak, they've also got him coaching the Ole Miss basketball team."

Willie also had some sport with his friend and writing colleague George Plimpton, when the founding editor of *The Paris Review* and the author of the best-selling football book *Paper Lion*—among others—came to Oxford at Willie's behest in February of 1980. Willie and Plimpton long had made much of a Civil War–era rivalry between their respective ancestors: Willie's great-grandfather, a Confederate colonel and a member of the Mississippi legislature, brought impeachment charges against one Adelbert Ames, Plimpton's "Yankee" great-grandfather—who had won the Congressional Medal of Honor for his heroics at the Battle of First Manassas (or Bull Run)—but who, as the appointed Yankee Reconstruction governor of Mississippi, was viewed by Willie's bloodline as the devil incarnate.

Willie conspired with Mississippi Governor William Winter to publicly issue a "pardon" to Plimpton, at a dinner, for the mischief Adelbert Ames had accomplished in Mississippi. What Plimpton was unprepared for was the several husky Mississippi highway patrolmen, in uniform, jangling with handcuffs, billy clubs, and pistols who rushed in shortly before the dinner was to end, announced loudly that Plimpton's "pardon" was only good for one more hour and that he would be jailed if still in Mississippi when it expired. The state cops rushed him out of the dinner, allegedly to the Memphis airport. Plimpton later claimed, in a letter to Governor Winter, that his minions had dumped him by a dirt road "bordered by ditches full of bellowing frogs" who were doing their croaking far from any airport though his Mississippi captors had told him the airport was "daid ahaid."

Truman Capote also visited Mississippi and Memphis, touting a book, and Willie spent some time with him, but they never got together on the specifics of a speech that "Tru" had promised to make—but never made—at Ole Miss. No doubt Willie would have set Capote up for some "surprise," too, had he made it to Oxford.

Willie called my home in that period quite often, always asking to speak to our three-year-old daughter, Lindsay. He would ask about her new baby brother, Blaine, and then say, "Go look in the refrigerator and see if you can find a Moon Pie and an Ara-Cee Cola for him. Then come back and tell me if you found them." When Lindsay reported failure, he would send her back to find "catfish heads and a turnip milkshake, because babies just *love* that." One Christmas he told far too many children and grandchildren of his friends that Santa Claus had confided in *him*—"Uncle Willie"—that he was going to bring them a pony for Christmas. This caused eventual kiddie uproars that not everyone appreciated.

Willie also loved, and was amused by, the workings of a small publishing house. When, in 1981, Yoknapatawpha Press brought out a new edition of Willie's *Good Old Boy*, a company hired to shrink-wrap the books did so without including the dust jackets, which they shipped separately. Larry Wells was more than slightly irritated, but Willie Morris got a kick out of cutting the shrink-wrappings with a knife and then putting the dust jackets on. "This is the Mississippi way of doing things," he said, grinning. "We were getting the books ready for a book-signing party for Willie and he was enchanted by his part in the physical preparations, which of course he'd never been involved in with big New York publishers," Wells said.

Willie would write in *Terrains of the Heart and Other Essays on Home* of his travels with the co-owners of Yoknapatawpha Press to push books in Memphis, Biloxi, Pass Christian, Tupelo, Yazoo City, Batesville, Clarksdale, Jackson, and Cleveland, in some of which no grown man had "held a book in his hand" since schooldays.

"Invariably, as we departed Oxford in Larry's car"—Willie wrote—

the trunk and back seat would be crammed with posters and boxes of books, so that the rear end sagged precariously with the weight, like the Okies' vehicles on their exodus to California. Our main problem was leaving enough room on the back seat for Dean. Since she is on the small size, as are all Faulkners, we usually managed. . . . Larry became known to us as "Boss," which I had never called [New York publishers] Cass Canfield, Alfred A. Knopf or Nelson Doubleday . . . to the Boss, Dean and I were "The Stable," with rights and privileges extending deeply into common law. One table, two chairs and an ashtray in all book stores; bourbon on the rocks in the car on lengthy trips, or for that matter short ones; no visits to bus stations (to pick up more books) after dark. . . . Not too long ago I read the three-part series in *The New Yorker* about the world of big publishers in this corporate age. No, they don't do things like this up there. I think the Yoknapatawpha Press has a Mississippi way of facing the world.

ONE OF THE HIGHLIGHTS in Willie's life in that period was the world premiere in Oxford of the movie of *Good Old Boy*. There was a party at the Hoka—a cinema-cum-coffeehouse-and-BYOB watering hole; a goodly crowd was on hand, some in formal attire, when Willie arrived in a car apparently being driven by a little dog, Willie wearing an unaccustomed tuxedo: two incongruous sights for the price of one. The little dog was Denver, who belonged to Dean Faulkner Wells's son John, who had ducked down and placed his dog's paws on the steering wheel. Such a loud cheer went up from the crowd that Denver got scared and tried to jump out of the car.

Willie got out, holding Denver's leash, and when Denver lifted his leg to water a nearby bush, Willie imitated the gesture as if to join him, much to the amusement of the crowd. "I think that was one of Willie's happiest nights in Oxford," Larry Wells said years later.

Willie also enjoyed the home-game football weekends. And why not? Everyone in Oxford partied hearty except the blue noses: cocktail parties in private homes, fraternity and sorority bashes, overflowing bars and restaurants, tailgating in The Grove, a tree-clumped glade near Hemingway Field—which, prankster Morris had assured two visiting French journalists, was meant to be named after William Faulkner until Faulkner said no, no, Hemingway needed the honor more than he did, so name it after Ernest. He enjoyed seeing the Frenchmen scribbling that "scoop" in their notebooks. (The Hemingway for whom the football field had been named actually had been dean of the Ole Miss law school in the distant past.)

Willie and his friends bought tickets together in the south end zone, and soon earned the sobriquet "The South End Zone Rowdies." History professor David Sansing was named president of the group, and immediately performed his only official act: He changed his title to "Emperor" and declared himself "sovereign for life." The Rowdies included Larry and Dean Wells, Barry and Susan Hannah, professor Ron Borne and wife Jane, Lib Sansing (who'd bought all those sweet potatoes from prankster Willie), David Rae Morris, John Mallard (Dean Wells's son), Ron Shapiro (owner of the Hoka), Jane Rule Burdine (a photographer and mayor of the nearby hamlet of Taylor), Richard and Lisa Howorth (owners of the Square Book Store), Elizabeth Dollarhide (now a Hollywood producer), writer Jim Dees, and occasional guests such as artist William Dunlap and photographer Bill Eggleston. "We had a mutant Visiting Lectureship program featuring such notables as Raad Cawthon and John Little, who delivered opinions (or toasts) at halftime," Larry Wells wrote in *A Century of Heroes: 100 Years of Ole Miss Football.* "On any given Saturday our number was swelled by movie producers, actors, magazine editors, literary agents, and former Rebel football stars. A writers and artists colony had sprung up in the south end zone."

Willie Morris being who he was, radio reporters sometimes brought their microphones into the south end zone to interview him; he got a kick out of watching the local radio reporter and one from Atlanta shoulder-bump each other for position when contesting to interview him during a Mississippi-Georgia game. Willie had such good time at the Rebel games, in fact, that a prominent Oxford physician, also a football fan—who had observed Willie's reveling at Rebel games—wrote a letter saying that he specialized in treating alcoholics and perhaps it would benefit Willie to make an appointment with him. Nothing indicates that Willie ever got in touch with him, or told anyone of the letter. It was discovered among Willie's papers after his death.

BUT, LITTLE BY LITTLE, the shine wore off Willie's homecoming—or, more accurately, his Ole Miss job. He hated grading papers, so he assigned few essays and included none in the exams he gave. Nor did he enjoy teaching the course in the American novel, the breaking down and analyzing of someone else's work having no appeal. Academia, he increasingly felt, spent too much time hunting for hidden meanings and symbolism and stressing dubious theories of writing. Willie's approach was more anecdotal, more practical.

Nor was he happy with his salary for two semesters of work in two courses. He was, in fact, given shamefully parsimonious wages; Princeton a full four years earlier had paid me $26,000 for less work, and Willie—getting not much more than half that— knew it. One might say, "Well, he knew the salary when he agreed to take the job as it was offered." True. As a native he also knew that poverty was, historically, one of Mississippi's larger problems. Willie's friend Ed Perry, chairman of the general appropriations committee in the state legislature, repeatedly complained, "There's no money. Anything we try to do, we have to juggle. There just ain't no money!" So he was forewarned, right?

Well, yes, but again, it was a case of Willie Morris not dealing with a problem in its early stages; he might have pressed his case for a little more money or a little less work or both. Since he had not, Ole Miss officials had no way of suspecting his festering resentment. Willie had a history of letting problems slide, as if somehow expecting the cavalry to ride to his rescue, bugles blaring. And, somehow, he always seemed surprised when no rescue occurred. Surprise, often, was soon replaced by anger and, eventually, quite often the anger led to careless or foolish actions.

AFTER TWO YEARS in the English Department, Willie wanted a change. Some faculty members in that department never warmed to him, even when he made periodic efforts to be accepted as "one of the boys."

He began, indeed, to get a bit paranoid. This was manifested when Ole Miss got a new chancellor, Gerald Turner, reputedly a conservative Methodist from Texas. Almost immediately Chancellor Turner left word with several sources that he would like for Willie Morris to come see him.

"Willie was scared to death," Ron Shapiro says. "He said, 'He's gonna know that I drink and stay up late, and he's gonna ruin me!' So Morris dodged the new chancellor for *months*. Wouldn't even *call* him."

Friends finally persuaded Willie that he simply must respond or matters likely would get worse. Finally, armed with numerous excuses as to why he hadn't seen the chancellor earlier, Willie with great trepidation went to his office. He didn't have to parade his excuses, however: The chancellor, an admirer of Willie's work, and who knew of his past as the crusading editor of both *The Daily Texan* and *The Texas Observer*, had merely wanted to shake Willie's hand and have a friendly chat.

Perhaps buoyed by this, Willie decided to make a move to transfer to the Journalism Department. He was delighted when told he could teach pretty much anything he wanted to in that department. It turned out, however, that he also was expected to supervise a student magazine. Okay—except that Willie, who had, after all, edited a magazine he'd once turned into the talk of New York and much of the nation, was appalled at the students' copy. One can see how Willie would have that reaction, having edited Mailer, Styron, Talese, Jones, Halberstam et al. What isn't so readily apparent is that Willie's solution was to rewrite just about everything himself. "It nearly killed him," Ron Shapiro said. "He had to work night and day because of that damned magazine." Willie, no fool, quietly folded the magazine after three issues. "The kids were not learning much from my rewriting them," he later admitted.

Willie found a unique—if costly—way to do his job without actually spending a great deal of time in the classroom. "He hit on the idea of having his journalism seminar—ten students—meet classes in his favorite restaurant, the Warehouse," Larry Wells reports.

Willie bought them steak dinners and wine, paying every cent out of his own pocket—money he didn't have, hell he was flat broke. You know, it would run a couple of hundred, maybe two hundred fifty bucks a meal! Bet your ass no student cut *that* class: a free steak dinner and wine, are you kidding?

Well, it was Willie's way of making his own dose of medicine go down: He'd grown really tired of teaching, and the dinners with the kids, and the wine and all, and the informal conversations, made it *fun* not *work*. Willie drank carafes of red wine and chain-smoked Viceroys, and laughed while the kids made table talk. He'd play word-association games with them, give them spot passages or biographical bits as clues to books or authors. The kids, of course, were in Heaven: no papers to write, no homework, no tests, and the professor gave them all A's. As for Willie, he could be the raconteur to his heart's content, with everybody hanging on to his every word.

At the same time, Willie gave the kids a sense of their own possibilities. *He* had been a small-town Mississippi kid, just like most of the students. They knew he had played in the Big Leagues, as it were, had become something of a star there. They saw him bring in other famous writers, accomplished friends who obviously respected Willie. The kids realized Willie had earned his success and there were possibilities for themselves. So Willie had a galvanizing effect on a lot of young people. Never forget that! It's something that should be stressed in any evaluation of Willie Morris.

INCREASINGLY, WILLIE FELT RESTIVE. Oxford might be a good little town, but the operative word was "little." With between 9,000 and 10,000 townfolk at the time, and about an equal number of students populating the Ole Miss campus, it fell far short not only of Manhattan but of the Hamptons in its teeming summers.

Oxford was a family town; wives expected their husbands to come home after work, probably have dinner in, and spend time in domestic pursuits. Locals who made the mistake of trying to keep up with Willie Morris after sundown found little but trouble. One of Mississippi's most powerful politicians, and a leading light in Oxford, began hanging out with Willie and one night, going home from a bar where he'd partied with his pal for hours, got arrested for driving under the influence—a personal embarrassment as well as the first stain on a spotless public record; he swore off booze forever, and thereafter dodged the nocturnal Willie as if Willie might be gunning for him.

When Morris first came to Oxford, many people opened their homes to him: *Welcome, Willie!* After a time they learned that perhaps they should have left the door only slightly ajar: Willie might come early and stay late, or come late and stay later. And he rarely, if ever, bothered to call to check whether a visit might be timely. So, after a while, there simply were not enough running mates to accommodate Willie, nor enough homes with their latch keys out—though a half dozen loyalists got together and each took an assigned night of the week they would host Willie if hosting he wanted. Often, after Oxford's bars closed, "designated hosts" who thought they been granted a "night off" heard a post-midnight rapping.

"Lining up somebody to have dinner with him, and then be willing to stay up all night drinking or talking, became Willie's biggest chore every day," said Larry Wells. "More and more he hung out with students because adults in Oxford, with their own jobs or businesses to attend, couldn't operate on Willie's upside-down schedule. He took to stocking beer in his refrigerator, though he had little taste for beer. Its function was to lure students home with him after the bars closed."

It was—a couple of Willie's friends decided—almost as if night represented death to Willie Morris, almost as if he felt it might smother him unless there were lights and noise and people, that he might cheat the Grim Reaper only by waiting for the deliverance of dawn. Not that Willie Morris himself ever said anything remotely like that, but his "desperation and near-panic if he couldn't find midnight companions," one friend said, had inspired their macabre speculations. And it is a fact that most of Willie's wee-hours telephone calls to friends all over the nation occurred when he was alone in the night, a disembodied voice from far away apparently being preferable to the awful sound of silence.

PART SEVEN

DEAD DOGS AND MELANCHOLY MADNESS: AT ODDS WITH UNCLE SAM, LOCAL COPS, AND A FEW OLD PALS

"I'm just a goddamned schoolteacher, so book talk is lost on me and isn't pertinent."

—AN ANGRY WILLIE MORRIS

to a startled David Halberstam
when Halberstam and Larry Wells, both writers,
were "talking shop" in Mississippi in 1981

CHAPTER 18

IN THE SPRING OF 1981, Willie Morris was receptive when David Halberstam, visiting in Oxford, suggested that he write what had the potential to be a "big book," one capable of delivering him from the miseries of debt and of being broke. But before that conversation occurred, Willie had suddenly—and for the first time ever—lashed out in anger at his old friend.

Halberstam did not know the particulars of Willie's obvious discontent, but he knew anger and frustration when he saw it. As Halberstam talked with Larry Wells about books and contracts—two book men innocently talking shop—Willie had suddenly exploded: He was only "a goddamned schoolteacher," he said loudly, so "book talk" was "lost" on him and "not pertinent." Halberstam was much taken aback, as was Wells: Neither of them had known how much resentment he harbored and neither knew the reasons for it. "I also hadn't realized he was as drunk as he was," Halberstam later said. "God knows I would have said nothing to hurt him." Halberstam tried to get the evening back on track with small talk and questions, but Willie was of no help, going into a conversational shell, sulking, answering only in monosyllables or not at all.

Halberstam, much distressed, kept talking to his uncommunicative friend, who was silently drinking in the back seat, as Larry Wells later drove Halberstam to the airport. "Willie," he said, "I think there's a book you should write. You know the subject matter, the complexities, better than anyone. It could be a big book, an important book.

And it's about that blue-chip high school running back you were talking about."

Marcus Dupree, a heralded All-Everything player for the Philadelphia, Mississippi, red-and-black-clad Tornadoes, was being wooed by college recruiters all across America. Notre Dame wanted him. Southern Cal. Oklahoma. Michigan. Ohio State. Hell, *all* the football powers—including Ole Miss.

You know the dark history of racism and murder in the Philadelphia area—Halberstam told his old friend—and you know the book can be about ever so much more than football; it's got your *name* on it.

Suddenly, Willie turned from "just a goddamned schoolteacher" into a hot-to-trot writer, grabbing at Halberstam's idea like a drowning man lunging for a rescue rope. Everyone in Mississippi—and many people elsewhere—who knew that a kicking tee wasn't a dance beverage knew who Marcus Dupree was. Dupree had been written up in magazines since coming to the fore as a fifteen-year-old high school sophomore sensation, and by 1981 was "a man among boys" in the opinion of sports writers who stopped just short of claiming he was faster than a speeding bullet and able to leap tall buildings in a single bound. But somehow Willie had not thought of writing a book about Dupree until Halberstam—almost desperate to cheer up his old friend, or offer him hope—suggested that he do just that.

Philadelphia, and Neshoba County, will forever live in infamy as the site where three young civil rights workers—on June 21, 1964— were shot to death for the "crime" of assisting black citizens of Mississippi register to vote. Two Jewish youngsters from New York, Michael (Mickey) Schwerner, twenty-four, and Andrew Goodman, twenty, and a twenty-one-year-old black native of Mississippi, Jim Chaney, were brutally murdered in an eighteen-person conspiracy involving, among others, the Neshoba County sheriff, his chief deputy, a former sheriff, the sheriff-elect, a Philadelphia city policeman, and the Imperial Wizard of the White Knights of the Ku Klux Klan. The victims were buried under a huge earthen dam, and their decomposed bodies were not found until August.

Tobacco-chewing Sheriff Lawrence Rainey, who looked the part of a redneck bully sent by central casting, and Chief Deputy Cecil Price, tried for murder, were acquitted by an all-male white jury in about the time it might take to drink two "Ara-Cee" Colas. Cecil Price later served four years for violating the civil rights of the three murdered martyrs, and four others got short jail terms. But, in effect, they—and others—got away with murder and everybody knew it. (Cecil Price, Jr., not so incidentally, was a 140-pound end on the Philadelphia Tornadoes football team with 222-pound star Marcus Dupree; they had entered first grade together and graduated together.)*

A contract was signed on June 28, 1981, under which Doubleday would pay Willie Morris $35,000—half then and half on completion of the book—plus 10 percent royalties. (The book later would become an alternate selection of the Literary Guild Book Club, for another $5,000 plus 7 percent royalties; the Jackson *Clarion-Ledger-Daily News* paid $600 for excerpts, advertising Willie's book as "Bringing to vibrant life the changing South of the 1980s." There was also a mass market paperback sale, though I haven't been able to learn how much in advance monies Willie received.)

Willie Morris knew that *The Courting of Marcus Dupree* might—just might, if all broke well—deliver him from pressures he had shared with nobody. His secret fear was that the Internal Revenue Service could swoop down on him any day, like a predatory chicken hawk, to demand thousands and thousands of dollars, plus penalties and interest. His darkest fear was that—since he had not even filed income tax returns for about a decade, much less paid any taxes to the Feds—he might be marched off to jail in lockstep should Uncle Sam want to be a hard-ass about it. But if he had the luck to write a really big book, he could perhaps pay his back taxes and rid himself of the crippling emotional and psychological burdens they imposed.

---

*On June 21, 2005—forty-one years to the day after Schwerner, Chaney, and Goodman were killed—an eighty-year-old former Ku Klux Klansman, Edgar Ray Killen, was convicted of three counts of manslaughter as the alleged ringleader of the killings. As he was wheeled from the courtroom in a wheelchair, an oxygen tube up his nose, he slapped two television microphones and a TV camera. He was sentenced two days later to twenty years on each of the manslaughter counts.

So Willie enthusiastically began two years of traveling around Mississippi, his observations and interviews producing a book that contained history, social change, folklore, small-town rituals, and the excesses of big-time college football. I rate it among Willie's better books; Willie himself always thought it was his best. *Dupree* won the Christopher Award, given in New York City, recognizing "those who have achieved artistic excellence in films, books, and television specials affirming the highest values of the human spirit."

Ah, but how much better it might have been in terms of money. If only, after a good, promising freshman season at Oklahoma University, causing speculation that Dupree might win the Heisman Trophy as early as his sophomore year, the Philadelphia kid had not fallen out with Oklahoma coach Barry Switzer over how he was being used. Saying that he was homesick, he went home after a bad game in 1983 and did not return to Norman. This happened the same week Willie's book was published and may have temporarily helped sales, but it was not a story that remained in the headlines long; soon Marcus Dupree plunged from sight as quickly as a stone dropped from airplane heights.

Willie had fallen behind schedule in delivering *The Courting of Marcus Dupree* by almost a year. Had the book been out while Dupree was still playing at Oklahoma, perhaps sales might have been better—but that is pure speculation. According to a former Ole Miss student, Robert Miskelly (self-described "friend, secretary, chauffeur, bartender, priest, father confessor and general flunky to Willie for four years, 1981–85") Willie's agent, Sterling Lord, had called him and said Willie couldn't seem to finish the book, and did Miskelly know what the trouble was? "I told him the trouble was drinking. A fifth or two of bourbon every day and sometimes some vodka. And that as long as Willie hung around Oxford, where he had so many drinking pals, he never would finish that book."

Miskelly, whom I have never heard accused of hiding his own light under a bushel, tells it that he secretly disabled Willie's car and drove him to an isolated cabin in the woods of a state park near Sardis Lake, giving him no radio, TV, books, or anything that might prove distracting and keep Willie from writing. "I took Willie one single pint of George Dickel bourbon each day and collected the pages he'd written, which averaged about six pages per day, or 36 pages per six-day week. He got a whole fifth of bourbon on Sunday, and the day off from work, but I wouldn't take him anywhere. It was too far to walk to any store or town, and there was no telephone in the cabin. And that's how *The Courting of Marcus Dupree* got finished."

Charles Henry, who says it was he who arranged for the Sardis Lake cabin for Willie, claims Miskelly's version is, in effect, so much bullshit.

> Willie wouldn't have stood for that kid bossing him around like that, holding him captive, dictating what he could drink. And Willie never bought a *pint* of anything in his life! The month it took Willie to finish that book, or however long it was, I had a steak dinner with him every Wednesday night at a cafè not too far from Sardis Lake. And Willie came to Oxford from that cabin two or three times while he was supposedly a captive and had a "disabled car." All that's just stupid! And as for finishing *Courting of Marcus Dupree* at the cabin, that's not right either; he finished it at his faculty house and we went to lunch to celebrate.

Well, who knows? Rocky Miskelly would probably try to dramatize a pie supper, and Charles Henry has trouble remembering anything at anytime that might put his great friend Willie Morris in a bad light.

Larry Wells believes that Willie had cut down on his drinking some time before going to the Sardis Lake cabin, for the express purpose of finishing his Marcus Dupree book, and that he was working well until a traumatic setback.

> Pete, his dog, was twelve years old and began to have failing health. He had trouble getting around. We all love our dogs, and some of us memorialize them or humanize them excessively, but Willie really made Pete an extension of himself. The students who attended his lectures that first year at Ole Miss will always remember Willie as the famous-writer-with-the-black-lab. Pete followed

him everywhere, rode in his car, curled up at the front of the stage in Willie's classes, sat by his barstool, napped by his feet at home.

Willie knew that his beloved dog was really on his last legs. One day he saw that Pete was struggling to get out the door, and he figured Pete wanted to die outside. So he carried him out, made him a soft pallet of leaves by the shrubs near Willie's front door, and then he hugged him and patted him and told him how much he loved him, how much he would miss him. It was an emotional and teary last goodbye. Maybe Willie didn't want to actually *see* Pete take his last breath, because he went in the house and began to telephone his friends. After a bit he went out to check on Pete, and found him dead. And he really cratered.

It was about midday, it seems to me, when I answered the phone to hear Willie say—in a curiously flat and almost robot-like voice— "Larry, I just found Old Pete dead in my front yard. I stooped down to pet him, and he was dead." I was not then a dog person; indeed I had been mauled by two large dogs as an eight-year-old and feared dogs much more than I liked them. So I issued only perfunctory condolences before inanely saying—because I felt in an awkward circumstance—"Hey, Willie, how's that Ole Miss football team looking?" He choked out, "I can't talk now," and hung up.

"Those calls were a cry for help," Larry Wells thinks. "Almost all of them went to old friends across the nation, many that he hadn't seen much of in years. I believe the realization that he had lost something irreplaceable in Pete brought it home that he was alone, had been alone a long time, no matter that he had a support group in Oxford with him every step of the way. And he wanted the world to *know* he was alone. Because he could think of nothing worse than being by himself. I don't know if he called Associated Press himself, but somehow the media got hold of the story right away." Yes: I had four or five calls—*bling bling bling!*—asking me for a quote about Pete. I found those interruptions while I was trying to work an irritant. And what was there to say about a dog I never had paid much attention to? "Just list me among the survivors as a first cousin," I snapped to one reporter.

Twenty years later, when I had to put down an eleven-year-old lov-able ball of long-haired ear-licking fluff—a Shih Tzu named Buster—I better understood Willie's loss and pain. But it was too late to tell him, because Willie was gone, too.

"WILLIE BEGGED MAYOR JOHN LESLIE to allow Pete to be buried in Oxford's St. Peter's cemetery," says Larry Wells.

Law, or perhaps just custom, forbids the burying of animals in sanctified ground. But "His Worship"—as Willie had nicknamed Mayor Leslie as added compensation for his honor's token $1-per-year salary—wanted to accommodate his friend. Not only did he like Willie personally, he thought that Willie attracted good peo-ple to Oxford and brought the town helpful publicity. So he put a grave digger to work on the property line at the rear of St. Peter's and Billy Ross Brown measured Pete and made him a little ply-wood coffin.

It was raining, not hard but steadily, when about a dozen of us gathered at the grave that afternoon in the February chill. At Dean's suggestion I read a short passage from the "Burial of a child" section in the Episcopal Book of Common Prayer:

"They shall hunger no more; neither thirst no more; neither shall the sun light on them, nor any heat. For the Lamb which is in the midst of the throne shall feed them, and shall lead them unto living fountains of waters; and God shall wipe away all tears from their eyes." Willie wept uncontrollably throughout, a kind of coughing childlike-can't-get-my-breath grief. I still have this incon-gruous image of a Viceroy stuck in one corner of his mouth, the smoke curling up, and the cigarette somehow staying lit despite the rain and Willie's tears.

Red-eyed and wild, Willie demanded a wake that would last the rest of the day and all night. A group of us, all males, took Willie to dinner at the Sizzler, and then went to the Holiday Inn bar. Seven or eight of us were attending Willie. The bar was moribund on a week night, with maybe a dozen other patrons. Our funereal decorum spread through the bar. The others glanced at us with empathy, not being aware of who the deceased was. And suddenly Willie got quiet and said, almost as if talking to himself, "I am a *writer!* None of you understand what that means. But I am a *writer!*" He glared at us. Why was he angry? Because we somehow weren't taking Pete's death seriously enough? Or that the wake, which had been going on much of the day was winding down and we were minutes away from "abandoning" him? Well, we didn't: despite half of us having been with him for twelve hours, leaving jobs or other responsibilities, when the Holiday Inn bar closed at midnight we all dutifully repaired to Willie's place on Faculty Row.

By three o'clock in the morning it was a chastened group of drunks who surreptitiously glanced at their watches and at each other, gauging who would leave first. One thing we knew: the *last* person wouldn't be permitted to leave! I confess I was one of the first to slip out of what turned out to be a three-day binge. It moved again from Faculty Row to the Holiday Inn, where Willie took a room because he couldn't bear to sleep in his house without Pete.

To get Willie off his drinking and emotional binge, and back to work, Charles Henry—or someone—arranged for that cabin at Sardis Lake. David Rae Morris believes Henry's version: "My father wrote me on October 15th, 1982, 'I'll go into real hiding after my speech in Memphis November 3rd, to get [the Dupree book] into shape—a cabin, probably at Sardis.' So my father probably had more control than some assume."

TWO YEARS EARLIER, Willie had written a friend in Yazoo City, Harriet DeCell, asking if she could use her influence to see that he and Pete were eventually buried side by side in Glenwood cemetery there. He even drew up headstones for them. Pete's read:

Pete
1971–198___
A big Yankee dog, a Black

Labrador, of rare tenderness
and beauty, who was Willie
Morris' friend and brother.

And Willie's read:

Willie Morris
1934–199—
American Writer and Editor
who, from his earliest childhood
as a boy, loved this beautiful
Cemetery.

It seems significant that Willie's "paper tombstone" for himself didn't anticipate his living to see the turn of the century though it was less than twenty years away. And, of course, he died about five months short of it.

"Everybody from Willie's friends to his students to his house-keeper wanted to give him a puppy after Pete died," says Larry Wells. "He wouldn't accept, saying 'I'll never have another dog. I'll get married first.' He was true to his word."

Well, says Ron Shapiro, he was sort of true to his word. Shapiro also had a black Labrador, named King,

And Willie kept kidnapping him. He'd take King home with him and after I'd closed up I'd have to go to Willie's house to get my dog no matter how tired I was. Willie would beg me to let the dog stay there, or want *me* to stay there too. It got to be a real pain and pissed me off. I told Willie he had to quit kidnapping my dog, but he paid no attention to me! And then one day when Willie had King, my dog chased a truck that hit him and he got killed. That lay between me and Willie. He felt guilty, and I felt anger; so, yeah, it came between us for awhile.

I told Shapiro it was history repeating itself: that a decade earlier Willie had "kidnapped" his son David Rae's black Lab, Ichabod H.

Crane, and that Ichabod, too, had been killed by a vehicle he may have chased. It blew Shapiro away. "No *wonder* Willie felt such deep guilt. I had no idea! I don't even know what to say . . ."

Also discovered in Willie's papers after his death was a long, rambling, rather flowery handwritten tribute to Pete that Willie intended to use on the first anniversary of the dog's death in placing a headstone at his grave. It mentions the deaths of people Willie had loved: Jim Jones, his own parents, "and all the others who were part of us in old mortality"; it included a poem by Edna St. Vincent Millay to be read and an instructive insert at a given point: "Unveil Memorial." None of the usual Oxford suspects recall attending such a ceremony, though the University Press of Mississippi book *Remembering Willie* has a picture of Willie in profile, nicely dressed in slacks, a blue blazer, and with his hair combed, sitting in profile near a grave marker reading: "Pete. 1970–1983"

Alas, someone stole that marker within months of Willie's having left Oxford.

The Courting of Marcus Dupree got better reviews in the South than it did elsewhere. "Yankee" publications, and reviewers, showed impatience with Willie's sometimes meandering side journeys into Mississippi history, early civil rights strife and crimes, and his personal memories of an earlier time. Some faulted him for sentimentality, and/or name-dropping. They seemed to want more of a straight "football story" and faulted Morris for not spending more time with Marcus Dupree and less time with the Philadelphia townfolk. Dupree, however, was rushing from college campus to college campus during the hot recruiting period at the beginning of Willie's interviews, and was under siege from recruiters, coaches, and the national media so that lengthy access was hard to come by.

A number of critics, after paragraphs of what the book lacked or had botched, came in the end to conclusions hard to rhyme with their opening blasts—e.g., David Bradley in *The New York Times Book Review:* "a well-conceived and well-crafted book that has topical impact, a luckily timed piece of publishing that is also a decision of significance and undeniable truth." Or Pam Lambert in *The Wall Street Journal:* "Despite these shortcomings, 'The Courting of Marcus Dupree' contains a story worth telling. In fact, several of them." On the other hand, Harry Crews—a Georgian writing in *The Chicago Tribune's Book World*—slapped Willie's literary jaws for excessive sentimentality and a general mishmash, ending, "Willie, I think you stayed in New York City just a shade too long." And Christopher Lehmann-Haupt of *The New York Times,* not normally a literary assassin, gut-shot Willie for "telling a story that already had been told, and told again, in several of Mr. Morris's previous seven books," a "disorganized narrative . . . prose [that] can't seem to get hold of itself . . . Instead of catching a story by the tail, Willie Morris staggers around, lunging after whatever happens to catch his eye." It was this review that caused Willie, who, again, often said he "never" read reviews, to grump, "I don't know what America is going to be reading this year, but it will not be the *Collected Reviews of Christopher Lehmann-Haupt.*"

WHATEVER HAPPENED TO MARCUS DUPREE?

The short answer is, regrettably, "not much."

After falling out with Oklahoma coach Barry Switzer, who later said he saw "a quitter" in Dupree, Marcus enrolled at Southern Mississippi, saying he never had wanted to leave Mississippi but the pressures had been too much. So why didn't you hear of his exploits at Southern Mississippi? Because he never played a down there. Instead, he joined the New Orleans Breakers of the short-lived United States Football League, where—in one season—he scored nine touchdowns but was not the leading running back on the team in yards gained or in touchdowns. He had knee operations in back-to-back seasons—1985 and 1986—and finally, in 1990, got a tardy NFL shot with the Los Angeles Rams. Over two seasons he played in but fifteen games and scored a grand total of one NFL touchdown. Yes, one. Dupree played a little semi-pro baseball, wrestled professionally for a short time, and briefly was a scout for the Washington Redskins. He may not be long remembered, though I think Willie's book about him—with its insights into Mississippi racial troubles and much more—certainly should be.

I once suggested to Willie Morris that he write a magazine piece on "The Failure of Marcus Dupree," analyzing what had gone wrong and why, but he quickly said, "No. I don't want to expose the kid to ridicule. He's been exploited enough and hurt enough." It was the kind of honest reaction and admirable compassion that Willie Morris was capable of even during his difficult periods.

CHAPTER 19

NEAR THE BEGINNING of the 1983 school year, Willie Morris decided that he simply could not teach any longer. It robbed him of writing time, he said, and, well, he simply didn't *care* for teaching. He was, indeed, sick of it and made that clear to a few intimates.

All too characteristically, he neglected to tell his faculty superiors of his decision. This could not have surprised many; the Ole Miss vice chancellor once had written Willie that trying to contact him by letter was comparable to sending a letter up the chimney to Santa Claus: "Perhaps it is received, perhaps not; one learns eventually from the event."

Larry Wells, Willie's unofficial plenipotentiary, rushed to negotiate with the Ole Miss muckety-mucks. Why not give Willie Morris relief from classroom teaching? Why not let him concentrate on using his fame and contacts to bring in guest lecturers no other Ole Miss source could supply? Why not let him serve as a university spokesman to put matters into "historical perspective" when critically inclined Yankees came to write about campus race relations, or about the Confederate flag still being waved at Ole Miss football games, or the presumed general "backwardness" of Mississippi? Willie was fast on his feet, Wells reminded, and had prestige and credibility not otherwise available. And above all, why not make Willie Morris the official writer-in-residence on campus? It was a position that most schools did not then have, but one that could in itself become prestigious for Ole Miss the moment Willie filled it.

All of that was agreed to—provided Willie would also give a single lecture on campus each year, open to the student body and faculty, the details of which would be worked out. It sounded wonderful: an arrangement that would benefit Willie Morris and Ole Miss. There were handshakes and back-slaps all around. Willie told a few that now, by God, he could resume being what he was meant to be: a writer, not a damned schoolteacher.

A Yoknapatawpha Press book of sports stories, *Always Stand in Against the Curve,* appeared that year (1983) as did *The Courting of Marcus Dupree.* The former, autobiographical pieces of Willie's young athletic days, sometimes helped along by a little lily-gilding fiction, was reviewed mainly in the South—although the *San Diego Union* called it "a slender volume full of riches . . . an exquisitely written search for the past" and the *Los Angeles Times* said, "Charm and mischief mark the best stories (and) all the pieces are deeply felt." Southern reviewers—especially sports writers—greeted *Always Stand in Against the Curve* with hand-clapping and some few hymns of praise. Willie was vastly pleased with the slim volume and with its reception.

How, then—with Ole Miss having cleared the decks so that Willie had ample writing time—do we account for Willie's literary creek suddenly running dry, not producing a visible drop for six long years? We can't, really: We can only guess. Maybe he had too much free time, robbing him of any sense of urgency. Maybe, for awhile, he was comfortable in his idleness; perhaps it felt good to have a breathing spell. But fairly soon, it became evident, Willie Morris climbed inside himself and became almost a full-time brooder; Dean Faulkner Wells believes that melancholy always lurked just under Willie's skin, and that even small setbacks caused it to break through. And JoAnne Prichard agrees.

This much is certain: Short of someone experiencing excruciating physical pain, there is no creature so miserable as a writer too long lying fallow. Most writers have a compulsion to write, no matter how much they claim to hate the process; it is as addicting as crack cocaine. When writers do not write for an extended period, simply cannot write, they are certain to feel as worthless as home-printed money. They will likely know guilt, or shame, or fear—or all three. Often they drink far too much, which robs them of time and energy and creativity and hurries the downward spiral. They do not know why they are blocked, or when the condition will go away—if ever. It is frightening, disorienting, and a torture no one else ever has been through. Or so it seems to the afflicted. Frustration erupts into anger, anger leads to foolish or harmful or outrageous conduct, and after awhile even some who love the afflicted seek relief from his whining, blame-placing, poor-little-me selfish conduct. Believe me, I've been down that lonesome road—and it's no place to tarry.

Some think the disappointing sales and mixed reviews of *The Courting of Marcus Dupree* closed Willie Morris like a winter tulip. "Willie believed he'd written a best-seller," Larry Wells says. "But in addition to his being late with the book, and Dupree disappearing into limbo, Doubleday's computers and distribution system crashed so that many stores didn't have the book in stock during the review and promo period. I personally think that's when Willie gave up, just said 'screw it' and went into a dark period that basically lasted six or seven years."

With each passing year, Willie's troubles seemed to grow; the larger they got the less he attempted to deal with them: an old pattern, one that caused him grief for much of his life. More and more he slept later and later—escapist sleep—a sure sign of chronic depression. He no longer seemed to enjoy the simple pleasures he delighted in when he'd first arrived at Ole Miss: little things that pleased his writer's eye, such as observing "The Goldfish," his descriptive name for Ole Miss coeds who put on complete cosmetic faces and fashionable attire even to jog around the campus for a few minutes; they were, Willie said, as much on display as goldfish in their glass bowls, and being on display was their main purpose since many—he told me—"were in college mainly to seek an M-R-S degree." Nor did Willie Morris play the role of merry prankster as in the past; indeed, as often as not he was snappish and churlish. "It was really painful to see the Mr. Hyde part of him dominate," says one who admired Willie Morris.

In that mode, Willie decided not to give the one lecture per year at Ole Miss that he had earlier agreed to. Under pressure, he ultimately consented to annually bring in an accomplished—read "famous"—outsider from among his contacts, introduce that speaker, and squire him or her through the town-and-gown social amenities. Not long afterward, he quit paying rent on his faculty quarters and, in effect, unilaterally divested himself of *any* visible responsibility to the school. Typically, he made no announcements: just quit attending to matters.

Friends—Mayor John Leslie, businessman Charles Henry, State Representative Ed (Third Most) Perry,* Larry Wells, and others— persuaded the administration to look the other way as to Willie's duties and to find a wealthy alumnus who would pay his back rent so as to keep the bean-counters happy. Look, they said, this is *Willie Morris,* a Mississippi legend who has done a lot for this state and has added prestige to the university. We have received tremendous publicity because of him, much better breaks in the media than before Willie came home. Allowances must be made! In a state that historically had been the national punching bag as many saw it—for a time the slogan on Mississippi car tags was *The Most Lied About State in the Union*—it was a smart and persuasive appeal. The wagons were circled.

ONE NIGHT as the Warehouse Restaurant closed, and Willie exited more than slightly tipsy with Rocky Miskelly on his right and Larry Wells on his left, an Oxford policeman on the sidewalk searched faces and gaits to see who might appear too drunk to drive. He looked at Willie Morris, already in a foul mood, a tad longer than Willie deemed appropriate. "DON'T YOU KNOW WHO I AM?" Willie shouted, without a word having passed between them. Then, inexplicably, he threw a punch at the astonished policeman. The punch would have done damage had it hit its target: Rocky Miskelly,

---

*Willie had bestowed the nickname on Perry since the news media almost automatically referred to Perry, he being chairman of the Mississippi legislature's Appropriations Committee, as "the third most powerful man in Mississippi" behind the governor and lieutenant governor.

not a small man, was almost lifted off the ground when he grabbed Willie's punching arm. Larry Wells jumped in to bridge troubled waters, stressing that Willie was the writer-in-residence at Ole Miss, much beloved in the community and a legend in the state, pleading that Willie had been upset by unspecified "bad news" earlier in the evening. He would personally see that Willie got safely home and to bed, Wells pledged. The policeman continued to stare at Willie as if he belonged in a cage, even as Rocky Miskelly hurried to lead Willie away, while Larry Wells soothed the policeman with handshakes and thank-yous and did everything but curtsy.

For all of Wells's peacemaking efforts, it was not a good moment between town and gown. The cops, it turned out, had an elephant's memory when it came to citizens who had the temerity to throw a punch at one of their number, whether hit or miss. So, not long afterwards, when Willie was driving home with his dog Pete after the bars had closed, he was pulled over by two policemen. When Willie asked if they knew who he was, and then told them, they apparently were so impressed they immediately handcuffed him, read him his Miranda rights, and took him to jail on charges of driving under the influence, despite Willie's pleas that he was only a hundred yards from home and should be permitted to take his dog there. But the cops took Pete into custody, too, as it were.

After being booked, Willie called His Worship the Mayor, John Leslie, who quickly was joined at the Cop Shop by attorney and State Representative Ed (Third Most) Perry. The two Poobahs quickly got Willie sprung. But Willie was incensed by his treatment; the cops, he said, had it in for him "because I took a swing at that policeman a while back and I don't even *remember it!*" (The logic of that loss-of-memory defense isn't as clear to me as it apparently was to Willie.)

Anyway, when Willie Morris learned that his driver's license would be suspended, that he must pay a fine, and also go to "drunk driver's school" he balked—loudly proclaiming he would move back to Long Island before he would suffer that "rehab shit." Nobody wants to talk about the details, but it seems that his friends provided Willie transportation while the heat was on, and that they also took up a collection to pay his fine. The order to attend "drunk driver's school" and the suspended driver's license? Well, the order apparently got misplaced or mislaid or misfiled or something and the driver's license shortly appeared by magic in Willie's mailbox. The Oxford cops, experienced readers of political tea leaves, didn't push the matter. It helped that although the whole affair became common gossip in Oxford, no newspaper in Mississippi or elsewhere published anything about the DUI arrest or its hush-hush aftermath. Drunk or sober, and licensed or otherwise, Willie was hardly a threat to win anybody's Best Driver Award. An Oxford friend recalls that he often left white splotches of paint, from his own car, on campus cars of other hues, as "his personal calling cards." And back on Long Island, in earlier years, people who knew both Willie and Truman Capote almost shuddered on seeing them together in a car no matter which one was driving: Capote's once-snazzy 1968 red Mustang convertible was so chronically dented it looked as if he parked it only in hailstorms and it was well-known that he disliked driving—except when he was drinking.

(David Rae Morris didn't know of his father swinging at the cop, and all that followed, until he read it in my manuscript: "NONE of his friends EVER came to me and said, 'We're worried about Willie' or 'We need to get him help' or 'He needs to take better care of himself.' I, personally, made two appeals to him to moderate his drinking—the first in 1983, when I moved to Mississippi, the second in 1989, in the midst of what you have referred to as a bad time for him. The first time I advised several of his friends what I had done, and received sympathy only from Dean Faulkner Wells. The problem was that his friends realized if they confronted him about his drinking, they would be immediately ostracized. So, instead, they continued to enable him.")

INTERNAL REVENUE SERVICE AGENTS ultimately found Willie, though with little help from the locals. After their dunning letters went unanswered, agents sought Willie in the Ole Miss English Department. Discovering him gone, they tracked him to the Journalism Department, but Willie, perhaps tipped off by someone, quit showing his face there. That was one reason he began holding his classes at night in a downtown restaurant. One would think the Feds might have discerned Willie's habits and tracked him to one of the several bars he frequented, and perhaps they tried, but questions as to his whereabouts or habits generally were answered "Willie *Who?*" or with other professions of ignorance. Ultimately, if tardily, the Feds found Willie's quarters on Faculty Row. Agents' cars began blocking his driveway, so he could not get his car out. Willie called friends to come rescue him, and Larry Wells recalls the Feds "perched like vultures" almost on Willie's doorstep. Soon the Feds began garnishing Willie's Ole Miss paycheck.

Willie then did a smart thing: He confided to his friend Charles Henry that he hadn't paid taxes or even filed an income tax return in more years than he could remember. Henry put his own CPA, Bob King, on the case and got a tax lawyer to back him up. Charles Henry recalls that the IRS said Willie Morris owed some $70,000 in back taxes, interest, and penalties. Henry's men offered a settlement of $15,000, with the proviso the Feds must clear Willie's books, a common practice in tax settlement cases. But the Feds decided to roll the dice: *No, we decline to accept $15,000; we'll wait until Mr. Morris gets a profitable book deal and we'll take more of it than you are offering.* Their greed backfired on the Feds, according to Charles Henry. When Willie eventually filed for bankruptcy—which came about after JoAnne Prichard wisely insisted on Willie's "dealing with your financial matters" before she married him—the Feds, because of having refused the earlier offered settlement, allegedly were left unprotected and never collected a dime. My CPA, however, seriously doubts that was the case; at least he never has heard of bankruptcy proceedings shielding debts owed to the IRS.

(Willie, by his own account, bamboozled the Feds in the early 1980s. Learning that an annuities fund his late mother had invested in had come due and that he was about to receive $20,000, he arranged to have the money paid to his son, David Rae, out of fear that should he receive the money, personally, the IRS likely would seize it all. He told David Rae, however, that the money came from an account he started in 1969, while editing *Harper's,* and that he simply had forgotten about it. He did mention "the damned IRS" to his son and said that "my accountant advised that this money be transferred to your name.")

IN 1988, with Herman Gollob at Doubleday encouraging him about the good work he was doing in *Taps* (alluding to Willie's astonishing literary powers that moved him both to laughter and tears, yada-yada-yada) while, at the same time, asking for numerous changes and more plot—a common carrot-and-stick editor's tactic—Willie Morris temporarily deserted Oxford and his drinking buddies so as to work on that novel unencumbered by social temptations. He took up residence in a cabin near McComb, where he holed up for several months. The cabin was owned by Dr. Vernon Holmes of McComb, a long-time Willie Morris fan; his son, Vernon Jr., was a friend of Willie's and often chauffeured him about.

Dr. Holmes, an M.D., owned several profitable nursing homes; he and his grown children also owned a bank. A trustee at Ole Miss, Dr. Holmes had shocked and angered many of his contemporaries by casting the only vote among the trustees in favor of James Meredith being admitted to the university in 1962. As time passed, he was more respected than censured for his Meredith vote, because—had his position prevailed—that obviously would have saved both Ole Miss and the State of Mississippi much grief and embarrassment as well as deadly violence. He still had Ole Miss's good at heart, and wanted Willie to succeed there. Consequently, Dr. Holmes not only gave Willie use of his McComb cabin but also, over a period of a few months, personally loaned Willie $12,000 out of pocket.

When the debt ultimately reached $20,000, Dr. Holmes required Willie to sign a bank note for that amount. So when Willie in 1990 received $25,000 for writing the text of a coffee-table book, *Faulkner's Mississippi,* he surrendered the lion's share to the Holmes family's bank.

There were a couple of very happy literary events in the fall of 1989. A book-signing signaling the publication of *Good Old Boy and the Witch of Yazoo*—which sold very well in Mississippi—was held at

Square Books on the Friday before an Ole Miss Rebels football game. Willie was established on a second-story outdoor balcony overlooking the town square and its familiar Confederate Soldier Monument, behind a big stack of his new books, while a musical trio played Delta blues and book buyers came outside to drink and mingle. "It was the most successful signing that Yoknapatawpha Press ever had," Larry Wells recalls, "not only in terms of books sold but also the unique atmosphere, the blues echoing off the buildings around the old courthouse and the alums shuffling along the sidewalks, visiting or dancing, some with drinks in their hands. It was almost like a carnival. Willie was beatifically happy." *Homecomings,* a collection of Willie's articles, mainly about Mississippi, with paintings by Mississippi artist William Dunlap, was published about the same time, and a gala reception and book signing at the Governor's Mansion in Jackson was hosted by Governor William Winter.

Willie also, a few months earlier, had an unexpected stroke of financial luck. National Geographic Books, preparing *Discover America: A Scenic Tour of the Fifty States,* offered Willie Morris $25,000 to write the Southern section: 40,000 words to be "personal, impressionistic and intimate." Willie did write the Mississippi chapter, but he cleverly got writer friends in Dixie to write about their favorite Southern places, then using his artful editorial skills, he melded their work with his. "In terms of labor for Willie, it was almost like an overnight paste-up job," says Larry Wells. "But Willie put it all together so well, giving it his special imprint, that it was seamless. No editor or reader could complain. And, of course, Willie was delighted with the quick money."

Willie also was feeling good about *Taps,* which—he thought—he had finished at long last. He told friends that the novel was the best thing he had ever written, that it contained all he knew. Then came possibly the hardest single blow Willie Morris ever was fetched as a writer: a letter from his editor, Herman Gollob, rejecting the novel and returning his manuscript. Willie could keep his $17,500 advance, but Doubleday had no interest in publishing the book. Sorry.

Willie was crushed. Anger soon followed disappointment. "I *hired* Herman Gollob to run Harper's Magazine Press when it was established," Willie grumbled. "It was the first time he had headed a publishing house, so I gave him a big career break. We have been friends for years, or so I thought, but now he's turned on me! Dammit, I *know* that *Taps* is a good novel!"

Gollob responds, "Let me say it again: We wanted a plot-driven novel. Willie wanted more of a lyrical, episodic book. It wasn't a matter of his novel being bad, it wasn't anybody's fault. We just wanted different books."

However gently worded, Gollob's rejection greatly depressed Willie. Perhaps his attendant anger was what caused Willie Morris suddenly to begin accusing Larry Wells—when Willie was in his cups—of "robbing him" of royalties due from his Yoknapatawpha Press books or to tell others he was being stolen from. Those who knew Larry Wells and Dean Faulkner Wells didn't credit Willie's story—including David Rae Morris. The Wellses had, arguably, done more for Willie than anybody in Oxford. During Willie's many lean times, in fact, Yoknapatawpha Press had doled out more than $20,000 in advances to help Willie keep the wolf from his door. Several times Larry Wells attempted to show Willie his meticulous records of those advances, and to discuss his accusations in general. But Willie, sober, would wave a hand and say, "Aw forget it, Boss," and then leave so as not to have to discuss the matter. This did not mean, however, that in dark moments fueled by grog Willie wouldn't accuse him again. One such midnight he threw rocks at Wells's house, after his friend and benefactor had denied him entry because of his angry demeanor, and demanded that his publisher come out and fight. Wells had the good sense to tell Morris to go home and get some sleep, then shut the door and turned off the lights. The next day—as always—Willie pretended the confrontation had never happened.

As hurt and upset with Herman Gollob as Willie had been when his friend rejected *Taps,* one would never have suspected his disenchantment by reading Willie's *New York Days,* published in 1993. In it he told several funny stories about Gollob, and summed him up thusly: "Herman Gollob . . . would go on to become one of the most respected and resourceful editors in book publishing." I was not surprised by that: Willie Morris, in many of his relationships, seems to have given more than he got.

THE END OF WILLIE MORRIS'S Oxford experience occurred—for all intents and purposes—in mid-morning in the spring of 1989. Like much in Willie's life, it wasn't planned so much as it erupted. The principles were Willie Morris, a Jackson lawyer, and his motorcycle buddies—accountants, lawyers, and other white-collar comfortables—who were a long way from being Hell's Angels but loved to pose as such, and Barry Hannah, a faculty colleague of Willie's.

You don't need to know much about the posturing Hell's-Angels-wanna-bes, but you do need to know about Barry Hannah, a truly outstanding writer of novels and short stories, recognized by the critics as a real comer when his first novel, *Geronimo Rex*, was published back in 1972. Hannah, in the words of Truman Capote, was "the maddest writer in the U.S.A." Hannah has been a finalist for a Pulitzer Prize and for two National Book Awards. He has won the William Faulkner Prize, a Richard Wright Award, and the Robert Penn Warren Lifetime Literary Achievement Award as voted by the Fellowship of Southern Writers. None of that is chopped liver.

Willie and Barry were "kindred spirits," in Hannah's words, and they worked closely together at least once, in helping Donna Tartt leave Ole Miss and her native state for a liberal arts college in New England.

But for all of that, it was generally thought in Oxford that Willie Morris and Barry Hannah each envied the other: Willie because Barry cut a dashing figure on his motorcycle, was more warmly eyed by the painted coed "Goldfish," had received more critical praise in high places, and more national honors than had Willie. Hannah, in turn, was rumored to be envious of Willie's popularity in Mississippi and the South.

"I don't recall feeling any envy of Willie," Hannah says, "nor was I aware that he envied me, though maybe there was a little tension between us at times." According to a tale Willie told, that tension may have increased one day when Hannah allegedly said to him, from a neighboring bar stool, "Willie, I write the truth and you write public relations." This was not out of character for Hannah when he was drinking: He often became aggressive and challenging at a certain stage. Willie said his first instinct was to belt Hannah in the snout, but he suppressed the instinct and claimed to have accompanied Hannah to a book signing a couple of hours later where he bought two of Hannah's books.

But, yeah, tension lingered between the two. "I did get a little pissed at Willie sometimes for chasing power," Hannah admits. Meaning? "Well, you know, if he got a chance to have dinner with the Lt. Governor or anybody in power, he'd drop everything to do that. And I felt that was foolish, unbecoming and a waste of time. It wasn't any of my business, but Willie's celebrity chasing irritated me."

On that late spring mid-morning in 1990, Barry Hannah irritated Willie in the extreme. "I was asleep," as Willie told it, "and this lawyer from Jackson, I didn't really know him very well, but he wanted to give his pals the impression he was tight with me. So they rode up to my faculty house, revving their engines, shouting for me to get up and go party with 'em." Willie later told a few Oxford friends he "roared at them like a bear" and slammed the door. He also locked his doors, both front and back, not a characteristic act. Willie returned to bed and just as he was dozing off—he said—he heard glass breaking.

Barry Hannah, by Willie's account, had broken a pane of glass in Willie's kitchen door, with a stick of stove wood, the better to reach in and unlatch the door—because he wanted to make a long distance call. Willie, much the bigger man physically, threw Hannah out. But Hannah shortly reentered, and grabbed the phone again. Willie, now truly aroused, gave Hannah a more emphatic heave-ho—but, in so doing, cut his feet on broken glass. Still, he flopped on the bed and tried to court sleep, just in time for a second motorized pass through his neighborhood by the bogus Hell's Angels who revved their engines, backfired them, tooted their horns, and yelled, in a deliberate disturbance of the peace to pay Willie back for his earlier rude reception.

That was all Willie could stand. He jumped up, "put on my only clean shirt," khaki pants, loafers sans socks, and grabbed his toilet kit, his Viceroys, and a six pack of beer before speeding straight to Jackson and putting up at the Sun 'N' Sand Motel. Though he stayed on the Ole Miss payroll almost a year longer and attended his duties, far less strenuous than they were originally—not resigning until February of 1991—his heart was no longer in Oxford, and he became a commuter. JoAnne Prichard, shortly after the incident with the bogus Hell's Angels and Hannah, cleared his Faculty Row house of some of Willie's clothes and other personal effects.

"*Stove wood?*" Barry Hannah says, astonished. "*Broken glass?* I really don't think so. It's been, you know, fifteen years or more and you're depending on the memories of a couple of drunks, but that's not what I recall. I *was* surprised to find Willie's doors locked, and I did break the lock, because I couldn't rouse him and I feared that something had happened to him, that he was sick or worse. So I broke in to use the telephone to call Willie's doctor."

Were *you* drunk, Hannah?

"Of course! That's the absurdity of it! And that's what pissed Willie off more than anything, my calling his doctor. He was very protective about his alcoholism. So *that's* why he threw me out!"

For the record, JoAnne Prichard didn't see any broken glass on the floor, no blood on the floor or sheets or elsewhere when she later fetched Willie's clothes and some personal gear from his Faculty Row house. "Remember," she said with a smile, "Willie was a writer. And writers love drama, even if they have to invent it." And also for the record, Barry Hannah gave up that ol' demon rum a number of years ago.

PART EIGHT

RECOVERY: FINDING A GOOD WOMAN AND JUMP-STARTING A STALLED CAREER

"Willie still stayed up at night, but there was another warm body in the house. He wasn't alone, *which was his greatest fear. He had that period of gentility he needed. Clean shirts. Clean bathroom. Snacks in the fridge. His own study. Those amenities had been missing from Willie's life for years. They seemed to anchor him. And he said to me, almost like a child relating some miracle, 'Look, Boss, I've even got my own Visa card!'"*

— LARRY WELLS

in 2004

CHAPTER 20

WILLIE MORRIS DID NOT TARRY LONG at the Sun 'N' Sand Motel, but commuted between Jackson and Oxford as need be. And when he was in Jackson, he found the living much more accommodating in a certain lady friend's house.

Something good had happened to Willie, and her name was JoAnne Prichard. Willie, while working on *Homecomings* with William Dunlap, began a romance with the woman who was editing that book for the University Press of Mississippi. JoAnne came to Oxford for a few days in 1989 to work with Willie and Bill Dunlap on an interview to be used in *Homecomings,* and during that trip romance not only blossomed but came to full flower. Willie found in JoAnne his most serious love since his romance with Barbara Howar had ended some sixteen years earlier.

Morris and Prichard had known each other for years, though only casually. They first met in 1967 when Willie read from his yet-unpublished manuscript of *North Toward Home* at Yazoo City High, where JoAnne, a native of Indianola, Mississippi, then was a twenty-three-year-old English teacher; both were married to someone else and no sparks were struck. "Every time Willie came to Yazoo City over the years I saw him at dinner parties or cocktail parties," JoAnne recalls.

> He wrote the foreword to a book that I co-authored with Harriet DeCell, a history of Yazoo County, and he spoke to my classes

three times in the 1970s. Harriet and I were in New York once and met Willie and his entourage at Elaine's. We even had tea with him at the house of his girlfriend, Muriel Murphy! So our friendship went back a ways, but it was never close and was intermittent. Willie later told me that he never knew I was funny, and that I had never flirted with him, so it was *my* fault that we didn't get together earlier!

On his frequent visits from Oxford to Jackson, while he was still treading water as the writer-in-residence at Ole Miss, Willie began to "case" the city where he had been born—but had spent little time in since childhood—to see if it might be a place he would permanently enjoy. He was wary of Jackson's reputation as a staid, standoffish place where the local powers—politicians, businessmen, so many lawyers they stumbled over each other—reputedly ran the town to suit themselves and to the exclusion of others. The state capital was not thought to have any of the laid-back qualities of Oxford, called by some "The Little Easy"—New Orleans, of course, being "The Big Easy." But Willie was eager to escape Oxford. He had, he said, suffered too many disappointments there, and he had "lost my privacy." He often remarked that his writing output had badly slipped in Oxford—as if, somehow, Oxford was more to blame for that slippage than he was; writers are often defensive, to say nothing of being irrational, when trying to explain away their lack of productivity.

"Somehow"—says Larry Wells, a faithful Oxfordian—

Willie seemed to forget his *good* times in Oxford. He was delighted with the town when he first came here. He made many friends who opened their doors to him and extended helping hands. He loved going to Ole Miss football games and the camaraderie of football weekends. He had a ball when Dean and I took him on the road to book signings. He enjoyed being the center of attention at just about any event that he went to. He loved showing the town to his visiting writer-friends. And though he tired of teaching pretty quickly, he enjoyed his students and he offered them, as well as faculty members and others here who wrote, his profes-

sional advice and tips about their own work, and he felt good doing it. I'm just sorry, I'm *saddened,* that Willie somehow forgot all
that as time passed and he grew restless.

("Willie never *forgot* the good times in Oxford," JoAnne Prichard
says. "He just somehow had trouble dealing with the memory of
them.")

For all of Willie's roller-coaster ups-and-downs, Wells thought
Willie was good for Oxford and vice versa. Even after Willie fled to
Jackson and became a commuter, Wells held out the hope he would
return: Willie had not relinquished his faculty housing, many of his
papers still being stored there, nor had he submitted a letter of resignation; he remained on the faculty payroll, and he did, indeed,
fulfill his contractual obligations to host three visiting writers per
year. As late as Halloween of 1990, Willie and Graham Prichard, one
of JoAnne's two sons, wearing hideous masks, met playwright Beth
Henley at the Memphis airport and drove her to Oxford, where
Willie gave her a tour of the campus and hosted a party in her
honor. She was the last of the many visiting writers he brought to
Ole Miss.

When Willie formally resigned his writer-in-residence position at
Ole Miss in February of 1991—"effective at the end of this semes-
ter"—Chancellor R. Gerald Turner (now president of Southern
Methodist University) praised him for his service to Ole Miss and
wrote that should Willie return to the Oxford area he would like to
"pick off where we left off" with the Writer's Program. And as late as
August of 1991, Larry Wells encouraged Willie to at least "retain the
lectureship job at Ole Miss. It's still yours if you want it. . . . You
wouldn't have to be on campus to make the phone calls to set it up.
Then you could simply appear for a couple of days and emcee the
program. Once they hire somebody else to do it, they'd be committed to him or her. So Dean and I hope you won't let it slide." Wells
even suggested that JoAnne Prichard—by then Willie's wife—surely
could find employment at Ole Miss and said she would be a good fit
in the Oxford community. But it was too late: Willie had increasingly
come to like living in Jackson; it was large enough that nobody

bothered him at home by popping in unannounced, yet small enough that when he felt like going out he almost certainly encountered people he knew. For a time, he considered building a weekend cabin in the woods near Oxford, on land then owned by Willie's friend Charles Henry, and JoAnne had gone so far as to draw up house plans.

THE CULMINATION OF Willie's and JoAnne's courtship occurred in April of 1990 in as public a place as it could happen. Senator Thad Cochran (R-Miss.) and his wife, Rose—old friends of Willie's— hosted a party in Washington for Willie and Bill Dunlap, celebrating the publication of *Homecomings* as well as the thirtieth anniversary of the University Press of Mississippi. Willie didn't let JoAnne Prichard know what he planned, but he told my wife, Barbara Blaine, in some excitement, "This is going to be a big night for me. I'm so glad many of my friends are here, because I have a big surprise in store for everybody."

Willie's sense of drama, and the awakening of his long-dormant romantic streak, caused him to make a surprise marriage proposal to JoAnne from the podium in the Senate Caucus Room in front of, literally, hundreds of people. JoAnne said "Yes" to great applause and cheers. "I was more surprised than anyone," JoAnne recalls. "Truth is, I had been mad at Willie about something or other and things were not at their warmest between us, so a proposal was the last thing I expected!" Willie always knew how to preen in the spotlight, and that evening he did so with the largest of smiles. "He was so obviously happy and pleased," Barbara Blaine recalls, "that everyone else felt good, too."

The betrothed couple settled on September 14 as their wedding day, and in contrast to their very public engagement decided on a small, private wedding on the deck of JoAnne's house, with only their respective offspring in attendance. "We never considered a big public wedding, having both been there and done that," JoAnne says.

After JoAnne had readied a stack of invitations to a post-wedding reception for mailing, Willie suddenly snatched them from her hand, said, "I'm not sure I'm ready for this," locked himself in a room and would not come out to talk about it. The next morning, appearing sleepless and haggard, he handed his bride-to-be the invitations, saying only, "Go ahead and mail 'em"—and then he went to bed! Well, he was not the first prospective bridegroom, or bride, for that matter, to have experienced tardy second thoughts about taking the final step toward the ultimate commitment.

The marriage came off without a further hitch after which the newlyweds went to the Ole Miss–Auburn football game in Jackson on—JoAnne later said—"the hottest day in the history of the world!" They then drove to Yazoo City for dinner at the Steak House and a one-night honeymoon in the less-than-posh old Yazoo City Motel. Pure Willie. The following day they returned to Jackson to celebrate with a large crowd of friends at their favorite hangout, Hal's and Mal's.

JUST ABOUT EVERYONE with any familiarity of their marriage at one time or another told me, "JoAnne saved Willie's life"—or least prolonged it—or got him back on track as a writer, or helped him regain his self-respect, or, simply, made him happier than he had ever been. She slowed his drinking a little, though it was impossible to stop it because Willie had no will to stop; she had less success getting him to quit chain-smoking his ubiquitous Marlboro Lights, a switch from his long-time Viceroys. Nor did JoAnne neglect Willie's ego: She welcomed his friends, cued him to tell his favorite stories, encouraged him to write, read his work, and discussed it with him. "Willie said I gave him serenity," JoAnne remembers. "But *he* gave *me* so much in return: fun and excitement, confidence as an editor, interesting and diverse social contacts, someone to talk with about the things that mattered to both of us, such as Mississippi, politics, literature, friends and family. It was a symbiotic relationship if ever there was one—each of us was more productive and happier together than we were apart. To put it in mathematical terms, two plus two equaled five."

"Willie still stayed up at night," Larry Wells says, "but there was another warm body in the house. He wasn't *alone*, which was his greatest fear. He had that period of gentility he needed. Clean shirts. Clean bathroom. Snacks in the fridge. His own study. Those amenities had been missing from Willie's life for years. They seemed to anchor him. And he said to me, almost like a child relating some miracle, 'Look, Boss, I've even got my own Visa card!'"

I know JoAnne Prichard gave Willie his happiest decade because he told me that personally and with obvious conviction, a sentiment he repeated to all who would listen. It showed in Willie's demeanor: The often idle and angry "Mr. Hyde" of the 1980s was replaced by the busy, mischievous, witty social raconteur of an earlier time. His son, David Rae, says, "Dad was a changed man, a different person, a *better* person." In the ways of fathers and sons, despite their love for each other, Willie and David Rae each had at times disappointed the other, quarreled, and were sometimes briefly estranged. But in Willie's last decade they healed old wounds, visited, traveled together, joked, even worked together: *My Mississippi,* a huge coffee-table book with text by Willie and photos by David Rae, was published in 2000; work on it had been completed only days before Willie Morris died.

Knowing that Willie was not by nature or instinct a great help around the house, JoAnne ran almost all of the family errands, paid all bills, filed all tax returns, did the yard work or made simple home repairs, or contracted to have them done. Author Jill Conner Browne of Jackson, a long-time friend of JoAnne's (who edited Jill's best-selling books *The Sweet Potato Queens' Book of Love, God Save the Sweet Potato Queens,* and *The Sweet Potato Queens' Big-Ass Cookbook and Financial Planner),* says, "What Willie wanted was to be carried around on a silk pillow and be waited on and doted on around the clock. JoAnne gave him a lot of that, but with the greatest sense of comedy. Once she was at work, facing a book deadline, when she got a mid-morning call from Willie. He usually slept until noon or mid-afternoon so she figured she had better take the call."

JoAnne picked up the phone to hear an excited Willie shout:

"COME HOME!"
"Uh, what? Why?"

"COME HOME! YOU'VE GOT TO COME HOME RIGHT NOW!"

"Why? What's wrong? Are you sick?"

"NO! A TREE FELL! A TREE FELL! COME HOME!"

"Where?"

"HERE! RIGHT HERE!"

"What tree, Willie? Where did it fall?"

"THAT BIG HACKBERRY TREE! IT FELL RIGHT ON THE HOUSE AND MADE A LOUD NOISE AND KNOCKED ME OUTTA BED."

"Well, Baby, are you hurt?"

"NO. BUT I'M ON THE FLOOR AND YOU'VE GOT TO COME HOME RIGHT NOW!"

"Whether she went right home was lost in JoAnne's helpless laughter as she told me the story," Jill Conner Browne says. "The idea of Willie flinging himself to the floor at the sound of the crash and calling *her* home to deal with the catastrophe, without his even *getting up off the floor*—well, a lesser woman such as myself probably would have wished the tree had hit him in the head, but JoAnne loved the pure *Willie-ness* of it."

JoAnne, it developed, did rush right home and arranged to get the tree off the roof and the roof repaired. Willie went back to untroubled sleep, secure in the knowledge that JoAnne was on the case. He had done *his* part by sounding the alarm: That's all Paul Revere did, isn't it?

WHATEVER ELSE, Willie Morris was working again. In the last decade of his life, he wrote as many books as he had in all his previous writing years.

Homecomings (University Press of Mississippi, 1989, edited by JoAnne Prichard) was widely reviewed and acclaimed. *The Chicago Tribune*: "The collaboration of Morris and [artist] William Dunlap seems to be especially fortunate, for the two men produce works that expand and improve with each viewing or reading. Morris aptly describes Dunlap's work as 'visual poems.' For a reader, though, it is Morris' own work that is worth the price of the book." *The Boston Globe:* "William Dunlap's art is somewhat commanding, and makes a handsome edifice for Morris' prose. The opening dialogue between the two men casts a telling glance at the internal and external landscapes that form the creative sensibility." Reviewer Gail Caldwell concluded that "there is damn fine life left in this man's prose." I did not find a single bad review of *Homecomings*—voted, in 1990, as the best nonfiction book of the year by the Mississippi Library Association. I think the book quite remarkable, both for Willie's prose and for Dunlap's art.

Faulkner's Mississippi (Oxmoor House, 1990; photographs by William Eggleston) was described as a "coffee-table book," but it was a good cut above that genre. (The "father" of the book—because he had the idea of doing it—is Larry Wells.) The New Orleans *Times-Picayune* praised Willie's "perceptive and beautifully written" prose: "Morris writes with understanding of this complex man. . . . This is a serious biographical and literary analysis, but Morris is also adept at writing in a humorous, and sometimes gently satirical tone. . . . Faulkner's Mississippi serves several functions: It is a deeply personal portrait of the writer, factual and informative, richly endowed with intimate glimpses of Bill Faulkner the man." *The South Carolina Review:* "This 'handsome' coffee-table volume is light years better than the average book of this type, even though parts of it seem to be aimed at an audience that likes to read biographical anecdotes about famous people but has no intention of reading Faulkner's novels. It is good that all writing about Faulkner is not aimed at specialists and scholars, and even better that someone as talented as Morris can communicate about Faulkner with the average reader."

Despite the subject matter, not many "serious" critics bothered to review this "coffee-table book"—or, if they did, they treated it in passing: *The New York Times Book Review* was content with a one-paragraph notice easy to overlook. Willie was disappointed, feeling that because he was, after all, writing about the giant Faulkner more top sources would pay attention. "He was almost *always* disappointed,"

JoAnne Prichard Morris says, "because he was always waiting for that big best seller. He really hungered for it."

In 1991, Willie took a break from writing his next "big" book— *New York Days*—to put together a sports book: *After All, It's Only a Game,* published by the University Press of Mississippi, with a foreword by sports editor Rick Cleveland of the Jackson *Clarion-Ledger* and illustrations by Lynn Green Root; JoAnne edited it. Barbara Liss, in *The Houston Post,* wrote that the book offered "a fine opportunity for anyone who hasn't met this intelligent, sensitive writer. Nobody has written more lyrical, lucid prose than Morris about sports as a rite of passage for boys—and girls, too, who cheered and twirled their teen-age hearts out—in a more innocent place and time, small Southern towns in the 1940s and 1950s." Ray Gamache in *Aethlon: The Journal of Sports Literature* gave Willie's new book a resounding cheer: "In this slim volume one man's love of sport, eloquently remembered, is given life as it must have happened in the back roads and locker rooms of his experience. Morris is able to breathe the Mississippi air, its people, and their love of sport into this work. By focusing on the simple, everyday aspects of sport, he touches a chord that rings true with clarity [and] reminds us that sport is best appreciated in our own memories, etched forever in our consciousness."

WILLIE REGAINED CONFIDENCE due to the receptions given to these books, and because JoAnne suggested that he was ready to write his oft-talked-of memoir, a companion piece to *North Toward Home.* She established an improved writing room for him in the basement, which he called "The Dungeon," as he liked to leave the impression that JoAnne often herded him into it. JoAnne says she never even had to give him a nudge, that he went to work on his own. Her encouraging words to Willie about the worth of what he was doing, however, and her specific recommendations, certainly played a large part in Willie's increased productivity in his final decade. Indeed, her deft touch with Willie reminds me of Willie's own talent in getting the best from his writers during the *Harper's* years.

In March of 1991 Willie sent his agent, Sterling Lord, a précis of *New York Days*—he already had titled the unwritten book—along with a letter recommending ways to interest editors in the proposed book. He suggested that copies of *North Toward Home* be sent to editors, some eight or ten of whom he named, and that quotes from reviews and ads of the earlier memoir accompany his précis. He left no doubt that he intended to write a "big" book: "I really want to get the most lucrative contract possible on *New York Days* and I think it deserves one." He suggested that competitive bids among publishing houses were in order—something writers do not do unless they believe they have a shot at grabbing the big brass ring.

Almost immediately, Willie began to write and call those who had known him best during his "New York days": a half-dozen of us from his *Harper's* crew and others to include George Plimpton, Edwin (Bud) Shrake, Norman Mailer, Bill Styron, Ed Yoder, Jean Stein, James Dickey, Gay Talese, Sara Davidson, soliciting memories, anecdotes, atmosphere—"Anything," he told me, "that will help bring those years back to life." Then, as if mentioning life recalled those who no longer had it, he added, "So many are dead. I wish I'd the foresight to talk with them." Willie later would say that *NYD* was harder to write than any other of his books. He was consoled by the advance Little, Brown paid him: $135,000, which provided the biggest payday of his career.

New York Days broke out of the gate like Seabiscuit. Elizabeth Hardwick, a respected novelist and New York publishing insider, wrote a lengthy and very positive front-page review in *The New York Times Book Review* of September 5, 1993—not only reviewing the book but judging Willie's accomplishments at *Harper's* as outstanding. Morris, she wrote, had "cast his story in the streets of the city with a fluent affection and an acute rendering of the turmoil of the years: the assassinations, the civil rights movement and the Vietnam War. . . . The book gives credibility to his aims and achievements. It is a mixture of pride and heartache." Although other biographies

and autobiographies had been centered around American magazines, "no other comes close to mind as having such a measure of
chagrin as *New York Days*. A certain naivete made Willie Morris care
too greatly and too painfully about the alliance with *Harper's*. A
fragility of temperament, beneath the sociability, inhabits his book
and brings, or can bring, the reader to much sympathy for this com-
position of nostalgia and hurting regret in Mr. Morris's total recall
of the lost days and nights." Ms. Hardwick's review also included the
boxed "A Provincial on the Upper West Side," three quoted paragraphs from Willie's book.

Elizabeth Hardwick's was far from the only review to praise *New
York Days: Booklist:* a "delectable sequel" to *North Toward Home* ("a delicious memoir") and "an extended essay on time and place, an especially beautiful piece of writing in which Morris attempts to
answer the question we all shy away from with regards to the roads
we have taken: 'What did it all mean?' . . . Journalistic memoirs
abound, but few are as full of heart and as gracefully expressed as
this one." Rust Hills, in *Esquire: Harper's*, when Morris edited it, "was
a truly remarkable magazine. His accounts of the creation of various
articles in that turbulent decade are fascinating. . . . Don't miss [this
book] . . . the tone is as down-to-earth American as its author."
Michael Swindle in *The Los Angeles Times Book Review* found *New York
Days* "enlightening, revelatory, touching and uproariously funny."

There were many "mixed" reviews; most of these began by finding merit in Willie's book but eventually retreated to a number of
"howevers" or "on the other hands" in finding him guilty of name-
dropping, stretches of purple prose, or perhaps not fully appreciat-
ing the hard business choices facing the Cowles family as America's
reading habits changed.

I thought Willie lacked introspection in failing to closely examine
what his New York days amounted to in the long run, in not digging
into what he might have done to better educate young John Cowles
in the realities of magazine profit-and-loss sheets, in not asking
tough questions of himself personally and professionally: *What might
I have done better? Where and why did I err? Why did I retreat from the*

world after the Harper's *fiasco, becoming close to a hermit for months on end, even though I had many attractive offers? Why, simply, didn't I fight back?*

In short, I think *New York Days,* while often entertaining, lacked meaningful candor and tough-minded self-examination. (The latter, especially, was never one of Willie's strong points.) In short, because of the faults here enumerated, I personally believe *New York Days* to be Willie's least effective nonfiction book. He was guilty of the literary crime of not bridging the wide gulf between what his book was and what it could have been.

Willie never said much of the overall reception of *New York Days,* but I think it was below his expectations in that area, as well as in sales. His publisher's springing for a promotional tour that included a party of literary and political and cultural Big Feet at Elaine's in New York, prepublication sales of excerpts to several magazines, and warm letters of praise from many who had received advance copies of the book—to include old pals William Styron and Ed Yoder—probably led Willie to anticipate greater personal satisfactions than actually occurred. But there was one definite positive: Unlike when *The Last of the Southern Girls* was ripped or when *The Courting of Marcus Dupree* disappointed or when Herman Gollob rejected *Taps,* Willie didn't go into a funk or self-destruct. It helped that he was awarded the third annual Richard Wright Medal for Literary Excellence, and that the Mississippi Institute of Arts and Letters named *New York Days* as the best nonfiction book of the year. But the big difference, I think, was that reinforcing encouragement and stability provided by JoAnne Prichard.

CHAPTER 21

WILLIE PUT ON HIS GOOD FACE when I twice visited him in Mississippi and met him on two occasions in Memphis, so I had been unaware of his bouts of what may have been clinical depression or other ills. Those familiar with his darker side, however, almost immediately noted his improvement in mood after he married JoAnne. He became much less the recluse, and when Willie and JoAnne visited Washington—as they visited New York, Hollywood, and Oxford, England, among other roamings—he was much more the social activist.

When we spoke together at the annual PEN-Faulkner dinner in Washington in the mid-'90s—along with Eudora Welty, Norman Mailer, Ken Kesey, Shelby Foote, and other writers—and the next day attended a luncheon honoring us in the U.S. Capitol, Willie was swarmed by senators and Congress members in attendance; he probably was more warmly greeted than any of us. "I guess they haven't forgotten me after all," he later said with a pleased grin that was good to witness.

In the 1992 race, not long before the election, Willie emceed in front of the Old State Capitol in Jackson, a Clinton rally that drew 15,000 people. Morris later told Jack Bales that then-Governor Clinton had whispered in his ear, "Willie it's going to be a tough few weeks, but I *think* we're going to make it." And at the invitation of President Clinton, Willie visited the White House. Willie also became more visible on the lecture circuit than formerly, speaking not only in his home state but also in Texas, Tennessee, Arkansas, and Virginia, that I know of, as well as invading a few Midwestern states.

In November of 1994, when Willie Morris turned sixty, he went to what he thought was a small birthday dinner with "a few friends" at Hal's and Mal's, a popular Jackson eatery. A "few friends" indeed: No less than 300 people, and some say perhaps as many as 500, showed up to fête him. Old high school "girlfriends" sang the Yazoo City High school song—lyrics once written by a sixteen-year-old student named Willie Morris—and others performed Willie's favorite song, "Darkness on the Delta," as well as "New York, New York." David Halberstam presented the guest of honor with an inscribed Tiffany silver box from his old colleagues and associates at *Harper's*, including Styron and Mailer. "Willie Morris was simply the best magazine editor ever," Halberstam told the assembled. "No one has ever done what he did as well, before or since." Novelist Barry Gifford said, "Willie, not a better man has hit sixty since Babe Ruth."

Football star (University of Tennessee) and coach (University of Pittsburgh) Johnny Majors, who had never met Willie Morris but had corresponded with him, was a legitimate surprise guest. Playwright Beth Henley sent sixty red roses from Hollywood. Messages were read from many writers, athletes, show-biz types, and politicians. Former Governor William Winter read a hand-written note of good wishes from President Clinton and First Lady Hillary. The show, months in the making, was produced by JoAnne Prichard Morris and emceed by David Rae Morris.

At a given point the Hinds County Sheriff entered, with several deputies, and bellowed over a bullhorn, "Willie Morris, you are under arrest." To the astonishment of some, Willie was handcuffed and charges against him were read, including "malicious mischief, shameless and habitual hyperbole, highfalutin' language, confusing and crossing the line between fact and fiction, perpetual childhood, corrupting and bankrupting the morals of the youth of Mississippi, and committing fraud against family, friends, acquaintances and strangers."

"Should we try him here and now?" the sheriff bellowed. Whistles, cheers, and shouts so signified. "Is there a judge in the house?"

Four authentic real-life judges came forward. "A prosecutor?" Up stepped Bobby DeLaughter, who had convicted Byron De La Beckwith for the cowardly back-shooting murder of civil rights activist Medgar Evers. "Is anyone willing to defend this man?" David Sansing, Ole Miss professor emeritus stood and said to the robed justices, "I am the only person here fool enough to attempt to defend this man. He is obviously guilty as charged, but I will do my best."

Writer Ellen Douglas testified as to Willie's use in his books of "highfalutin' language" and "even foreign language, such as *raconteur* and the like." Three youngsters testified that reading Willie Morris's books had led them to lives of troublemaking and mischief. Ron Shapiro, disguised as the Witch of Yazoo, attested that Willie had committed fraud in not sharing profits from his book about her and also accused him of crossing the line between fact and fiction; Shapiro additionally indicated that Willie's reputation was such that "five hundred people came here just to watch him drink whiskey." Harriet DeCell of Yazoo City, who had known Willie longer than anyone else present, testified, in effect, that he had never been much good even as a child. "Defense" attorney Sansing regretted that he couldn't put on defense witnesses because "nobody could be found who could think of anything good to say about the defendant." Little wonder that his client was quickly found guilty.

Judge E. Grady Jolly, of the Fifth Circuit Court of Appeals, imposed sentence:

> WILLIE WEAKS MORRIS, you are hereby sentenced to a continuing prodigious memory for all historical events that happened before your life began 60 years ago and for all that has happened during your life, and to the retelling of all of those wonderful stories, time and time again, each and every time your friends ask, world without end.
>
> WILLIE WEAKS MORRIS, you are hereby sentenced to continue to see forever the essential goodness in the world around you and in the people that populate that world and constantly to express and paint that world in color for all of your more cynical, jaded and pessimistic friends.

WILLIE WEAKS MORRIS, you are hereby sentenced never to grow up, never to regress to a sophisticated indifference, but always to be astonished by each new day, by each new experience, by each person you meet, and by every college football game you attend.

WILLIE WEAKS MORRIS, you big-hearted, sentimental old ragamuffin, you are hereby sentenced to be smothered in the love, affection, and mirth of your thousands of fans and friends for the *next* sixty years.

Willie, obviously touched, responded, "My name is Jimmy Stewart and this is the movie *It's a Wonderful Life*."

"A"-list celebrants, of which there were many, repaired to the handsome yellow house Willie and JoAnne had bought in northeast Jackson, a genteel place of trees and other soothing greenery near a bubbling creek in the aptly named Meadowbrook section, close to the home of their friend William Winter. It was billed as a "coffee and cake" party with a sing-along around a piano, but bourbon and other strong wet goods somehow got introduced to enliven both the singing and a general camaraderie that went on well into the wee hours: no surprise there, considering who the guest of honor was.

"It was a kitchen floor type of party," David Rae Morris said. Beg pardon? "Well, I don't think anybody actually passed out on the kitchen floor," Willie's son said, "but they might have." And Willie himself claimed, for months, that he was still finding guests from that party snoring in the hedges. It seems self-evident that a good time was had by all.

IN 1995, WILLIE PRODUCED *A Prayer for the Opening of the Little League Season,* his tribute to kiddie baseball, with watercolor art by Barry Moser. But miles ahead of that, in the same year, was *My Dog Skip,* though when I told Edwin (Bud) Shrake the title of Willie's work in progress he thought I was joking and even David Halberstam said, "We've got to get Willie to quit writing about goddamned dogs!" And Texas writer Gary Cartwright and yours truly—having read Willie's assertion in *North Toward Home* that he had buried Skip in his Yazoo City backyard, wrapped in his high school letter jacket—wrote a smart-aleck song about it beginning, "Skip may be dead but he's still mean / We wrapped him in the white and green / He'll never slobber anymore / Nor run a punt back for a score. . . ." Willie had the last laugh: His "dog project" turned out much better than any of us thought it would.

The project began when Willie's new agent, Theron Raines, whom Willie had hired on the recommendation of Winston Groom, suggested that Willie write an entire book about his boyhood dog. Raines felt that if Willie included his boyhood stories of the World War II era, exploiting the nostalgia people were feeling about the last "good war," a movie sale might result. Willie jumped at the opportunity and later said that *My Dog Skip* was the only book he ever truly enjoyed writing. Theron Raines had such confidence in the book that he put it up for bids, Random House winning with an advance of $100,000 for both hardback and paperback rights; it was, behind *New York Days*, Willie's second largest career payday.

Skip became a Book-of-the-Month Club alternate selection and, sure enough, the movie rights were bought by Warner Brothers. Kevin Bacon played Willie's father, Rae Morris, and Diane Lane was his mother, Marion. Young Willie was played by Frankie Muniz, who soon became the star of the TV series *Malcolm in the Middle*. The real-life Willie Morris and the movie Willie Morris got along famously, the actor calling the writer "Big Willie" and the writer calling the young actor "Little Willie." There were six or eight fox terrier "Skips" of various sizes and ages, since the movie played out across a number of years.

The movie was shot not in Yazoo City but in smaller and older-looking Canton, Mississippi. This was misunderstood by some in Yazoo City; they complained that Willie Morris had not used his influence to have the film made in his *real* hometown; disturbed, Willie wrote an article for the *Yazoo Herald* explaining the situation: He had tried to persuade the Hollywood folks to film in Yazoo City, but Yazoo City had not preserved much of its older sections, clearing old buildings to make way for more modern structures. While

this may have helped promote "progress," it had not helped historically. An official of the movie company said, "You could not look any
direction in Yazoo without seeing the *recent* past, rather than the *distant* past."

Willie loved visiting Canton during the shooting of *My Dog Skip*,
hanging out with the cast and crew, director Jay Russell, and even
the bit-part players and extras. Early on, the comely Diane Lane
asked Willie what he could tell her or show her that might assist in
her role as his movie mother. With a mischievous gleam Willie said,
"Well, I used to kiss my mother a whole lot." Seeing a reasonable fac-
simile of portions of his childhood being created was, he said, "*Déjà
vu* of the most stunning kind." The production paid attention to historical accuracy: In the Dixie Theater—actually an outside façade
superimposed on a restaurant in a building that had the virtue of
looking old—a small sign below the ticket booth read "For Whites
Only." Replicas of 1940s advertisements for soft drinks, bread,
headache powders, and other products were painted on Canton
Buildings. Most of the filming took part in the town square with its
1855 courthouse and in the vicinity of its well-preserved antebellum
homes. The look was truly authentic. Willie's only criticism was,
"Most of the kids would have been barefoot back then."

Canton was but a short drive from Jackson, so Willie and JoAnne
held a "Southern party" in their backyard for the cast, crew, a few Yazoo City visitors, Canton officials, and their own special friends. The
menu: Moon Pies, R.C. Colas, boiled peanuts, crawfish, and fried
chicken. Yum yum, y'all. Willie and JoAnne went to New York in late
July of 1999 to attend a special private screening of *My Dog Skip*.
And the movie simply blew Willie away. He called several friends late
in the evening to tell them how great it was. "I cried in the taxi all
the way from the theater to our hotel," he said. "That was *my whole
life* on that screen!" Well, not really: It was Willie's greened-up version of his boyhood, aided by a great deal of Hollywood hokum,
though the hokum was so smoothly injected that former Texas Congressman Charles Wilson, an old friend of Willie's, said, "I cried
when they wanted me to."

As family entertainment *Skip* was a good show; the reviews were almost all favorable, and the *Today* show critic, Gene Shalit, said, "Don't be put off by the title. This is a grown-up movie for adults that young people will also cherish." And he particularly commended Frankie Muniz, saying he had given "as splendid a performance by a youngster as I have ever seen." The movie was a commercial rarity: It grossed more at the box office in its second week than in its opening week, meaning it had great word of mouth, which almost always helps the box office more than good reviews. Despite Hollywood's voodoo bookkeeping—to legally conceal that a movie has crossed into profit, so as to prevent the thieves-in-charge from having to share said profit with the writer or writers without whose creation there could *be* no movie—I have no personal doubt that *Skip* made money. I wish Willie could have known that the Broadcast Film Critics Association honored *My Dog Skip* as Best Family Film of the year 2000. "If Willie had lived to see its national success," JoAnne Prichard Morris has said, "he likely would have told everyone, 'Everything in that movie is absolutely true.'"

BY THE TIME THE FILM OF *My Dog Skip* was made, Willie had chalked up an earlier Hollywood experience. Indeed, he was almost single-handedly responsible for the filming of *The Ghosts of Mississippi,* about the trial in which Byron De La Beckwith, thirty years tardily, was convicted of having fatally shot from ambush with a deer rifle—and in the back—virtually on his own front steps, civil rights activist Medgar Evers.

Willie Morris had attended that trial in Jackson and had become friendly with the prosecutor, Bobby DeLaughter, who had gained a conviction other prosecutors had been unable to get in an earlier time, due to two hung juries no doubt influenced by racist indifference. As a sixth-generation Mississippian, Willie felt a need for that story of justice long denied—but finally attained—to become known to a larger audience. He thus incessantly campaigned with a Hollywood producer he knew, Fred Zollo, to make a movie about how that trial—and conviction—came about. Once Zollo decided to produce the film, and had hired Rob Reiner to direct it, he hired Willie Morris as an advisor—for his knowledge of the case, of Mississippi, and for his obvious passion for the story.

It was natural for Willie to keep notes from the outset, which he turned into a nonfiction book—at the suggestion of both George Plimpton and Winston Groom—*The Ghosts of Medgar Evers: A Tale of Race, Murder, Mississippi and Hollywood* (New York: Random House, 1998). His book reveals his surprise that what he saw as a good movie—though perhaps he was too involved in it for objectivity—not only was slammed by critics, but by some of Medgar Evers's descendants and old friends, who thought Bobby DeLaughter was given too much credit and Medgar's widow, Myrlie Evers, not enough credit in persisting in seeking justice over three decades. *USA Today*'s critic, under the headline "Black Hero Missing in Movie," wrote, "DeLaughter's story is but a historical footnote to the campaign Evers led in Mississippi against racial bigotry and discrimination—and the efforts of his widow to put his killer in jail." (Willie was hurt by the alleged criticism by Myrlie Evers because, according to JoAnne, "He knew that she had been in on the movie planning from the start.") Richard Corliss in *Time*: "*Ghosts of Mississippi* is not really about the black civil rights struggler. It is about the white liberal's burden." I thought the movie not very good, and Willie's book about it—despite his passion for the movie and the story—unfocused and rather slapdash.

What seemed to surprise, and pain, Willie most was so many white people in Mississippi resenting the stirring up of old passions and history. He recounts numerous cases of whites saying that sleeping dogs should have rested undisturbed, that young Bobby DeLaughter was a "nigger lover" and should be run out of town and similar verbal poison darts.

Despite good notices for James Woods as murderer Byron De La Beckwith, and an Academy Award nomination for him as Best Supporting Actor, the film was a box-office flop. It grossed less than $10 million—much below its actual costs—and came nowhere near attracting the large audience Willie had almost desperately wished to see.

"There was a noticeable backlash in portions of the state's white community that was absolutely racist in origin and extended to the box office, and this amounted to something of a boycott," Willie wrote.

I myself was severely disappointed by this "boycott mentality" in my state but not surprised, for the current outcroppings of the pre-1960s white mentality are smug and tangible and ultimately sorrowful and will be with us here forever, little matter what is ever said or done or whoever conceivably says or does it. When a friend of mine asked a well-heeled Jackson businesswoman if she had seen *Ghosts,* the woman replied, "My husband and I have seen enough of nigger movies." And the editor of the *Jackson Business Journal,* under the headline of KEEPING THE GHOSTS IN THE CLOSET, trashed it solely on that basis (though in slightly cleaner language), then admitted that he had not seen the movie, nor did he intend to.

That was very strong language for Willie Morris to use about his beloved Mississippi, or even the erring people in it.

ON JULY 17, 1999, Willie Morris turned in to the University Press of Mississippi the roughly 80,000 words he had written for *My Mississippi,* a collaboration with his son, David Rae, who took the many pictures—almost all in color—illustrating and complementing the book. The editors had asked Willie not to recycle old material, more or less, but to consider his native ground with a new and inquiring eye. I believe Willie Morris did that. His prose offered the most complete thumbnail history of Mississippi that I had read, the state's quirks and peculiarities, its poverty and old sins, its gains and losses and fumbles and strivings.

Though reviews of *My Mississippi* largely were confined to the South, they were respectful at worst and sometimes idolizing. John R.

Kemp in the New Orleans *Times-Picayune* wrote that despite Willie's long love affair with his native state, he had not failed to recognize Mississippi's flaws, such as its legendary racism: "Willie's engagingly written, impressively researched 103-page text gives readers a thorough, passionate view of Mississippi today. He explores the land and the people, and the dark ironies and tragic contradictions that have plagued the state for generations. David Rae's 96 superb color photographs give a sensitive glimpse of ordinary Mississippians going about their lives." Kemp said Willie's prose "speaks to the intellect" and that David Rae's photos "stare you in the face." *Library Journal, The Atlanta Journal-Constitution,* and the Jackson *Clarion-Ledger* were among the publications leading the cheers.

Willie was on a roll, quickly going from one book to another, as if to make up for the years he had lain fallow. *My Cat Spit McGee* was completed in January of 1999. It has been well-documented that Willie was a "dog man"; what has been much less advertised is that in JoAnne Prichard he married a "cat woman"—a fact he himself did not know until JoAnne's then teenage son, Graham, gave her a stray kitten for Christmas with a red ribbon tied around its neck. Willie claimed that he saw from JoAnne's reaction that he had cat troubles: "Her features became flushed and joyous. Never had I seen such a happy female." He didn't know the half of it. That stray, in time, had a litter of kittens of her own. One of them would become Spit McGee.

My Cat Spit McGee documents Willie's "conversion" to cats—though he by no means ever disavowed his love for dogs—after eleven-year-old Bailey Browne, daughter of Jill Conner Browne, suggested that he write about how Spit McGee had changed him from a cat hater to a cat lover.

"Spit McGee," named after a character in Willie's *Good Old Boy* books, was a tiny white anemic kitten with one blue eye and one golden eye. Spit's mother, after three others of her litter had died, apparently quit nursing him and hid him under the house where Willie found him all but dead. JoAnne drove him to the vet but as a cat lover was too shook up to attend to matters, so Willie held the kitten in the palm of his hand and took him into the animal hospital. One vet said the kitten had no chance to live, the other vet on duty said wait a minute, a blood transfusion just might give the kitten a fighting chance. The kitty did live, and Willie began to feed it with an eye dropper and otherwise care for it. A mutual attachment occurred, though Willie was slow to admit it. JoAnne knew he was hooked when he named the little kitty after one of his own book characters.

My Cat Spit McGee is a charming little book, funny in Willie's frustrations when the cat won't behave as a dog and—always—full of new knowledge and growing love. It is, really, a book about interdependence, adjustments, and personal growth. I dare just about anybody not to like it; no critic I read had harsh words, the worst being a comment in *The Arizona Republic* that "a little Spit McGee goes a long way." Now a report from friendly precincts: *Kirkus Reviews:* "a tender, melodious tribute," the stories "flash with humor" and the book "draws a deeply affectionate portrait of the evolution of [their] friendship." *Publishers Weekly:* "A quirky iconoclast, Spit will win the hearts of both cat lovers and those who are cat-neutral in this enjoyable sequel" to *My Dog Skip. The Seattle Times:* "with Morris and Spit you cross many emotional intersections on this free-spirited ride, where the author delightfully channels energy into charisma. A trusting faith, infused with spirit and confidence, surfaces time and again between the pair."

Spit McGee died in 1994, and such was his fame that the Associated Press noted his death on its national wire.

JoAnne Prichard Morris thinks that the book Willie planned to write next was the one he was most excited about since he had first conceived of *Taps* many years earlier. It would be called "One for My Daddy: A Personal Memoir of Baseball." Willie had written a friend on July 3 that the book would "go into my relationship with my father, and baseball and dogs were our strongest bond." He often said that one of his earliest memories was of his father trying to teach him to attack a baseball with a level swing when batting "and I couldn't have been more than three." He said that in a long-ago softball game on Long Island, in 1972, he had a flashing thought, just before taking a healthy cut at a pitched ball thrown by movie star Dustin Hoffman, *This one's for you, Dad!* That, he said, was precisely when he hit an inside-the-park home run—and broke a severely turned ankle as he crossed home plate. That phrase had stuck in Willie's mind; he knew that "one day" he would write a book using that title or something close to it. (Indeed, he used the title for an article in his 1983 book, *Always Stand in Against the Curve.*)

Surely that book would have included Willie's memories of his own high school and American Legion baseball days, the few trips he made with Rae Morris to Memphis to witness minor-league pro games, his graduation to major-league games in New York, perhaps his takes on the great ones: Babe Ruth, Willie Mays, Stan Musial, Joe DiMaggio, Mel Ott, Jackie Robinson, Mickey Mantle, Ted Williams, Willie having seen the younger among them play in the flesh. More intriguing still, we might have learned much more than we know of Rae Morris, as Willie worked through his memories and his subconscious began to surface. But, alas . . . we will never know.

Willie planned to start his baseball book on August 2, 1999. Just before JoAnne went to bed Willie asked whether plenty of paper and freshly sharpened pencils had been placed on the table in his writing study; JoAnne assured him all was in readiness. She knew that, as always, Willie had plotted his upcoming book on a sizeable stack of 3 x 5 cards, lined up across a long table near his writing desk and ancient manual typewriter, though he wrote mainly in longhand. Willie had never made peace with computers; JoAnne claimed he closed his eyes when passing hers.

When he finished "One for My Daddy," Willie told his wife, he would get back to work on *Taps.* It needed—as always—just a little touching up. Willie was having a drink and thumbing through music albums when JoAnne went upstairs to bed; all seemed right in their world.

PART NINE

ADIOS, AMIGO

"When I heard the news, the first thing I thought of was how much fun we'd had together, sharing so much when we were young, and how Willie had opened the door for me and all the others at Harper's, *giving us so much freedom."*

—DAVID HALBERSTAM

in a letter to the author in early 2005

CHAPTER 22

THE NEXT MORNING—almost noon, in fact—JoAnne was talking in her living room to two friends about a book she was editing when "Willie called out my name pretty loudly. I didn't pick up on any sense of urgency, and was finishing my sentence when he called out again—louder. My friends looked startled, so I hurried to our second-floor bedroom. Willie was sitting on the edge of the bed, gasping. He said, 'I can't breathe.'"

JoAnne tried to calm her husband: "If Willie's temperature got to 99 degrees, he was petrified. I could see fear in his eyes that morning. I assured him that all would be fine, but that I would call for help to be on the safe side. He said, 'I've got to write my baseball book!'"

"You will," JoAnne said. "Just take it easy." She called for an ambulance and asked that portable oxygen be brought.

Willie said, "If anything happens to me, get *Taps* put together."

JoAnne reassured Willie that everything would be fine, but said she would do that.

He said, "If anything happens to me, don't grieve. Well . . . grieve a little." JoAnne laughed, but Willie—still serious—said, "I want you to be happy and fulfilled"; he made a remark about what a good wife she was. Then, suddenly, he began to sweat profusely and tear at his pajamas. "I never got my will written," he gasped.

It seems obvious, from Willie's comments, that he had a strong premonition he might die, although JoAnne says, "He *always* thought he was going to die soon—every day that I knew him!" Perhaps that is why JoAnne on that fateful day "wasn't thinking death" but how to give Willie comfort: "Willie was always excitable and I was concentrating on calming him and keeping him covered, as my two friends had come up from downstairs." The paramedics arrived and placed Willie on a stretcher, then carried him downstairs. As they loaded him in the ambulance, Willie Morris spoke his last full sentence: "Where's my wife?" "Right here," JoAnne said, climbing into the seat by the driver as paramedics gave Willie oxygen and checked his pulse.

In the St. Dominic Hospital emergency room, Willie was hooked up to varied IVs and given a shot of morphine. He tried to talk but all he got out was "Dog . . . Skip." JoAnne said for Willie's benefit, as much as for the hospital workers, "This is my husband, Willie Morris. He's a great writer, and a movie of his book *My Dog Skip* will get a world premiere here soon. Willie wants to invite all of you to it." Willie nodded, as they wheeled him away to a private room. JoAnne was told she couldn't come in just yet.

Soon a "gruff doctor" told JoAnne that her husband had suffered a heart attack. JoAnne remembers only snatches of what the doctor said: ". . . heart so weak we can't tell . . . congestive heart failure . . . clear fluid from his lungs." But she still didn't think Willie was dying; her mind apparently refused to accept that possibility. What she thought was, *This should be a wake-up call for Willie. Maybe now he'll cut down his smoking and drinking and take better care of himself.*

Within a half hour a nurse told JoAnne, "You might want to call his family and friends. He's very serious." JoAnne's first call was to David Rae Morris in New Orleans; then she called Jill Conner Browne, who relieved JoAnne of her chore and began to call others; soon friends were flocking to the hospital. "I remember one of the first was William Winter, the ex-governor and our close neighbor," JoAnne recalls. "Then it's all a blur."

Willie was in a coma, JoAnne was told, but, no, she couldn't see him just yet. She immediately called a friend from childhood, Dr. Walter Jones, who rushed to the hospital and spent a few moments at Willie's bedside. Then he told the doctor and nurses on duty to let JoAnne—and anyone she wished—into Willie's room. "And that," JoAnne says, "is when I realized Willie likely would die.

"I had read that hearing is the last of the senses to go," JoAnne recalls. "So I got on Willie's bed and told him private, loving things. And I hugged him and kissed him." She then opened the door to their assembled friends. One by one, they held Willie's hand, or touched him, and said their private farewells. David Rae arrived from New Orleans but did not see his father before he died.

"For a while Willie's vital signs improved," JoAnne says. "His blood pressure got better. I almost got my hopes up. Then a nurse told me that he had suffered irreversible brain damage. I snapped, 'Maybe not! You don't know how smart he was to start with!'" But Willie, as will be the case with all of us in time, had run out of tomorrows. At 7:12 P.M. on August 2, 1999, sixty-four-year-old Willie Morris breathed his last; his big, sentimental heart was stilled forever.

I WAS SHOCKED when I got a call telling me of Willie's death, so much so that I now cannot recall who told me. I immediately called several people to pass the sad news, and all seemed as shocked as I was. Perhaps we should not have been. Ed Yoder put it into perspective in his excellent memoir published in 2004, *Telling Others What to Think: Recollections of a Pundit:*

> I say that his death was unexpected, but that isn't quite true . . . for years Willie had lived close to the edge, burning his candle at both ends. Often in his later years his gathering embonpoint and a once handsome face now red, puffy and splotched, reminded one on his bad days of the more sybaritic Roman emperors, and prompted friends to fear for his life. He had enjoyed an Indian summer decade of survival—physical revival—under the loving care of his second wife, JoAnne Prichard ("She saved my life," he once told my wife Jane). But the damage done by years of hard drinking and smoking, bohemian hours and habits, could hardly be undone. And while he seemed at times almost to court death, it nonetheless came as a terrible blow to us all when it did come.

Some of his friends, including my wife Jane, had a reaction not unmixed with anger, knowing as they did how recklessly Willie had lived for so long. "Willie has cheated us of his company far too soon," she said and meant it literally, for he was the most entertaining of companions. Her sentiments were echoed at Willie's lying-in-state in the old Mississippi state capitol building by another close friend, Dean Faulkner Wells. "The son of a bitch went and died on us," she said in the soft voice that sounded so much like that of her immortal uncle, tears welling in her eyes.

"When I heard the news," David Halberstam wrote me, "the first thing I thought of was how much fun we'd had together, sharing so much when we were young, and how Willie had opened the door for me and all the others at *Harper's,* giving us so much freedom. . . . Going back to the funeral was much harder than going to visit Willie in earlier times. It's difficult to deal with the death of someone you've known when you were young and you shared all your dreams and talked about them with such youthful innocence."

Willie Weaks Morris became the first writer ever, and only the third person in the twentieth century, to lie-in-state in the rotunda of the distinguished Old Capitol Building in Jackson, the city of his birth. (The others: former Governor J. P. Coleman, in 1991, and former U.S. Senator John C. Stennis, in 1995.) "*Not* Senator James Oliver Eastland," David Halberstam later wrote. "I could almost hear Willie's voice saying *How do you like them apples, Jim Eastland?*

"The crowd that came to pay their respects was immense—it stretched as far as the eye could see. And there were a bunch of young Black reporters working for local television stations interviewing people, and that was something different, something that could not have happened in the Mississippi I knew nearly a half century ago. There was a great sweetness to the ceremonies."

Rick Bragg would write in *The New York Times* of the "hundreds of people [who] circled around and around, gazing at the closed dark-wood coffin, before moving on to hug his wife, JoAnne Prichard, her tired face drifting somewhere between a smile and a sob. 'Willie would have loved this,' she said. 'Oh,' said his 39-year-old son, David Rae Morris, 'he does.'"

It was no stretch to believe that Willie Morris, who may have believed in ghosts, had become one; surely that ghost would not have failed to attend its own funeral, as Tom Sawyer and Huck Finn had done, after premature reports of their deaths, in the imagination of Mark Twain. Of Willie's friends, who laughed and told "Willie Stories" even in the presence of his mute form, Rick Bragg added: "His ghost, they say, or his spirit, or—this being Mississippi, where people talk about God without feeling funny about it—his soul, will fly free every time someone cracks open one of his books about home, about family, about dogs and cats and finding peace in all of it."

The funeral, in the Methodist church in Yazoo City that Willie had attended as a boy, was billed as "A Celebration of the Life of Willie Morris," and an effort was made to keep it as "light" as possible under the circumstances. Harriet DeCell Kuykendall, who was a Yazoo High teacher when Willie was a student, opened by saying, "Willie always said he liked me better than he liked algebra," then read passages from *North Toward Home*. David Halberstam, William Styron, and Winston Groom, writers who spoke, stressed amusing stories. Other speakers were former Governor William Winter and former Secretary of Agriculture Mike Espy (the first black Mississippi congressman of the century). The official in charge was Will Campbell—in Halberstam's words—"the heroic minister of the Civil Rights movement, who once had been the chaplain at Ole Miss, and had been run out of town in 1955 by the segs."

President Clinton sent a lengthy eulogy that was read aloud:

It was early in 1968 when I met Willie Morris in New York. Morris was editor of *Harper's* and had been a Rhodes Scholar. I wrote to him shortly after I got my Rhodes, and to my surprise, he agreed to see me. He was wonderfully wry and funny—the classic Southerner. He wrote a great book about his dog. He wrote a fascinating book about the role of football in the South and the racial barriers, *The Courting of Marcus Dupree*. You know, most Southerners thought they'd be looked down upon if they went up to the Northeast. The cultural elites would all think they were hayseeds—although that was kind of phony; *The New York Times* was largely run by Southerners—but there was always this sensitivity about how you would be seen. Willie gave us another way of thinking about the South.

You know, for most of my generation of Southerners who went north, the book that stuck in their minds was [Thomas Wolfe's] *You Can't Go Home Again*. Willie's *North Toward Home* was a beautifully written, evocative portrait of one person's love for the South who had profound regret over the racial situation. It helped a lot of people like me who wanted to see the world but also come home and live in the South. He showed us how we could love a place and want to change it at the same time. It really was an important thing he did for me. He showed us we could go home.

Then came the touch that must have made Willie's ghost grin: As pallbearers came forward, the Reverend Campbell asked the assembled to stand and reward Willie Morris for all the good things he had done by giving him one last standing ovation. As the casket was carried down the aisle, "We rose"—Curtis Wilkie would write in his book *Dixie*—"and applause beat across the crowded sanctuary like a warm summer rainstorm." Somebody whistled, a few openly wept, and others smiled despite the lumps in their throats. "It was unbelievably cathartic," JoAnne Prichard Morris would later say.

Willie was buried where he would have wanted to be: in the old part of Greenwood Cemetery, where he had wandered as a boy with his beloved dog, Skip; where as a young father he ran foot races with his small son, David Rae; where he played spooky jokes on his youthful contemporaries; and where as a teenager he blew "Taps" for Korean War dead. As Willie himself was laid to rest, two buglers—one the traditional "echo man" far away from the gravesite—blew "Taps" for Willie Morris; one of them—the bugler nearest the grave, as Halberstam said, "was Winston Groom, a lovely man and a lovely writer. . . . It had all come full circle."

I like it that Willie's grave is exactly thirteen measured steps from that of the "Witch of Yazoo," whose legend he artfully embellished and made famous. I like it that he returned home to Mississippi on his own, before they had to bring him back in that pine box his friend Truman Capote had talked about.

R.I.P., Ol' Willie. *Adios, Amigo.* R.I.P.

A FEW DAYS LATER Edwin (Bud) Shrake e-mailed from Austin that he had read that the corneas of Willie's eyes had been donated and benefited two blind black men. "Too perfect!" Shrake wrote. "Too perfect to be true."

In time, I checked with JoAnne Prichard and then called Bud Shrake. "It's even *more* perfect," I said. "A black man got one of Willie's eyes. White man got the other. Now they both can see, and the black dude says he wants to read Willie's books. How's that for down-home racial integration?"

"*Absolutely* perfect!" Shrake said. "But I wouldn't dare write it as a screenplay. The Hollywood fops would say 'too improbable!'"

We shared a laugh over that, and later I thought, *Well, hell, maybe Ol' Willie's life* was *stranger than fiction.* Looked at over all, the Yazoo Kid had quite an exhilarating ride.

IT WOULD PROBABLY BE EASIER to name the publications in America that did *not* write tributes to Willie Morris following his death than those that did. Many websites joined in the chorus, no matter that Willie might have closed his eyes while passing computers. There was everything from signed columns to straight obits to feature stories to editorials, to cartoons—all commendable. My favorite was the final graph of a signed column written by Sid Salter, editor and publisher of *The Scott County Times* in Forest, Mississippi: "In Willie's Heaven there will be Pete, Skip and Mamie—and Rae and Marion. Ole Miss and LSU will play football in the mornings, and State and Alabama will play baseball in the afternoons. At night, there'll be some étoufée at the Hoka with a bottle of Bolla and some chicory coffee. And what stories [Willie] will tell—stories that God will want to hear."

WHAT STANDS OUT MOST IN MY MIND is the day of Willie's funeral, although, alas, I was on August 6, 1999, a long way from Mississippi. I was, indeed, in Italy—in Rome—on a long-planned family vacation. On waking I suddenly knew what I must do.

Thirty-odd years earlier I had written a *Harper's* piece for Willie, "Requiem for a West Texas Town," about my Texas birthplace and how it had been reduced to 103 people down from its peak population in my childhood, when I had assumed it would be eternal and never-changing. One sentence ran, "For some three thousand salts-of-the-earth Putnam would still be standing when Rome had only a general store and an old stadium." Something about that line tickled Willie's fancy; he mentioned it many times, always with a chuckle or a smile.

So I went to the ruins of the Colosseum, built in A.D. 75–80, and said to Willie's ghost, *Willie, I'm here at this old stadium in Rome. I doubt they'll sing "Jesus on the Five-Yard Line" at your funeral today, Mississippi having too many tight-mouthed Baptists. But I'm gonna sing it now, Willie, to you and for you—one last time.*

And I did. Loud and clear, if not excessively tuneful, never mind a few strange looks from Colosseum visitors. It seemed to help where I was hurting.

AFTERWORD

FEW WRITERS HAVE HAD as many works published posthumously as has Willie Morris. *My Mississippi, My Cat Spit McGee,* the novel *Taps,* and a nonfiction collection of essays, selected and edited by Jack Bales, *Shifting Interludes,* were published within four years after Willie's death. All were well received critically, as was *My Dog Skip,* the last of his books published during Willie's lifetime.

Though some have lamented Willie's writing only of minor themes in his last years—often specifying dogs and cats—I think they overlook the fact that larger themes were present within the confines of those stories: growth, changes both in people and places, some of the old eternal verities. Willie was generally happier in his work than ever before during his last decade, more productive, better paid, and with a few grumpy exceptions more critically acclaimed. All that gives me the gratifying feeling that Willie Morris himself—had he time to think about it—probably would have felt that he went out near the top of his game.

JoAnne Prichard Morris did, indeed, get *Taps* in shape for publishing as she promised her husband she would in his final hours. "I did very little," JoAnne insists. "*Taps* was truly Willie's book. You know, he began writing that book even before he wrote a line of *North Toward Home.* So it was almost a life's work. I think the book had been ready for some years, but Willie seemed reluctant to let it go; it was his baby; he felt that his literary reputation hinged on *Taps,* and so he obsessively sought perfection."

Willie didn't attain that impossible perfection, but from the raves of most critics he came close. *Publishers Weekly* in a red-starred review called *Taps* a worthy companion of *North Toward Home* and "a deeply affecting swan song by one of America's most beloved writers. Echoing Faulkner and [Erskine] Caldwell, and Dan Wakefield's *Going All the Way,* it plays a fitting 'Taps' for a literary genius cut down in his prime."

Bryan Woolley, *Dallas Morning News:* "a novel that's simultaneously warm and terrifying, sentimental and tough, funny and heartbreaking . . . *Taps* is a story that stays in the heart a long time, like the notes of the song itself." Harry Levins, *St. Louis Post-Dispatch:* "When Morris was good—oh Lord, he was really good . . . his final chapter—on Swayze's final performance of 'Taps' at his final funeral—is just wonderful." Michael Swindle, *Memphis Commercial Appeal:* "The song Morris plays in *Taps* he has played before, but like a jazz trumpet genius he has found an imaginative variation on the theme. He has made the old new again." Brad Buchholz, *Austin American-Statesman:* "Reads like a 'Mississippi *Gatsby.*' The tenderness of language, the compelling and foreboding symbolism, the wistful voice of its narrator all evoke the spirit of F. Scott Fitzgerald's most famous novel." Michael Pearson, *Atlanta Journal-Constitution:* *Taps* is Morris's "best book, a story written with genuine passion and soulful understanding. It is an old-fashioned Dickensian sort of novel, but with a Southern accent, filled with main characters one is compelled to love and hate and minor characters one is unable to forget."

I found not a single scathing review, or what some writers call "killer mean" reviews, of *Taps,* though David Conrad in *The Christian Science Monitor,* Richard Eder in *The New York Times,* and Scott Brown in *Entertainment Weekly* managed to contain their enthusiasm. *Taps* certainly won many more than it lost, though I suspect its postmortem publication caused it to be judged a bit more kindly than it otherwise might have been.

THE QUESTION I HAVE BEEN ASKED MOST about Willie Morris is "After the *Harper's* fiasco"—or incident, or blow-up or fratricide or whatever—"why didn't Willie Morris fight back?" Or "Why didn't he take one of the many good jobs he was offered?" "Why did he exile himself?" "Why did he go into a shell for so long?" Those are questions, you'll recall, that I had hoped Willie would himself answer in *New York Days*, but he chose not to go there.

I have no single conclusion that will please everybody—or even myself. He was wounded. He was bereft. He was angry and felt somehow betrayed. He felt he had given much to *Harper's* and got little back. He was sore ashamed of what he saw as his failure, and failure had been such a stranger to him that he didn't know how to react. It was almost as if a bomb had exploded in his hand and it took him more than months—it literally took *years*—for Willie to recover from the resulting wounds; if he ever completely healed, I think, it was not until the last decade of his life. So, originally, he hid from almost everyone, like a hermit in a cave, among his whiskey bottles.

There is another factor that occurred to me a bit tardily—David Halberstam first suggested it, after talking with Will and Patty Lewis of Oxford, who knew Willie Morris long and well—and that is that Willie likely was subject to clinical depression from a young age. There are clues dating back to his honeymoon trip with Celia when, on the ship to England to continue his Rhodes Scholar work, he turned his back on his bride and faced the bare bulkhead, often sleeping while Celia and other Rhodes Scholars were socializing. When Willie had what he called "the flu" and stayed abed—again, hiding in sleep, for two or three days at a time—that was conduct common to the clinically depressed. His disappearance just before Congressman Mo Udall and I were to visit him on Long Island for our first "peace meeting" after our fist fight, his failing to show up to take David Halberstam and another friend to a World Series game he had invited them to, his not appearing for Barbara Howar's thirty-seventh birthday party when he was proclaiming her to be the love of his life, his standing up young John Cowles when they were to have dinner together just before Willie resigned his *Harper's* editorship, are among many typical to-hell-with-it desperate moments the depressed often cannot deal with. Even Willie's not responding to the many job offers he received in the wake of the *Harper's* blowup are easier to understand if one sees him as paralyzed beyond action, as often happens with the truly depressed.

Willie also had a certain dependency on others not foreign to the depressed. If, unlike Blanche DuBois, he failed to "depend on the kindness of strangers," he damn sure depended on the kindness of friends: Charles Henry bailed him out of his tax problems; Larry and Dean Faulkner Wells paid his auto insurance and bought his football tickets each season, as well as giving him advance royalties on books when it wasn't always easy for them; no way to number, really, the many favors done for Willie Morris by perhaps two dozen people in Oxford. "He was much prone to dependencies of various kinds," says JoAnne Prichard Morris.

> He hardly did anything for himself; he always managed to have someone else do everything for him. I had a strong sense that he should do things *himself,* no matter how small, because he had lost all sense of himself as a functioning individual. A tiny example I remember from our courtship—it's silly, and maybe unbelievable—but representative. We went out to cut a Christmas tree at my favorite Christmas tree farm. When we found the right tree, I could sense that it hadn't occurred to Willie that *he* might have to cut down the tree, that he was waiting for *me* to do it. So, I just handed him the saw and casually said, "I'll hold the tree and you cut it as close to the ground as possible." He did, and after that, he always loved getting down on his knees to cut down the Christmas tree.

Little by little, JoAnne got Willie functioning in other ways: She weaned him from eating out every night and, to her surprise, he decided he wanted to learn to cook. JoAnne persuaded him the cook should also buy the groceries; Willie did, particularly enjoying the farmer's market in the summertime, where he often asked sources how to cook items he bought from them. "He was far from a gourmet chef," JoAnne says,

> but he did have certain specialties: spaghetti, which for some strange reason he always topped with slices of boiled eggs; pot roast with pota-

toes, onions and carrots, beef short ribs; steaks; chicken he broiled in a clay pot. He liked having friends in to eat "his" meals—though, being Willie, he sometimes *claimed* he had cooked barbecued ribs, homemade lemon ice box pie and other dishes he had, in reality, bought and sneaked home. Disasters? I recall a couple. He cooked a goose for visiting Yazoo City friends, but when he took it out of the oven there was nothing but a huge pan of grease and about three bites of goose. And once he worked *so* hard to cook a squash and cheese casserole he was very proud of—but it was dropped on the kitchen floor, the pyrex dish broke and scattered casserole everywhere.

Doing things for himself—becoming a self-starter—extended to Willie's work as a writer, which was what JoAnne hoped for when she encouraged his participation in as many activities as possible. "He liked to say I 'drove' him to work in 'the dungeon,' but, in fact, Willie did his work without my ever having to give him even a nudge. He continued to stay up half the night, drinking and smoking while listening to music, and he slept until noon or later, but he did his work and he was happy in his work."

That was something that could not have been said of Willie Morris during far too much of his career.

DEAN FAULKNER WELLS, who knew Willie Morris as well as anyone during times both bad and good, recently said, of his Oxford days,

It seems in retrospect as if Willie could hold hurt and anger at bay only until he drank enough to let the demons loose. For forty-eight hours at a time, he would be monster-ridden. "The flu," he called it. Then, twenty-four hours later, Willie would be himself again, full of fun, planning an adventure, playing another practical joke. Everything he did, from arranging a dinner party to planning an excursion to a football game in Jackson, was a herculean effort rife with detail. He turned ordinary gatherings into events that sparkled, yet gave to a three-day drunk the same energy, concentration and stamina. He lived in the fullness of time, but sometimes everything went on too long.

I believe that Willie always hoped, deep inside himself, that somehow the better angels of his nature would prevail.

He was so much a part of history, had such an immediate sense of participating in major events, as commentator or observer, that those of us privileged to be his friends were pulled into currents where we might never have had the opportunity, or courage, to venture.

I miss Willie Morris at least once every day.

"He was our Buddha," Larry Wells adds. "And we loved him."

I LOVED HIM TOO, and I owed him, but his complexities—his maddening *contradictions*—sometimes made Willie Morris the object of my wrath, leading to all those sentences beginning "God*dammit,* Willie! . . ." He could be selfless when it came to helping others, and he could be as selfish as a kid in a candy store when he decided on a course of action benefiting himself, and the devil take the hindmost. He wouldn't have stolen a single one of John D. Rockefeller's many dimes, but he seemed strangely untroubled about not promptly paying his debts: Real money appeared to have no more value to him than did Monopoly money—though that, I know, is at odds with his always looking for the big best seller, unless it was the fame and acclaim he hungered for rather than money. He could tell a few people he loved them, but with most it wasn't easy for him to show it or sustain it. He could call his mother "crazy" and say he could never live in Mississippi until she died, close proximity being more than he could handle, yet when she died he felt, and showed, true grief.

Though he could read most other people with the ease that he read books, he seemed wary of the sort of serious self-examinations most of us make in our thirties or forties, trying to better understand ourselves, our world, and our place in it. Not only did Willie hold "shrinks" in contempt—holding psychiatry to be as phony a science as Tom Cruise has come to believe—he often was dismissive of those who attempted to talk with him of self-examinations; if he participated at all he used his well-honed skills as a raconteur, hiding behind standard one-liners ("I'm the world's oldest sixth-grader" or "They say I have a bourbon problem, but I don't. I can get all the bourbon I want") more to filibuster and evade than to impart or exchange information. At other times he would grow sullen or say, "I don't want to talk about that stuff," or stare stone-faced over his inquisitor's shoulder, or perhaps, simply walk away. Though much was often awry in his life, he was for many years obsessive, I think, in fighting not to change it. I don't pretend to understand the "why" of that.

Two absolutes remain, both of which were earlier stated, but neither of which I can improve: (1) I shall miss Willie Morris so long as I have breath and (2) Willie Morris will mainly be remembered, and *should* be mainly remembered, for his many and unique contributions to American letters during his time on earth.

BIBLIOGRAPHY

Applebome, Peter. *Dixie Rising: How the South Is Shaping American Values, Politics and Culture.* San Diego: Harcourt Brace, 1996.

Bales, Jack, ed. *Conversations with Willie Morris.* Jackson: University Press of Mississippi, 2000.

_____, ed. *Shifting Interludes: Selected Essays of Willie Morris.* Jackson: University Press of Mississippi, 2002.

Bellows, Jim. *The Last Editor: How I Saved The New York Times, The Washington Post and The Los Angeles Times from Dullness and Complacency.* Kansas City, Mo.: Andrews McMeel Publishing, 2002.

Blount, Roy, Jr. *Crackers: This Whole Many-Angled Thing of Jimmy, More Carters, Ominous Little Animals, Sad-Singing Women, My Daddy and Me.* New York: Knopf, 1980.

_____. *Roy Blount's Book of Southern Humor.* New York and London: W. W. Norton, 1994.

Carr, John. *Kite-Flying and Other Irrational Acts: Conversations with Twelve Southern Writers.* Baton Rouge: Louisiana State University Press, 1972.

Cobb, James C. *The Most Southern Place on Earth: The Mississippi Delta and the Roots of Regional Identity.* New York: Oxford University Press, 1992.

Corry, John. *My Times: Adventures in the News Trade.* New York: G. P. Putnam's Sons, 1993.

Doyle, William. *An American Insurrection: The Battle of Oxford, Mississippi, 1962.* New York: Doubleday, 2001.

Eubanks, W. Ralph. *Ever Is a Long Time: A Journey into Mississippi's Dark Past.* New York: Basic Books, 2003.

Frady, Marshall. *Wallace.* New York: World Publishing Company, 1968.

_____. *Southerners: A Journalist's Odyssey.* New York: New American Library, 1980.

Goulden, Joseph C. *Fit to Print: A. M. Rosenthal and His Times.* Secaucus, N.J.: Lyle Stuart, Inc., 1988.

Graham, Don. *Giant Country: Essays on Texas.* Fort Worth: Texas Christian University Press, 1998.

Hart, Henry. *James Dickey: The World As a Lie.* New York: Picador USA, 2000.

Hendrickson, Paul. *Sons of Mississippi.* New York: Knopf, 2003.

Hotchner, A. E. *Everyone Comes to Elaine's: Forty Years of Movie Stars, All Stars, Literary Lions, Financial Scions, Top Cops, Politicians and Power Brokers at the Legendary Hot Spot.* New York: HarperEntertainment, 2004.

Manning, Robert. *The Swamp Root Chronicle: Adventures in the Word Trade.* New York: W. W. Norton, 1992.

Miller, Char, ed. *Fifty Years of The Texas Observer.* San Antonio: Trinity University Press, 2004.

Milner, Jay D. *Confessions of a Maddog: A Romp Through the High-Flying Texas Music and Literary Era of the Fifties to the Seventies.* Denton: University of North Texas Press, 1998.

Morris, Celia. *Finding Celia's Place.* College Station: Texas A&M University Press, 2000.

Morris, Willie, ed. *The South Today: 100 Years After Appomattox.* New York: Harper & Row, 1965.

_____. *North Toward Home.* Boston: Houghton Mifflin, 1967 (reprint, Oxford, Miss.: Yoknapatawpha Press, 1981).

_____. *Yazoo: Integration in a Deep Southern Town.* New York: Harper's Magazine Press, 1971.

_____. *Good Old Boy: A Delta Boyhood.* New York: Harper & Row, 1971.

_____. *The Last of the Southern Girls.* New York: Alfred A. Knopf, 1973 (paperback edition, Baton Rouge: Louisiana State University Press, 1994).

_____. *A Southern Album: Recollections of Some People and Places and Times Gone By.* Edited by Irwin Glusker. Birmingham, Ala.: Oxmoor House, 1975.

_____. *James Jones: A Friendship.* Garden City, N.Y.: Doubleday, 1978.

_____. *Terrains of the Heart and Other Essays on Home.* Oxford, Miss.: Yoknapatawpha Press, 1981.

_____. *The Courting of Marcus Dupree.* Garden City, N.Y.: Doubleday, 1983.

_____. *Always Stand in Against the Curve and Other Sports Stories.* Oxford, Miss.: Yoknapatawpha Press, 1983.

_____. *Homecomings*. Art by William Dunlap. Jackson: University Press of Mississippi, 1989.

_____. *Good Old Boy and the Witch of Yazoo*. Oxford, Miss.: Yoknapatawpha Press, 1989.

_____. *Faulkner's Mississippi*. Photos by William Eggleston. Birmingham, Ala.: Oxmoor House, 1990.

_____. *After All, It's Only a Game*. Jackson: University Press of Mississippi, 1992.

_____. *New York Days*. Boston: Little, Brown, 1993.

_____. *My Dog Skip*. New York: Random House, 1995.

_____. *The Ghosts of Medgar Evers: A Tale of Race, Murder, Mississippi and Hollywood*. New York: Random House, 1998.

_____. *My Cat Spit McGee*. New York: Random House, 1999.

_____. *My Mississippi*. Photographs by David Rae Morris. Jackson: University Press of Mississippi, 2000.

_____. *Taps*. Boston: Houghton Mifflin, 2001.

_____. *Shifting Interludes: Selected Essays*. Chosen and edited by Jack Bales. Jackson: University Press of Mississippi, 2002.

Norris, Kathleen, ed. *Leaving New York: Writers Look Back*. St. Paul, Minn.: Hungry Mind Press, 1995.

O'Connell, Shaun. *Remarkable, Unspeakable New York: A Literary History*. Boston: Beacon Press, 1995.

Pearson, Michael. *Imagined Places: Journeys into Literary America*. Jackson: University Press of Mississippi, 1991.

Plimpton, George. *Truman Capote: In Which Various Friends, Enemies, Acquaintances, and Detractors Recall His Turbulent Career*. New York: Doubleday, 1997.

Polsgrove, Carol. *It Wasn't Pretty, Folks, But Didn't We Have Fun? Esquire in the Sixties*. New York: W. W. Norton, 1995.

Smith, Steven A. *Myth, Media and the Southern Mind*. Fayetteville: University of Arkansas Press, 1985.

Unattributed. *Remembering Willie: A Collection of Tributes Memorializing Willie Morris, the Acclaimed Southern Author*. Jackson: University Press of Mississippi, 2000.

Walton, Anthony. *Mississippi: An American Journey*. New York: Vintage Books, 1996.

Wells, Dean Faulkner. *The Ghosts of Rowan Oak: William Faulkner's Ghost Sto-

ries for Children, Recounted. Foreword by Willie Morris. Oxford, Miss.: Yoknapatawpha Press, 1980.

West, James L. W., III. *William Styron: A Life.* New York: Random House, 1988.

Wilkie, Curtis. *Dixie: A Personal Odyssey Through Events That Shaped the Modern South.* New York: Scribner, 2001.

Yoder, Edwin M., Jr. *Telling Others What to Think: Recollections of a Pundit.* Baton Rouge: Louisiana State University Press, 2004.

INDEX

PUBLICAFFAIRS is a publishing house founded in 1997. It is a tribute to the standards, values, and flair of three persons who have served as mentors to countless reporters, writers, editors, and book people of all kinds, including me.

I. F. STONE, proprietor of *I. F. Stone's Weekly,* combined a commitment to the First Amendment with entrepreneurial zeal and reporting skill and became one of the great independent journalists in American history. At the age of eighty, Izzy published *The Trial of Socrates,* which was a national best-seller. He wrote the book after he taught himself ancient Greek.

BENJAMIN C. BRADLEE was for nearly thirty years the charismatic editorial leader of *The Washington Post*. It was Ben who gave the *Post* the range and courage to pursue such historic issues as Watergate. He supported his reporters with a tenacity that made them fearless, and it is no accident that so many became authors of influential, best-selling books.

ROBERT L. BERNSTEIN, the chief executive of Random House for more than a quarter century, guided one of the nation's premier publishing houses. Bob was personally responsible for many books of political dissent and argument that challenged tyranny around the globe. He is also the founder and was the longtime chair of Human Rights Watch, one of the most respected human rights organizations in the world.

. . .

For fifty years, the banner of Public Affairs Press was carried by its owner, Morris B. Schnapper, who published Gandhi, Nasser, Toynbee, Truman, and about 1,500 other authors. In 1983 Schnapper was described by *The Washington Post* as "a redoubtable gadfly." His legacy will endure in the books to come.

Peter Osnos, *Founder and Editor-at-Large*